Music to the Glory of God

HUMPHREY DOBSON

Music to the Glory of God

Why You Should Think About Music

Learned and thoughtful, interesting and insightful, Humphrey Dobson has given us a helpful reflection on music and Christianity. This study looks at issues related to church music, but has much more on the cultural and spiritual significance of music. Very valuable.

—W. ROBERT GODFREY, PHD,
Ligonier Ministries Teaching Fellow and Chairman of Ligonier Ministries; President Emeritus and Professor Emeritus of Church History at Westminster Seminary, California

Like literature, art, architecture, philosophy, politics, and culture, music is an expression of worldview, for good or for ill. In this very insightful primer, Humphrey Dobson explores music from a Christian worldview perspective. Historically informed, biblically grounded, and musically adept, this incisive book is must-reading for pastors, teachers, parents, and music lovers alike. You will love this book. Tolle lege.

—GEORGE GRANT, PHD,
Pastor, Parish Presbyterian Church, Franklin, Tennessee

. . . the most thorough and comprehensive treatment of the subject I have come across. . . . Since, as Bach himself believed, God is the only true creator, it follows that music cannot simply be subjective, whose beauty is solely in the ear of the listener. There is something objective about it; it is not neutral. . . . We can all use some clear biblical guidance, and this is a book which provides it. It admirably lives up to its name. Take it and read—and sing and play with sanctified understanding.

—PETER BARNES, THD,
Retired Presbyterian Pastor from Revesby; Author; Lecturer in Church History at Christ College, Sydney, Australia

Relativism has won the day in the modern world and, unfortunately, even most evangelical Christians have bought into aesthetic relativism, believing beauty is in the eye of the beholder and art forms carry no inherent meaning and are morally neutral. I'm thankful for Humphrey Dobson's biblically robust and philosophically sound corrective to the powerfully seductive secular view of music and the arts. This book is a must-read for all Christians."

—SCOTT ANIOL, PHD,
Executive Vice President, G3 Ministries; Author; Professor of Pastoral Theology, Grace Bible Theological Seminary

Music is one of God's greatest gifts to his creatures, and especially to his church. Though opinions about music are never in short supply, biblical thoughtfulness on the matter is sorely lacking. In *Music to the Glory of God,* author Humphrey Dobson offers a helpful corrective to the musical illiteracy of the modern church. In fact, there is more to this book than what the title lets on: in these pages you'll find a helpful theological primer, not only on music, but on aesthetics and beauty. I am certain the careful reader will be better equipped to take every thought captive to Christ and worship the Lord in the beauty of holiness.

—JONATHAN LANDRY CRUSE,
Pastor, Hymnwriter, Author, *What Happens When We Worship* and *Sing in Exultation!*

Music to the Glory of God

Why You Should Think About Music

Humphrey Dobson

ISBNS:

Paperback:	978-1-63342-346-6
Hardback:	978-1-63342-351-0
ePub:	978-1-63342-347-3

Unless noted otherwise, Scripture quotations are taken from the King James (Authorized) Version of the Bible

Cover design and typeset by www.greatwriting.org

Shepherd Press
P.O. Box 24
Wapwallopen, PA 18660
www.shepherdpress.com

Printed in Colombia

To Amanda:

Godly wife
Beautiful helpmeet
Dearest earthly friend

Foreword 11
Preface 13
1 Mark the Music 15
2 Music in Creation 21
3 Christians and Music 29
4 Thinking about the Arts 33
5 Objective Beauty 39
6 Thinking about Music 47
7 Surveying Composers 55
8 Applying the Principles of Beauty to Music 97
9 Bach and Beauty 105
10 Reflecting on Bach's Music 119
11 What Went Wrong? 123
12 Music as Mass Entertainment 131
13 Taste in Music 141
14 The Bible and the Soul 149
15 Music and the Soul 157
16 Bringing Disorder to the Soul 163
17 Music and Character 171
18 Three Questions 177
19 Music in Church History 185
20 Calvin and Corporate Worship 193
21 Worship or Entertainment? 199
22 Reforming Church Music 209
Conclusion 217
Musical Examples 225
Endnotes 229
Index 247

Foreword

Why read a book on music?

FIRSTLY, music is a *good gift from God.* As Creator of the universe, God has ordained the eternal, unchangeable, and objective principles behind it. The scientific basis of music lies in the mathematical patterns embedded in the core of creation. The Indian author Vishal Mangalwadi observes that God has "encoded music into the structure of the universe."[1]

God himself sings with delight over his people (Zeph. 3:17). Songs of praise were heard at the dawn of creation when the Lord laid the earth's foundation (Job 38:7).

Music is a wonderful gift from our kind and generous God. It has the power to sooth, comfort, inspire, embolden, and more besides.

SECONDLY, we are *commanded to praise God with music and song.* We have an absolute duty to praise our Creator. Praising him in song engages our emotions and our body, as well as our mind.

Psalm 100 summons all people on earth to worship the Creator with *joyful* songs. As divine image bearers, we are here on earth to represent God, and to be like God. He endowed us with the capacity and ability to praise him in song and instrumental music.

At the Passover meal before his crucifixion, our Lord Jesus Christ sang with his disciples (Psalms 113–118 were usually sung as part of this festive meal).

1 Vishal Mangalwadi, *The Book that Made your World* (Nashville, TN: Thomas Nelson, 2011), 12.

Heaven will be filled with songs of praise to God as Creator and Redeemer (Rev. 5:9–10; 14:1-3; 15:2–4).

THIRDLY, as believers we are to do ***all*** *to the glory of God* (1 Cor. 10:31). That includes music!

All this suggests that we should think carefully about music (both inside and outside the church).

This book serves both as a guide and a challenge. Humphrey Dobson is a trained musician, with a degree in music from the historic Durham University in England. He has reflected deeply over many years on how to engage with music for the glory of God. He writes in an accessible style, with plenty of examples. The pen portraits of many notable composers are particularly engaging.

Whether you consider yourself musical or not, reading this book will provoke you to reflect on how to engage with music for the glory of God. Our enjoyment and appreciation of music can, and should, lead us to a deeper love and enjoyment of our Creator God. But most importantly, we can be spurred on to more joyful, intelligent, and heartfelt worship of the One who is alone worthy of all our praise.

SHARON JAMES,
London, Summer 2024

Preface

It was a sunny, early summer evening in the city of Durham, Northeast England. Together with friends, I sat down on the hard, unyielding wooden pews of the historic Norman cathedral. I was a young undergraduate, taking the evening off to attend the university orchestra's end-of-term concert and had not thought much about the music awaiting us. It being the north of England, sunlight was streaming in through the high clerestory windows until nearly 10 p.m. and bathing the massive tan pillars in a warm, radiant glow.

I only remember one piece of music performed that night—the third symphony by Camille Saint-Saëns, often known as his *Organ* symphony. It was new to me. I was immediately enthralled. The soaring, beautiful lines of music from the orchestra combined with the immense power of the Cathedral's pipe organ made an indelible impression on my soul.

Music leaves a mark on our lives. The great Reformer Martin Luther said of music that he was "overwhelmed by the diversity and magnitude of its virtue and benefits."[1] Andrew Marvell, the seventeenth-century English poet, called music "the mosaic of the air" in his poem *Music's Empire*. Have you ever seen a Roman mosaic made of hundreds or thousands of tiny stones, tiles, or other fragments? Like a mosaic in sound, music carefully pieces together a multitude of disparate notes to compose a beautiful whole.

It shapes whole communities and music has often been seen as an indicator of cultural health: "Plato teaches that, in order to take the spiritual temperature of an individual or society, one must 'mark the music.'"[2] It was not only the ancient Greeks who thought so. Throughout the history of Western civilization, this has been the judgment of thoughtful people. Music has a powerful yet mysterious effect on the soul. For this reason, music is much more than a hobby or entertainment. There is an urgent need to reflect on the music all around us.

Why should you think about music? How can you glorify Jesus Christ in your music choices? The Bible teaches that Jesus died on the cross to save his people from their sins (Matt. 1:21) and they are to respond in loving obedience (John 14:15). But how does this apply to music? This book explores biblical principles, ranging from the character of God and the danger of idolatry, to the heart of what it means to be human. It is written with the simple conviction that all of life should be directed to the glory of God, including our music. In the words of 1 Corinthians 10:31: "Whether therefore ye eat, or drink, or whatsoever ye do, do all to the glory of God."

The Bible teaches that the ultimate purpose of music is the praise of God, and mankind should rejoice with song in the glory of our Creator and the works that God has done. We are all exhorted to sing praises with understanding (Ps. 47:7). Essential to considering music is actually listening to it—above all, beautiful music. The twentieth-century composer Aaron Copland once wrote,

> All books on understanding music are agreed about one point: You can't develop a better appreciation of the art merely by reading a book about it. If you want to understand music better, you can do nothing more important than listen to it. Nothing can possibly take the place of listening to music.[3]

This book seeks to provide a biblical perspective on music—so that music takes its proper, God-given place in each of our lives. It sets out principles to guide our understanding and enjoyment of music, which have particular importance for the church's corporate worship. I have used sources and quoted authors spanning the centuries, but the views expressed and any errors are my own. I set forth this work in reliance on the grace of God in Jesus Christ and with the prayer that it will prove a blessing to many people.

1

Mark the Music

How sweet the moonlight sleeps upon this bank!
Here will we sit and let the sounds of music
Creep in our ears: soft stillness and the night
Become the touches of sweet harmony. . . .

The man that hath no music in himself,
Nor is not moved with concord of sweet sounds,
Is fit for treasons, stratagems and spoils;
The motions of his spirit are dull as night
And his affections dark as Erebus:
Let no such man be trusted. Mark the music.

(*The Merchant of Venice* by William Shakespeare, Act 5, Scene 1)

Mark the music. Music is all around us, but few pay attention to it. Background music is played in homes, cars, restaurants, retail stores, events. Many people are not even aware that it is there. The careless man is drenched in the sounds of music, but pays little attention to its impact on him.

Perhaps Shakespeare was exaggerating when he wrote that the man who is not moved by music should not be trusted. Thankfully, those cases are rare. Plenty of people attend live music, and some sing or play instruments themselves. People in the Western world attend performances by folk bands, orchestras, barber shop, and rock groups. Limitless amounts of recorded music can be streamed online. A lot has changed since Thomas Edison invented his phonograph in 1877 for recording sound.

Children usually start learning about music by taking lessons. With the full support and encouragement of my parents, I had piano lessons starting at the age of six-and-a-half, and later organ lessons as well. My longtime teacher was Mrs. Jenkins, a kind, elderly Welsh lady. Mrs. Jenkins was originally from Aberystwyth, on the coast of Wales, but for many years had lived in northern England in the town of Leyland, Lancashire, two doors down from my family home. She taught me to play accurately and expressively, and I did not escape her reproach when I failed to practice! Her teaching was my grounding for a lifelong love of music.

Two other childhood musical experiences affected me in different ways. My family attended an evangelical Church of England church in Leyland that preached the gospel and used mostly pop-style music in its services.[1] One of the churchwardens (elders) played the guitar in the music group, along with a keyboard player and a few singers. For a time, my Sunday School classes were dominated by singing one modern song ("chorus") after another.

In stark contrast, between the ages of eleven and eighteen I was a member of my school's chamber choir, along with my brothers. We learned the traditional liturgical music of the Church of England, especially the Psalms and different settings of the *Magnificat* and *Nunc Dimittis* for Evensong. The chamber choir regularly sang in magnificent ancient cathedrals across northern England, such as York Minster, Durham Cathedral, and Carlisle Cathedral. The music was nuanced, refined, and brilliant.

As the years have passed by, I have reflected on these contrasting experiences. Was all the music "good music"? Is music neutral? Should you just choose what you like? Are there principles for discerning between good and bad music? What music should be used in church worship?

Some aspects of life are morally neutral: whether you prefer blue or yellow, beaches or hiking, apples over oranges. Yet the thinking Christian sees that so many things in life have a moral dimension: the friends we choose, how we spend our money and our time, even what clothes we wear. Just open the book of Proverbs to see how many aspects of life need right decision-making.

Music wields great power to move and shape people. It would

be strange if it were morally neutral. Our money, friends, and business decisions all have a moral dimension. So does music. It definitely affects our behavior. Why else do companies pipe recorded music throughout their retail stores?

The Reality of the Soul

Perhaps our age is not able to properly assess music because music relates to the soul. The Bible plainly teaches that mankind is made body and soul in the image of God. But, as theologian J. Gresham Machen (1881–1937) once said,

> In thus affirming the existence of the soul, the Bible is in direct conflict with many powerful tendencies in modern unbelief. Great hosts of unbelievers deny not only the existence of a personal God but also the existence of the human soul.[2]

Everywhere today in the West, the reality of man's soul is denied. Naturalism, evolution, and materialism proclaim that only the physical world is real. Against this stands the entire Bible. Genesis 2:7 recounts that God created man on the sixth day as a physical and a spiritual being; when God breathed into him, man became a living creature. Jesus clearly taught that man is body and soul (Matt. 10:28), and this is reflected in the writing of the apostles (e.g., 1 Peter 1:9, 2:11, and 2:25).

John Calvin (1509–1564) explained that the soul of man is "an immortal yet created essence, which is his nobler part." In the *Institutes,* he writes that "the many pre-eminent gifts with which the human mind is endowed proclaim that something divine has been engraved upon it; all these are testimonies of an immortal essence." Mankind has been made in the image of God (Gen. 1:26–27) and Calvin argues that "although God's glory shines forth in the outer man, yet there is no doubt that the proper seat of his image is in the soul."[3]

The English Puritan John Flavel wrote: "The soul of man is a vital, spiritual, and immortal substance, endowed with an understanding, will, and various affections; created with an inclination to the body, and infused thereinto by the Lord." He went on to affirm that "All the affections and passions of hope, desire, love, delight, fear, sorrow, and the rest, are all rooted in it, and springing out of it; and for habits, arts and sciences, it is the soul in which they are lodged and seated."[4]

The Huguenot author Philippe de Mornay located the ability to identify musical harmony and discord in the soul, rather than the sense of hearing that merely absorbs the sounds.[5] This completely accords with the Bible's teaching about the soul. And it points to the fact that performing or listening to music involves both body and soul. Scripture and general experience show that some music can soothe a troubled mind and calm the weary soul (see 1 Samuel 16:23 and 2 Kings 3:15). This was recognized in antiquity.[6] In our own time, witness the popularity of listening to "smooth classics" to wind down at the end of the day.

Is Music Morally Neutral?

Music is one of the arts. And art is shaped by the worldview of the artist. This is more obvious in writing or painting, but it is no less true in music. Does this mean Christians should only listen to music composed by other Christians? That would be very limiting and, as we will see, God has not only given the gift of making good music to Christians, but to unbelievers as well.

Mark the music. Christians are called to be transformed by the renewing of our minds (Rom. 12:2). A biblical worldview should shape every aspect of our lives, including the different types ("genres") of music we can listen to. Music must be considered in the light of God's Word and we should pray for his wisdom as we seek to understand it better.

Angelic beings in heaven are described as singing and carrying harps, making sweet harmony to the glory of God (Revelation 5:8–9). Heaven is perfect and the angels play music there. God is even described as rejoicing over his people with singing (Zeph. 3:17). Music can clearly be used for good on earth, but this earth is corrupted by sin. It is still God's world, but since mankind's fall, it is a theater of conflict in which Satan is active; the whole world lies in wickedness (1 John 5:19). So is it not possible that the devil can also use music for his wicked ends? He is, after all, a fallen angel who is capable of masquerading as an angel of light (2 Cor. 11:14).

This book contends that there is objectively good-quality music and bad-quality music, and that music in some forms is being corrupted in our day. Music is not neutral. There is an urgent need to awaken people to this reality. At the same time, thanks to its Christian heritage, Western culture has bequeathed an unparalleled musical legacy to the world, which, when performed and appreciated, brings great glory to God.

2

Music in Creation

Music is a gift from God in creation and is clearly intended for his glory. The psalms often exhort us to sing; for example, Psalm 92:1 states "It is a good thing to give thanks unto the LORD, and to sing praises unto thy name, O most High." Or take Psalm 96:1–2: "O sing unto the LORD a new song: sing unto the LORD, all the earth. Sing unto the LORD, bless his name; shew forth his salvation from day to day."

Jesus sang a psalm with his disciples the night before his death (Matt. 26:30), as no doubt he had done throughout his earthly ministry. Later in the New Testament, Colossians 3:16 commands: "Let the word of Christ dwell in you richly in all wisdom; teaching and admonishing one another in psalms and hymns and spiritual songs, singing with grace in your hearts to the Lord."

Yet the Bible does not come with sheet music. It does not include an approved list of music. Neither does it tell us how to build the best bridges, tend the most magnificent orchards, or paint the loveliest pictures. But in his written Word, God reveals himself. He shows us his character and provides us with principles to apply to every aspect of our lives. We must always begin with the character of God. He is the God of order, not chaos. The Genesis creation account demonstrates this and it is evident throughout Scripture. He designed all things in this world for his own glory.

Theologians acknowledge that God is the source of everything that is good, true, and beautiful. Augustine of Hippo taught that God is the highest truth, the highest good, and the highest beauty (see Chapter 4—*Thinking about the Arts*).[1] It is because mankind is made in his image that we can appreciate what is good, true, and beautiful.

The Bible shows that God cares about beauty, even in his requirements for making the robes of the priests in the Old Testament—they were to be "for glory and for beauty" (Ex. 28:2, 40). R.C. Sproul commented: "God was concerned not only to use artists in the building of His sanctuary in the Old Testament but also to endow those very artists with the power of His Holy Spirit to make sure that what they were doing met the standards of excellence that He Himself wanted."[2]

Birdsong

Where do we find beauty in God's creation? Everywhere. Stunning sunsets, vast oceans, monumental mountains, tiny flowers, precious gemstones. Beautiful music is also built into creation. Listen to birdsong. Stand outside for a few minutes in the countryside and you are likely to hear birds making melodies. Some of them are too high-pitched or rapid for humans to perceive accurately. But others, like the cuckoo, are very clear.

Many people down the years have noted the influence of birdsong on Beethoven, including one of his pupils, Carl Czerny. As well as his sixth symphony (*Pastoral*), which features the songs of the nightingale, quail, and cuckoo, there is debate about which bird inspired the famous four-note motif that opens Beethoven's fifth symphony—the yellowhammer or perhaps the Ortolan bunting.[3] Jean-Philippe Rameau, the French Baroque composer of an earlier generation, imitates birdsong wonderfully in his keyboard piece *Le Rappel des Oiseaux*—"The Calling of the Birds."

The Puritan Thomas Watson wrote: "Look into the air, the birds, with their chirping music, sing hymns of praise to God." Watson also believed that God made the birds for music.[4] Martin Luther cited Psalm 104:12 with its praise for "the astounding art and ease of the song of birds."[5] Commenting on the same verse, the American theologian W.S. Plumer later wrote, "Without intellect or heart, the birds of the air were the first and have been the most constant to sing the praises of Jehovah."[6]

Engineer and scientist Stuart Burgess, in *Hallmarks of Design—Evidence of Design in the Natural World,* reviews the amazing range of musical ability of different birds, including hermit thrushes singing the pentatonic scale (that's equivalent to playing only the black notes of a piano), nightingales producing harmonics to enhance sound, and the amazing ability of blue jays to sound three notes in harmony at once (musically speaking, a "major triad").

Stuart Burgess adds:

> One of the most astonishing musical abilities of birds is their control of the key in which the song is sung. Many birds have what is musically known as "absolute pitch" which is the ability to know exactly what key they sing in without any reference to other sounds. Absolute pitch is such a sophisticated skill that very few human singers have it even after training.[7]

This is all clear evidence that God has built melody and harmony into creation itself. But John Calvin, in his preface to the Genevan Psalter (1543), reflected that mankind is capable of greater singing than the birds:

> . . . it is necessary to remember that which St. Paul hath said, the spiritual songs cannot be well sung save from the heart. But the heart requires the intelligence. And in that (says St. Augustine) lies the difference between the singing of men and that of the birds. For a linnet, a nightingale, a parrot may sing well; but it will be without understanding. But the unique gift of man is to sing knowing that which he sings. After the intelligence must follow the heart and the affection, a thing which is unable to be except if we have the hymn imprinted on our memory, in order never to cease from singing.[8]

The Bible commands thoughtful singing in the church's worship: we must sing with the spirit and with the understanding also (1 Cor. 14:15). That chapter of 1 Corinthians explains at length the importance of engaging our minds during corporate worship (see Chapter 21—*Worship or Entertainment?*). And using our minds is essential to all musical appreciation, which we will consider later.

Science and Order

Where else is there evidence that God has hardwired music into creation? Have you ever realized that your ears were designed by God to hear music? British scientists Andy McIntosh and Stuart Burgess have shown, in great detail, that the range of sounds heard by the human ear far surpasses what is necessary for merely functional use, and that our ears are precision designed so that we can hear subtle changes of sound.[9]

The range of frequencies we can hear (around nine octaves covering 20–20,000 Hz) allows mankind to appreciate a range of beautiful musical sounds as well as human speech. There are many components to the workings of the human ear, from the precise length of the ear canal, to the eardrum, to the tiny bones that amplify the signal and pass the vibrations into the cochlea. Inside the cochlea is the basilar membrane that converts each frequency into a precise electrical signal for the brain. Without this elaborate mechanism, we could not appreciate or distinguish the tones and timbres that are essential to hearing music. God made our ears to enjoy great music: "Such a system involving air vibrations, mechanical, chemical and electrical engineering confirms the intelligent design of the ear."[10]

Another obvious example of God's design in creation is the connection between music and mathematics. This has been recognized since at least the time of Ancient Greece, and today can be seen in the whole science of acoustics. A musical pitch, or note, is a regular pattern of sound. The science shows that regularity and order is intrinsic to the musical notes themselves.

Philosophers in Ancient Greece saw musical design in what for us are unexpected places. Above all, they talked about the "music of the spheres." As R.C. Sproul explained, "Plato, following the Pythagoreans, was concerned to discover the harmony of the world, particularly the heavens, where the ancient astronomers believed that the so-called harmony of the spheres resided. They believed that the stars, in their order, spelled out a certain majestic harmony that could be known . . ."[11] Aristotle, Plato's successor, was skeptical about it, but the possibility of this sound of the spheres fascinated philosophers and inspired poets down the centuries.[12] Our scientific understanding of the cosmos makes it impossible that the planets (or stars) should be striking literal notes of music, yet scientists have seen ways of comparing mathematical proportions in planetary orbits with mathematical proportions inherent in the sound of music.[13] However this comparison is interpreted, mathematical order is obviously displayed in both planetary motion and music theory.

Eminent theologians such as Augustine carried the connection the Greeks had made between music and mathematics into the Christian era. In *How Christianity Transformed the World,* Sharon James draws attention to Augustine's six-volume work *De Musica,* which laid out "a theology of music, and showed that God providentially ordained the rational, eternal, unchangeable and objective principles behind it. The scientific basis of music lies in mathematical patterns embedded in the core of creation."[14] (See Chapter 14—*The Bible and the Soul.*)

In medieval learning, music took its place alongside other mathematical disciplines (arithmetic, geometry, and astronomy) in the Quadrivium. Many aspects of musical composition, including rhythmic patterns, the development of themes, the use of certain musical structures ("forms"), have mathematical relationships even if it is not consciously intended by the composer.[15] At its simplest, the organized timing of a piece of music is based on mathematics. Think of a march, which goes one-two, one-two etc. The notes of a musical scale also have a mathematical relationship to each other. The fact that humans and some birds organize sound in this way to make music is clear evidence of design in creation. This order cannot have originated by chance or random processes, which is all evolutionary theory has to offer.

Common Grace

Music exists in every known culture around the world. It is a "common grace" blessing, given by God to all people in creation. It is noteworthy that the first musician mentioned in the Bible is Jubal from the ungodly line of Cain (Gen. 4:21). Yet he is credited with being the inventor of string and wind instruments. So those who do not follow God can make good music. As Calvin commented on this verse: "[T]he excellent gifts of the Spirit are diffused through the whole human race."[16] He expands on the point in his *Institutes of the Christian Religion*, saying, "[T]he knowledge of all that is most excellent in human life is said to be communicated to us through the Spirit of God."[17] Calvin goes on to clarify that such abilities are not the work of regeneration, but they do come from the Holy Spirit, warning: "[I]f we neglect God's gift freely offered in these arts, we ought to suffer just punishment for our sloths."

Later, the theologian Herman Bavinck (1854–1921) said: "[A]n artist is an artist by the grace of God. . . genius does not come completely from special gifts but is an unusual strengthening of ordinary gifts found in all people. Nevertheless, we still are faced with an original power that is not explained by any law of nature, and it points back to a divine, creating Almighty."[18]

The doctrine of common grace explains that God, in his infinite power and understanding, chooses to work through Christians and also non-Christians. This is despite the fall of all mankind into sin, which has corrupted every part of our nature (the doctrine of total depravity—see Genesis 3:6–8; Romans 3:23).[19] The Lord Jesus upheld this truth, saying to his audience in Luke 11:13, "[Y]ou then being evil," yet earlier in Luke's Gospel (6:33) also teaching that sinners can do good to each other.

The outworking of common grace is obvious all around us. God endows authors, architects, and astrophysicists with amazing talents and abilities which they can use to write classic works, design impressive structures, and analyze the depths of space. When their output is well done, this reflects the glory of God—even if they personally do not believe in Christ. Since Jesus is eternally God the Son through whom all things were made and in whom all things are held together (John 1:3; Col. 1:17), we can be sure that Christ is intimately acquainted with all mankind's activities, including music.

The famous pastor and theologian Jonathan Edwards wrote his treatise *The Nature of True Virtue* in 1755, only three years before he died. In this work, Edwards delves beneath people's outward actions to examine their attitudes and motivations for doing good. He distinguishes true virtue from natural conscience and the moral sense, saying in chapter seven, "Natural conscience is implanted in all mankind, to be as it were in God'[s] stead, as an internal judge or rule, whereby to distinguish right and wrong." Men may do the right thing because of their conscience, but this is not true virtue. It is, though, God-given and can be used by God for good: "The present state of the world is so constituted by the wisdom and goodness of its supreme Ruler, that these natural principles, for the most part, tend to the good of mankind. So do natural pity, gratitude, parental affection, etc."

Jesus teaches about common grace in the Sermon on the Mount, drawing our attention to his Father's provision of sunshine and rain for those who are just and those who are unjust (Matt. 5:45). The apostle Paul describes the important role of man's conscience in Romans 2:14–15. The doctrine of common grace has massive implications. It means that God is constantly at work in the whole of his creation, restraining sin and maintaining order, and also enabling mankind to do what is good, true, and beautiful. All of this points to the LORD and is for his glory.

3

Christians and Music

If music is a common grace gift to people throughout the world, is there such a thing as distinctively "Christian music"? How does a composer's worldview affect the music he writes?

There have been great musicians who believed in God and followed him. King David was renowned as the "sweet psalmist of Israel" (2 Sam. 23:1). He played the harp from early in life (see 1 Sam. 16:16–23) and composed many of the psalms. Later, King David appointed chief musicians from among the Levites, as he was instituting musical accompaniment for the worship of God (see Chapter 19—*Music in Church History*).

Martin Luther (1483–1546) loved music, played the lute, and composed pieces himself, including the famous hymn tune *A Mighty Fortress Is Our God*.[1] He wrote: "I would certainly like to praise music with all my heart as the excellent gift of God which it is and to commend it to everyone . . . next to the Word of God, music deserves the highest praise. . . . But when [musical] learning is added to all this and artistic music which corrects, develops, and refines the natural music, then at last it is possible to taste with wonder (yet not to comprehend) God's absolute and perfect wisdom in his wondrous work of music."[2]

In later centuries, the lives and musical output of distinguished composers such as Heinrich Schütz, J.S. Bach, and Felix Mendelssohn provide clear evidence of their faith in Christ. Yet this has not been the case for many of the most distinguished composers (or performers). The works of Mozart, Beethoven, and Schubert, to pick three names, are widely admired, but they were certainly not Bible-believing Christians. You do not need to read much about the lives of many famous composers to realize that their personal lives were marked by immorality.

Can you separate the art from the artist? No—art is not neutral. As Albert Mohler has said: "Christians understand that we have no art without the artist, and you never have an artist of any kind, because you never have a human being of any kind, who is not a moral creature. And that morality is going to show in every dimension of the individual's life."[3] This is undoubtedly true today, when non-Christian artists in the West often use their work to proclaim their unbiblical worldview. We only need to think of the ugliness and despairing character of much modern art.

R.C. Sproul taught that changes in art reflect changes in people's philosophy or outlook on life. He explained:

> It's the artists who are the real change agents that introduce ideas into the culture. We don't want to think for a minute that the popular music, literature, or paintings that we see have no philosophical content. On the contrary, these styles and forms of art are delivery mechanisms to awaken people to new ways of thinking and acting. This is why we have to be careful about what we borrow from the secular world and bring into the Christian life, not just in terms of music but also in terms of painting, architecture, and literature.[4]

Worldview Matters

Before the rise of modern secularism in the West, the Christian worldview was dominant over life and learning, and this shaped the art and music of both believers and unbelievers. The existence of one Creator God was fundamental to the tapestry of life. In the times of the well-known composers such as Bach, Handel, Mozart, and Mendelssohn, few people in Europe were avowed atheists. These composers operated in a Christian worldview, which prized order and beauty.

Take an example from the realm of architecture. We could speculate that Sir Christopher Wren (1632–1723) was partly motivated by pride in designing St. Paul's Cathedral in London—it would only come naturally to a sinner, but we cannot make a window into his soul. Whatever the case, St. Paul's is still a magnificent piece of architecture, which was built when the Christian worldview was dominant. Likewise, whatever the personal characters of composers living in that era, the order and beauty prized in their music can only have developed from the Christian worldview. Sir Christopher Wren famously said that "architecture aims at eternity."[5] It was during the nineteenth century in the West that a secular, godless worldview began to predominate.

Beethoven is a complex case, personally and, to an extent, musically (e.g., his late string quartets—see Chapter 7—*Surveying Composers*). He did not go to church and sometimes expressed skeptical beliefs about God to those around him.[6] Yet it is significant that Genesis 4 records that it was the ungodly line, those not worshipping the living God, who first made musical instruments. So we should recognize that sinful men, who are guilty before God, can use their talents to create good quality works of art, engineering, or science. Likewise good music can be appreciated by anyone. It is not a gift only for Christians. This is the doctrine of common grace in action, and it shows that Christians can freely enjoy music composed by non-Christians.

We cannot use a simple equation: Christians make good music; non-Christians make bad music. In fact, from Jubal in Genesis 4 to the evidence from recent centuries, we see that unbelievers are just as capable as Christians of composing excellent music. God will one day judge the sins of those who reject him, but in the meantime they are able to make music of high quality.

Those who believe in Christ cannot simply compile a list of "good" and "bad" composers based on the personal lives of these men, and only listen to the former. No, we have a more challenging and exciting task. Being transformed by the renewing of our minds, Christians need to apply objective principles to different pieces of music, whatever genres they belong to (in music, a "genre" is a type or class of music with similar features; e.g., symphonies, tone poems, or violin concerti are different genres). We need to be alert to each individual piece and be thinking about its impact on us.

In the background to this conversation lies the profoundly important question of how Christians should relate to the world, which can be traced throughout church history. The polar opposites are monks on one side who have advocated total withdrawal and, on the other, those who have surrendered to their culture entirely. We need wisdom and the right application of Scripture to avoid either retreat from the world (1 Cor. 5:9–10) or succumbing to the thinking and practice of the world (Rom. 12:2).

Much has been written over the past century or so about the relationship of Christianity to culture. J. Gresham Machen outlined three different approaches: Christianity can i) be subordinated to culture, ii) seek to destroy culture by indifference or open hostility, or iii) "consecrate" the culture. Commending the third option to Christians, Machen explained how the Bible should be confidently applied to every area of life:

> Instead of destroying the arts and sciences or being indifferent to them, let us cultivate them with all the enthusiasm of the veriest humanist, but at the same time consecrate them to the service of our God. Instead of stifling the pleasures afforded by the acquisition of knowledge or by the appreciation of what is beautiful, let us accept these pleasures as the gifts of a heavenly Father. Instead of obliterating the distinction between the Kingdom and the world, or on the other hand withdrawing from the world into a sort of modernized intellectual monasticism, let us go forth joyfully, enthusiastically to make the world subject to God.[7]

4

Thinking about the Arts

God has installed music in the world he created. There is a lot of science behind the formulation of music. Mathematical patterns are inherent in it. Yet mankind's composition and performance of music is better thought of as one of the arts.

When I was at school, "art" lessons included painting, drawing, and sculpture. But when people talk about "the arts," they mean more than that. In the modern era, the term "the arts" generally describes a specific range of activities, e.g., "painting, sculpture, music, theatre, literature, etc., considered as a group of activities done by people with skill and imagination" (Merriam-Webster).

Those of us brought up in the West recognize and have probably learned about specific paintings, statues, poems, and perhaps some pieces of "art music," or "classical music." But at the same time, when you reflect on it, this definition of the arts is not completely satisfactory—there is an artistic dimension to many other aspects of life from the design of clothes to home furnishings, and from the design of cars to houses. In the ancient world, the concept of "art" was applied broadly, including any purposeful human activity—as we sometimes say of a difficult task, "There's an art to that." The Greek philosopher Aristotle defined art as the ability to make, which could include anything from shipbuilding to governing a city.[1]

The Lutheran scholar Gene Edward Veith helpfully distinguishes between everyday objects which are made with aesthetic beauty in mind (e.g., houses, home furnishings, clothes, etc.,) and "fine arts," things that are made solely for the purpose of admiring their beauty. A painting in a museum exists solely to be appreciated in its own right. Veith argues convincingly: "In the fine arts, aesthetics and meaning are expressed in their most intense and purposeful way. Fine art demands close attention. Whereas the musak played in the grocery store is only soothing background noise, a Beethoven symphony should be listened to in its own right."[2]

The philosopher Sir Roger Scruton (1944–2020) explained that "Works of art are expressly *presented* as objects of contemplation" and he described the appreciation of art in this way: "As soon as we are engaged in generating and appreciating objects as ends in themselves, rather than as means to our desires and purposes, we demand these objects be ordered and meaningful."[3]

Let's note that the arts flourish in times of peace and prosperity. It is when a community generates sufficient wealth through trade that the middle and lower classes can afford to spend money creating or appreciating fine arts, and have sufficient time away from daily toils to do so.[4] Without this expansion of opportunity, the fine arts would remain confined to the elites of society and mostly hidden from view.

The consideration of "fine art," something worthy of contemplation for its own sake, is very important to understanding "classical music." Many pieces of classical music were composed for their own beauty and enjoyment—without any additional practical purpose like dance or military music—and yet, when those classical works reflect God's order and design, they have intrinsic importance. As Martin Luther wrote, "I would like to see all the arts, especially music, used in the service of him who gave and made them."[5]

(Although, strictly speaking, the "classical" era in Western music refers to music composed from the mid-eighteenth to early nineteenth centuries, this book uses the term in the common way to describe art music—serious music as distinguished from popular or folk music.)

Appreciating Beauty

Abraham Kuyper (1837–1920) was a leading Dutch theologian and statesman. His lecture *Calvinism and Art,* one of six lectures he gave at Princeton Seminary in 1898, is a brilliant and profound exploration of the biblical view of the arts. Kuyper argues that mankind is capable of being artistic because he is made in the image of God, who is the source of all beauty. We may "imitate God's handiwork. . .the beautiful is not the product of our own fantasy, nor of our subjective perception, but has an objective existence, being itself the expression of a Divine perfection."[6]

Kuyper insisted that an appreciation of beauty ("the aesthetic life") has a valuable and independent place as an aspect of human personality: "Our intellectual, ethical, religious and aesthetic life each commands a sphere of its own. These spheres run parallel and do not allow the derivation of one from the other." He went on to describe how this is given by and inseparable from God our Creator.[7]

In this, Kuyper takes his lead from John Calvin directly. Commenting on Exodus 31, in which God calls Bezaleel and Aholiab to make the Tabernacle, Calvin says: "No one excels even in the most despised and humble handicraft, except in so far as God's Spirit works in him." [8] This is not only true of the spiritual gifts given to those who are born again, but also to people generally in every area of life by God's common grace.

Kuyper summed up Calvin's view that art is a gift of God and artistic endeavors should imitate God:

> In view of all this we may say that Calvin esteemed art, in all its ramifications, as a gift of God, or, more especially, as a gift of the Holy Ghost; that he fully grasped the profound effects worked by art upon the life of the emotions; that he appreciated the end for which art has been given, viz., that by it we might glorify God, and ennoble human life, and drink at the fountain of higher pleasures, yea even of common sport; and finally, that so far from considering art as a mere imitation of nature, he attributed to it the noble vocation of disclosing to man a higher reality than was offered to us by this sinful and corrupted world.[9]

Looking ahead by faith to the new creation, Kuyper asserted that art can remind us of the beauty that was lost at Eden and which will be restored when Christ makes all things new: "Standing by the ruins of this once so wonderfully beautiful creation, art points out to the Calvinist both the still visible lines of the original plan, and what is even more, the splendid restoration by which the Supreme Artist and Master-Builder will one day renew and enhance even the beauty of his original creation."[10]

True, Good, and Beautiful

Herman Bavinck was another Dutch theologian and teacher of vast learning, who systematically applied the biblical worldview to all of life. Bavinck's essay *On Beauty and Aesthetics* is particularly helpful as we consider a biblical perspective on music and the arts in general (the philosophy of beauty is called "aesthetics").[11] Bavinck explains that what is good, true, and beautiful comes from God because they are aspects of his character. Although the ancient Greeks taught similar ideas, Christian theologians such as Augustine defined them biblically. In fact, later Protestant theologians would define the "beautiful" more in terms of God's majesty or glory.

Bavinck argues that the form or content of beauty in creation is derived from what is true and good, so that beauty cannot be independent from them or placed on the same level. His definition of beauty is illuminating: "Beauty consists in the agreement with content and form, with essence (idea) and appearance; it exists in harmony, proportion, unity in diversity, organization, glow, glory, shining, fullness, perfection revealed [*perfectio phaenomenon*] or whatever one wants to name it. But beauty always is in relation to form, revelation, and appearance."[12] Later he comments that "because it deals with appearance and observation, it is tied more closely to the luxury of life than the true and the good, and it reached freedom and independence much later."[13]

A biblical theology of the arts establishes that what is good, true, and beautiful is given by God. It is therefore objective. It is not relative, dependent on our feelings. However, man's appreciation of beauty varies. Bavinck explores this in elevated prose:

> We cannot express in words what a valuable gift the Creator of all things has granted to his children. He is the Lord of glory and spreads his beauty lavishly before our eyes in all his works. His name is precious in the whole earth, and while he did not leave us without a witness, he also fills our hearts with happiness when we observe that glory. Beauty and the sense of beauty respond to each other, as the noble object

> and the knowing subject, the *religio objectiva* [responding] to the *religio subjectiva*. Truly, awareness of beauty cannot be fully explained as "empathy"; when observing and enjoying true beauty, it is not man who bestows his affections and moods on the observed object, but it is God's glory that meets and enlightens us in our perceptive spirits through the works of nature and art. Humanity and the world are related because they are both related to God. The same reason, the same spirit, the same order lives in both. Beauty is the harmony that still shines through the chaos in the world; by God's grace, beauty is observed, felt, translated by artists; it is prophecy and guarantee that this world is not destined for ruin but for glory—a glory for which there is a longing deep in every human heart.[14]

Beyond Our Emotions

Writing thirty years later, the Christian apologist C.S. Lewis in his polemical work *The Abolition of Man* made a similar case for the objectively created order that determines standards of right and wrong, worthy and unworthy: "Until quite modern times all teachers and even all men believed the universe to be such that certain emotional reactions on our part could be either congruous or incongruous to it—believed, in fact, that objects did not merely receive, but could *merit* our approval or disapproval, our reverence or our contempt."[15]

Lewis saw that the Western world was increasingly turning within and making man, specifically the feelings of the individual, the measure of all things. But he reaches back to antiquity, citing Augustine and also the Greek philosophers: "St. Augustine defines virtue *ordo amoris,* the ordinate condition of the affections in which every object is accorded that kind of degree of love which is appropriate to it. Aristotle says that the aim of education is to make the pupil like and dislike what he ought."[16]

Plato taught that children, by learning to distinguish between good and bad, valuable and worthless, would develop good character: "In the *Republic,* the well-nurtured youth is one 'who would see most clearly whatever was amiss in ill-made works of man or ill-grown works of nature and with a just distaste would blame and hate the ugly, even from his earliest years and would give delighted praise to beauty, receiving it into his soul and being nourished by it, so that he becomes a man of gentle heart.'"[17] (See Chapter 17—*Music and Character.*)

The non-Christian philosophers of ancient Greece could see that beauty is an objective reality. But only the Christian looks by faith to the triune God as the source of all beauty and responds, by God's grace, with a thankful heart. As Herman Bavinck concluded, "Because beauty is such a rich, divine gift, it also must be loved by us."[18]

5

Objective Beauty

Beauty is an objective reality given by God, but how do we describe what is beautiful and distinguish it from what is ugly? Let's now look in more detail at how we can assess beauty.

You have probably heard someone say he or she likes a particular piece of music because "it makes me feel good." This is not an objective description of the quality of the music, but it could tell us a lot about his or her taste. It also points to an important truth—good music should not be judged by our feelings, but by using our minds.

R.C. Sproul once wrote: "I am convinced that if we look in the Scriptures we'll see that God is a God of beauty. He's the ultimate foundation of beauty, and his character is beautiful. Part of the task of man is to mirror and reflect the character of God. That means we are called to produce art and that that art be excellent."[1] Dr. Sproul taught that Western civilization has recognized four "transcendent norms of beauty":[2]

- Proportion
- Harmony
- Simplicity
- Complexity

He noted "these basic principles of proportion, harmony, simplicity, and complexity can be found in the art of painting, sculpture, dance, music, literature, and all the other various art forms that we know."[3]

These are the four essential ingredients which unite in something that is beautiful. Christians recognize these norms to flow from the character of the God who created the cosmos, who is the source of the good, the true, and the beautiful. But the modern secular worldview rejects all ultimate standards of beauty. This is not surprising, because it rejects God the Creator. The popular view today in the West is that everything is relative and there are no grounds for saying one thing is more beautiful than another. Yet, as creatures made in the image of God, the capacity for people to appreciate beauty has not been completely erased. In fact, it still reemerges in surprising ways.

In late 2018, controversy erupted in the United Kingdom when its government appointed the "Building Better, Building Beautiful" commission. The then Housing Secretary said: "It is not just about personal taste. There are basic things that make a good building—elements of design and principles of beauty."[4] In the US in 2020, the then presidential administration issued an executive order promoting classical styles of architecture over modernist styles in new Federal buildings. It is rare in the modern era for political elites to acknowledge what should be obvious—the worldview of secularism has bequeathed us many ugly modern buildings which defy the principles of beauty.

Aspects of Beauty

From Genesis 1 onward, our Creator is revealed to be the God of order, not chaos. Wherever we look in creation—to the heavens above or to the earth beneath—we see proportion and harmony in what God has made. In his work *The Nature of True Virtue*, Jonathan Edwards describes this "natural beauty" in creation. This beauty "consists in a mutual consent and agreement of different things, in form, manner, quantity, and visible end or design; called by the various names of regularity, order, uniformity, symmetry, proportion, harmony, etc." In this, Edwards is expounding the classical understanding of beauty endorsed by Augustine and dating further back in antiquity.[5] As examples, Edwards gives the pattern on a chess board, the human body or face, and the "various notes of a melodious tune."

Edwards goes on to talk about beauty as unity in diversity. He cites his contemporary Francis Hutcheson's observation that the greater the variety is in equal uniformity, the greater the beauty[6] and comments, "Which is no more than to say, the more there are of different mutually agreeing things, the greater is the beauty. And the reason of that is, because it is more considerable to have many things consent one with another, than a few only."

The unity and diversity all around us in creation leads us back to the triune God, who is one-in-three and three-in-one. As Herman Bavinck explained a century later, "The unity and diversity in the works of God proceeds from and returns to the unity and diversity which exist in the Divine Being. That Being is one being, single and simple. At the same time that being is threefold in His person, in His revelation, and in His influence. The entire work of God is an unbroken whole, and nevertheless comprises the richest variety and change."[7]

Let's continue thinking about architecture as an example of human invention. Some buildings have greater levels of unity in diversity than others, and this affects how we think about them. A vast, ancient cathedral draws together many different elements in one united building. It is more beautiful, for example, than a homely log cabin which is both small and has little diversity. While a log cabin on the American frontier may have charm, we do not tend to say it is breathtaking when we step inside.

Jonathan Edwards put it this way: "Thus, the symmetry of the parts of a human body, or countenance, affects the mind more than the beauty of a flower. So the beauty of the solar system, more than as great and as manifold an order and uniformity in a tree. And the proportions of the parts of a church, or a palace, more than the same proportions in some little slight compositions, made to please children."[8] He is saying that we may think a doll's house is cute, but a magnificent old palace far surpasses it in beauty. I have visited beautiful old palaces and castles in the United Kingdom and continental Europe, and there is a lot to take in. I have also enjoyed looking round old cottages connected to famous people (e.g., William Shakespeare or the engineer George Stephenson), but it doesn't take very long because there is not actually much to see.

Diversity without unity is not beautiful. Edwards gives the example of seeing random columns scattered around the countryside. With nothing to unite them, or bring them together, they cannot be called beautiful. (The modern Scottish Parliament Building in Edinburgh exhibits this affliction.) In the realm of music, we can equally say that random notes played by different orchestral instruments cannot be considered objectively beautiful. Yet such performances continue to be promoted today by the avant-garde movement. Iannis Xenakis (1922–2001), an architect and avant-garde composer, wrote works that give the deliberate impression of random noise and shifting shapes. In fact, the musical score for his piece *Metastasis* (1953) exhibits the same shapes as the Philips pavilion building that Xenakis designed at the same time.[9]

Music and Architecture

We can compare musical compositions to architecture in important ways. As diverse physical materials are gathered and put together to construct a building, so the sounds of instruments and voices are organized to build a piece of music. Earlier we considered the beauty of St. Paul's Cathedral in London. Its columns are not scattered randomly throughout the building, but rather are measured and selected to fit into the united whole of the structure. There is a clear parallel here to the balance, order, and harmony of renowned pieces of classical music, such as Bach's Mass in B minor, the Beethoven piano concerti, or Brahms' symphonies. Pick up the music study score to one of these great works and you can see the patterns and shapes as the musical lines rise and fall, and how the different groups of instruments make up the structure of the piece.

Music is building with sound. The connection between music and architecture has been commented on for centuries. Indeed, the nineteenth-century German philosopher Schelling called architecture "frozen music." The conductor Sir John Eliot Gardiner illustrated this in writing about J.S. Bach's *St. John Passion*: "I would suggest that the multi-layered structure underpinning Bach's Passion can be 'felt', if not immediately seen or heard, by the listener in the same way that flying buttresses, invisible to the visitor when entering a Gothic church are essential to the illusion of lightness, weightlessness and the impression of height. In fact, the longer you study them, the more numerous seem to be the geometric patterns of repetition, symmetry, and cross-referring, varying in the sharpness or thinness of their outlines."[10]

If you are new to architecture, Quinlan Terry's captivating book *The Layman's Guide to Classical Architecture* will open up new horizons for you. Terry—one of the leading present-day classical architects—explains that our pleasure in a building "will be enhanced by understanding how each part relates to the rest, in the same way that those who understand Classical music know what to expect when they enjoy listening to a great symphony."[11] Sir Roger Scruton noted particularly how the details in music and in architecture are set within an overall form that holds it all together. For example, the moldings, window-frames, and subsidiary columns of a great building can each be viewed as a small-scale unit yet they are in harmony with the whole: "In just such a way," he wrote, "the large-scale organization of keys and harmonic structures will cause us to hear the musical details in relation to them."[12]

Moreover, both good music and good architecture rely on traditions, patterns established by those who have gone before us, who have worked out down the generations "what works" and what does not work.[13] As music critic Jay Nordlinger has written, "composers are a family, learning from one another, borrowing from one another, building on one another—all intertwined."[14] This is very different from other aspects of life such as Latin grammar or algebra, which are intrinsically based on specific rules. It's why we can think of music and architectural design as arts, which require good judgment and taste.

Another helpful parallel is to consider that a piece of music stands in its own right, as does a building. Since the Romantic era, it has been popular for instrumental music to be "program music," which describes a story, a picture, or place (for example, Beethoven's sixth symphony—*Pastoral*). But music does not need an external meaning to validate it. It should be listened to for what it is. We should appreciate a piece of music for the music, as we admire a beautiful palace for being a palace or a fine castle for being a castle.

The great pieces of classical music were composed, and many of the world's finest buildings were made, in the West where the worldview was shaped by the Bible. Scripture teaches that the creation is real and the God-given place for work (Genesis 1 and 2 onward). This truth was accepted in much of the Western world for the past thousand years and has led to immense advances in scholarship, technology, and manufacturing. All combined so that human inventiveness developed an advanced system of musical notation and more varied and more refined musical instruments than ever before. And therefore musicians composed in more complex ways than ever before. Many of those involved may have been benefiting from the biblical worldview by God's common grace, without themselves being born-again Christians. And today people globally can enjoy this musical heritage—witness how many leading conductors and performers of classical music are from east Asia or other parts of the world.

Perceiving Beauty

Christians must insist that beauty is objective, real, and not a matter of personal choice—because true beauty has been set in this world by God. We often hear the saying, "Beauty is in the eye of beholder," but that is pure relativism. Some people are better at perceiving beauty than others, but that does not make all concepts of beauty relative. We should learn to exercise taste and discrimination in identifying what is objectively beautiful by learning more about the different arts.

Gene Edward Veith writes that the ancient Greek philosophers, followed by major Christian theologians such as Augustine and Thomas Aquinas distinguished two faculties of the mind—the *ratio* and the *intellectus*. *Ratio* is the mind's ability to think rationally, to use logic to draw conclusions. The *intellectus* is the faculty of "immediately perceiving truth, intuitively and directly."[15] These are deep waters, but for our purposes this is helpful because these authors locate the appreciation of beauty in the *intellectus*, in the mind. Although it involves feelings, "beauty is perceived by the intellect. . . . When we see something beautiful, our intellects experience a flash of satisfaction and joy."

The mind is a faculty of the soul (see Chapter 14—*The Bible and the Soul*). Contrary to some popular authors today, our minds are not simply biological processes of the brain. The mind is that aspect of our soul that we use to form judgments and make decisions. This underscores the importance, as we considered earlier, of realizing music's impact on man's soul. It also explains why sometimes non-Christians are prone to use spiritual expressions to describe their appreciation of music (e.g., "transcendent" or "heavenly").

Why has God given humans the capacity to appreciate beauty? As Herman Bavinck reflected, ". . .beauty always awakens in us images, moods, and affections that otherwise would have remained dormant and not even known to us. Beauty thus discloses us to our ourselves and also grants us another, new glimpse into nature and humanity. It deepens, broadens, enriches our inner life, and it lifts us for a moment above the dreary, sinful, sad reality; beauty also brings cleansing, liberation, revival to our burdened and dejected hearts." [16]

6

Thinking about Music

Music is given by God in his common grace to people throughout the world. A countless number of songs, instrumental pieces, and other works have been composed and performed down the millennia. Since beauty is objective, how do you identify beauty in music? How do you know what to listen for? Which pieces are worth getting to know well?

The human voice is the original musical instrument for mankind. Martin Luther waxed eloquent about it, saying, "So abundant and incomprehensible is here the munificence and wisdom of our most gracious Creator. Philosophers have labored to explain the marvelous instrument of the human voice."[1] In light of all we have considered about the central place of music in the created order, we can be certain that mankind has sung since the days of our first parents, Adam and Eve, in the garden of Eden. Those days of perfection inevitably included singing songs of praise to God, as commanded throughout the Scriptures (e.g., Ps. 47:6; Ps. 105:1–3; 1 Chron. 16:9).

Solo songs have been sung through the ages about love, hope, happiness, grief, or to relate truths, myths, stories. Various folk tunes have survived in most cultures down to today. Some have a memorable simplicity such as the Appalachian carol, *I wonder as I wander, Scarborough Fair* from England, or the spiritual *Swing Low, Sweet Chariot.*

Since the days of Jubal, mankind has been making instruments using pipes or strings, either to accompany song or dance or to perform purely instrumental music. Archaeologists have uncovered many animal bones bored with holes to be played as flutes from centuries ago in America, the British Isles, and elsewhere. There are depictions of harps dating back thousands of years in Egypt. Sadly, we usually have little idea what the instrumental music of now-lost cultures actually sounded like.

Looking around the world today, different types of traditional music have survived, including gamelan in Indonesia that uses tuned and untuned metal percussion such as gongs and drums. Traditional Chinese music employs plucked stringed instruments such as the qin or the zheng, together with voice and percussion. There is evidence for bagpipes being used by different cultures around the world for thousands of years.

You may have noticed that I have not so far defined *music*. That is because people generally know what the word means. Yet the degradation of music over the past century in the West makes it important to distinguish music from mere sounds. It is not simply the organization of sound—because noises can be organized in many ways that are not recognizably *music*. Think of the repetitive beep of a reversing truck or an emergency siren. In contrast, music is designed to be beautiful.

> *Music is the organization of sound according to the objective principles of beauty.*

This definition is important to understanding the nature of music and how it should be appreciated. We will return to this later and also ask if everything labeled "music" today is really music, or actually a distortion of music? Some avant-garde compositions over the past century are openly presented as assortments of noise rather than music.

Tonality

While the best solo songs are undoubtedly attractive, they do not reach the same heights of beauty as one of the great works of classical music. Why is that? Consider the essential ingredients of beauty: proportion, harmony, simplicity, and complexity. Old solo folksongs may possess a simple charm and a proportion in their constituent phrases, but there is little complexity. Alone, they do not have a unity in diversity that comes from combining with other voices or instruments. Thinking back to the analogy with architecture, they are the equivalent of a pleasant English cottage rather than a royal palace.

The great, palatial works of classical music are built by combining many different voices or instruments harmoniously in one united whole. A casual listener today may not realize it, but the existence of this music is only possible because of the discovery of *tonality*. The development of modern Western music is inseparable from the establishment of the tonal system, which allows melody and harmony to work together in almost infinite variety.

Tonality as a concept has been defined in different ways, but, at its core, it is music that revolves around a *tonic*. When a passage of music returns to its tonic, it feels like it has returned "home." Whatever tonal regions may be explored during the piece, there is a sense of completion when it ends in the tonic key.

The tonic note gives the name to the scale which is based on it, e.g., C in C major, or G in G minor. The tonic triad, composed of the tonic plus the third and fifth notes above it, provides the defining chord of a piece. The keys (C major/G minor etc.,) show what scale a piece is based on and so which notes should be used.

Today, it is easy to take the tonal system, with its orderly arrangement of keys, for granted, but it is a priceless inheritance that allows different musical lines or voices to combine in harmony. The invention of the tonal system allowed for music to blossom as never before.

There are clear indications in creation that God has provided for melody and harmony (for example in birdsong). Many of the oldest folk tunes rely on the pentatonic scale (this is based on five rather than seven notes), and you can hear it by playing only the black keys on a piano. The pentatonic scale is also evident in birdsong, such as hermit thrushes (see Chapter 2—*Music in Creation*).

The oldest tune to have been reconstructed, a Sumerian song dating back over 3,000 years, clearly points to similar harmonic patterns we recognize today.[2] Traditional music in some other non-Western cultures does not use scales as we know them, divided into whole tones and semitones. There are greater complexities and tonal subtleties in classical Arabian music and Indian scales, yet they are still ultimately tied to the concept of an octave with notes in between that its musicians recognize as either in or out of tune.[3]

The tonal system operates with two distinct types of scale—major and minor—the arrangement of whole tones and semitones is different between the two. It developed over time from the modal system of the medieval world, which in turn had its origins in early Christian church music in Byzantium.[4] Each mode had a different arrangement of tones and semitones; for example, the Dorian mode can be played on a piano by starting on D and playing only white notes for one octave.

The modal system was developed for early medieval plainchant, sung by clergy and religious orders throughout Christendom. Over time, the singing gradually became more elaborate with different notes being sung simultaneously. A major advance came with the building of Notre Dame Cathedral in Paris (begun AD 1163), which led to the rise of full *polyphony*. Composers Léonin and Pérotin (flourished c.1150–c.1200) exploited the vast spaces of the new cathedral to compose motets with independent vocal lines singing simultaneously (polyphonic music).[5]

The Notre Dame school is only one notable example of when the physical space of a great building influenced the composition of music in specific and new ways. Later, around AD 1600, the Gabrieli family in Venice developed antiphonal music using different groups of instruments and voices answering each other in the surroundings of St. Mark's Basilica. A thousand years earlier, the Hagia Sophia in Constantinople (modern day Istanbul) was the inspiration for eastern Orthodox chant and song.

Léonin and Pérotin are remarkable examples of quite complex polyphony, but their reliance on only intervals of fourths, fifths, and octaves between voices gives an "empty" sound to the music. Another century passed before the beginnings of tonality can be heard in some harmonic passages of the French composer Guillaume Machaut (c.1300–1377 AD).[6] Harmonic progressions built on parallel intervals of thirds and sixths were in wider use in fourteenth-century England, but they were popularized by the "full euphonious" music of English composer John Dunstable (c.1385–1453 AD).[7] Little is known about his life, but his music was well-known across Europe. This was profoundly important in the move towards polyphony combined with harmony.

The move toward what we now recognize as harmony was a big departure from the "bare" sounds of earlier composers. Medieval music was bound by mathematical theories and ratios, dating back to the followers of Pythagoras in ancient Greece[8], which rejected harmony in thirds and sixths. For example, the intervals of a fourth and a fifth were considered beautiful, or "perfect," for reasons related to the science of sound (acoustics) and mathematics. It is surely no coincidence that the development of harmony took place in the Renaissance era in the West when mankind's own perception of the world became more important and movement in thirds and sixths, which is more pleasant to the ear, was allowed to take center stage. (This is not to belittle medieval music, which, for example, saw important and sophisticated developments in the use of rhythm.)

The writing of a more harmonic polyphony was continued by composers in the following hundred years so that the basic contours of tonality were set by the end of the Renaissance by great composers such as Palestrina (c.1525–1594) and Lassus (c.1532–1594). In the mid-1500s, the Swiss Humanist Henricus Glareanus proposed additional modes to reflect current musical practice—the Ionian mode, the major scale as we know it today, and the Aeolian mode, our minor scale (without the raised seventh note). The music of Palestrina, for example, typically employs what Glareanus identified as the Ionian or Aeolian modes and so uses tonal language that is familiar to us today.

But the full elaboration of tonality was made possible by the definitive move to equal temperament in the first half of the eighteenth century, of which J.S. Bach was a key exponent. This involves tuning musical instruments so that each octave is divided into twelve equal semitones, rather than tuning for the natural intervals that occur acoustically. Where semitones are not equally divided, various keys differ widely in how they sound. In some keys the music's harmonies can become very strained to the ear (look out for recordings of organ music, for example, played on instruments with the older "meantone" or "just" intonation). Yet, even in equal temperament, keys "by virtue of their physical properties within the equal system of tuning and its corresponding overtone series, have colors and qualities. Some are more powerful than others; some are brighter, while others are more melancholy."[9]

Although there is scholarly debate about to what extent Bach fully practiced equal temperament, he clearly favored tuning that allowed music to move freely in all twelve major and all twelve minor keys. Bach's famous keyboard work *The Well-Tempered Clavier* was written for this purpose and in total has two pairs of preludes and fugues in all twenty-four keys, hence it is also known by musicians as "the 48."

Reflecting on Tonality

The tonal system organizes sound to allow for great harmonic and melodic complexity. In the hands of the best composers, tonality provides the palette of sound for the most magnificent music of voices and instruments, as you would expect from the principles of objective beauty. Tonality in the time of Bach saw the composition of complex and impressive pieces for voices and for organ, but the full flowering of its potential came with the invention and refinement of the instruments that make up the symphony orchestra.

I do not say that only tonal music can be beautiful. Modal music such as solo folk songs and plainchant can be exquisite. However, they are not as objectively beautiful as the great pieces in the canon of classical music because they lack the complexity of uniting with other voices or instruments in harmony. (Several early twentieth-century composers used modes to provide contrasting color to their work.) Neither do I say that all tonal music is beautiful; it can be bland, offensive, peculiar, and worse—as a building made of great stones can be dull, ugly, or badly constructed.

God gave man the capacity to invent and have dominion over the world by using its resources (Gen. 1:28). Organizing sound as music is one demonstration of this, like organizing the materials needed to build a house. In particular, the discovery of tonality by the inventiveness of composers allowed the greatest expression of music by uniting polyphony and harmony in ever greater complexity.

The opposite of harmony in music is discord, a combination of notes that clash together, sounds that are not in harmony. Usually in tonal music, composers resolve a discord into notes that harmonize together. In fact, composers well know that a discord, such as a suspension, which then resolves in the next chord, can be very beautiful. The apotheosis of a great piece of music is, in many cases, the wonderful resolution of a suspension. For example, *Crucifixus* by Antonio Lotti (1667–1740) builds a series of suspensions, which continually resolve, reaching a high point about two-thirds of the way through the piece.

Perhaps, in this fallen world, music which resolves discord into harmony is looking forward to the new creation, where God will transform this creation into a new world where everything is in perfect harmony.

7

Surveying Composers

We have inherited a rich tapestry of music in the tonal system. These treasures comprise pieces from different countries, with abundant variety of music for instruments and/or voices. The great works of the classical music canon have an enduring quality that is widely recognized, and their composers are justly famous. That is not to say that all pieces by well-known composers of the past are objectively beautiful, but starting with their works that are still performed today provides the surest ground for appreciating good music.

Remember, the only way to learn about beautiful music is to listen to, or, better still, to perform great works. Reading about music is no substitute for experiencing music itself. We can be thankful that for the past 150 years, since Thomas Edison invented the phonograph, recordings of musical performances have been available, and by our day in amazing quality. While even the best digital recordings do not have the thrill and immediacy of being in the audience during a live concert performance, they do open up a world of music to anyone who makes the time to listen. So, especially if you don't yet read music, search online for the pieces mentioned below and listen to some of them!

There are four basic elements of music: pitch, melody, harmony, and rhythm. When you listen to a piece of classical music, this is what you hear. The American composer Aaron Copland (1900–1990) wrote a book called *What to Listen for in Music* and in it he also focuses on tone color (or "timbre"), recognizing how different musical instruments have distinct sounds—for example, a violin is easily distinguished from a trumpet.[1] It is unusual for a composer to write a book about how to listen to music, and Copland's stated purpose was particularly to encourage people to listen to what is actually going on in the music rather than simply to enjoy the superficial effect a piece has on them. Copland's book includes a guide to different musical structures ("forms") that composers use to build pieces of music, e.g., variation, fugue, or sonata form.

The objective principles of beauty are manifested differently in Western music over time and as different genres develop (e.g., the concerto, symphony, or opera). What follows is a survey of works by great composers in Western music history. It is, of course, impossible to capture centuries of music in a few pages, and a survey cannot explore the cultural context of each composer's life and output. But the men mentioned here are significant signposts on the way from the Renaissance to the modern era, and this tour is offered as a launchpad for further exploration of classical music.

Although there are not sharp dividing lines between the different musical periods (Renaissance, Baroque etc.), these categories can help place where composers and their works belong chronologically and identify developments over time.

Renaissance (1400–1600 AD)

The Renaissance took place later in music than in the other arts.[2] While folk music of the era was certainly varied, with songs either unaccompanied or accompanied by instruments such as the lute, the most enduring pieces were typically those for choir, either sacred (usually masses or motets) or secular (e.g., madrigals). One of the earliest of the Renaissance composers was Englishman John Dunstable (c. 1385–1453), whose persuasive adoption of harmonies based on thirds and sixths paved the way for tonality. Significant composers of the early/mid-Renaissance era include Guillaume Dufay (1397–1474) and Josquin des Prez (c. 1450–1521).

Giovanni Pierluigi da Palestrina (c. 1525–1594), who was born in the town of Palestrina, Italy, was probably the greatest composer of the Renaissance. His choral works have been preserved, performed, and studied since his death. The smooth polyphony, in which each voice part has an equal footing and often moves stepwise between notes, sounds effortless, but shows his technical mastery of counterpoint (the art of composing for two or more voices at once).

Palestrina's motet *Super Flumina Babylonis* is a setting of Psalm 137 and poignantly portrays the grief of the Israelites exiled in Babylon.

Musical Example 1: Palestrina, *Super Flumina Babylonis*

A famous contemporary of Palestrina, who died in the same year, was the Flemish composer Orlandus Lassus (c. 1532–1594). Lassus was also a master of sacred polyphony, but his settings of secular songs are a more well-known part of his output. His music can be more intense and vigorous than typical Palestrina. This is a sparkling madrigal *O occhi, manza mia.*

Musical Example 2: Lassus, *O occhi, manza mia*

Two of the best-known English composers of the Renaissance are Thomas Tallis (c. 1505–1585) and his pupil William Byrd (c.1540–1623). Tallis was principally a church musician and his settings of liturgy for choir have been preserved to our time; they are of quite different styles, depending on the twists and turns of the Reformation in England. His motet *Spem in Alium* for 40 individual voices is one of the most extraordinary pieces of any era. The short anthem, *If Ye Love Me, Keep My Commandments,* based on Jesus' words recorded in John 14:15, has a beautiful simplicity.

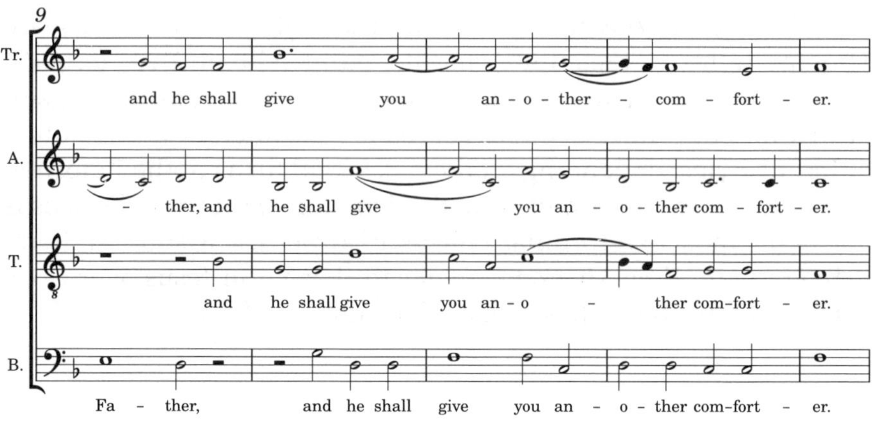

Musical Example 3: Tallis, *If Ye Love Me, Keep My Commandments*

Christians today do not usually think of the early Protestant hymn tunes as examples of Renaissance music, but that is the era in which they were composed. The Reformation impacted music as much as everyday life. The rediscovery of the Word of God in the days of Luther, Tyndale, Calvin, and Knox drastically changed the music used in worship.

The Reformers recognized the New Testament emphasis on congregational singing in worship (see Chapter 19—*Music in Church History*). This led to the composition of hymn tunes and psalm tunes. Thomas Tallis provided tunes for a psalter published c.1567, including the one we know today as *Tallis' Canon*. (A "canon" is a musical device in which the same melody is sung by different voices beginning at different times. In this case, the tenor copies the treble line, entering four beats later.)

Martin Luther himself composed early chorale (congregational hymn) tunes, most notably *Ein Feste Burg* ("A Mighty Fortress"). Louis Bourgeois (1510–1559) worked with John Calvin in Geneva and composed several new tunes to accompany the psalms, playing a part in the development of the Genevan Psalter. The most widely known psalm tune attributed to Bourgeois is *Old Hundredth*, typically set to Psalm 100 ("All People That on Earth Do Dwell").

Musical Example 4: Bourgeois, *Old Hundredth*

In succeeding decades, composers began to arrange and develop chorale tunes on a larger scale. The German Michael Praetorius (1571–1621) composed and arranged many of these tunes; some are quite elaborate and require eight to twelve voice parts. The Christmas carol *Lo, How a Rose E'er Blooming,* sung in many churches today, is an arrangement by Praetorius of an earlier German melody.

The Roman Catholic Counter-Reformation of the sixteenth century sought to adjust its church music so that the words were not submerged by the polyphony. Yet Roman Catholic music for worship services remained much more elaborate than that of Protestants. During this era, music at St. Mark's Basilica in Venice was led by Andrea Gabrieli (c. 1532–1585), then by his nephew Giovanni (c. 1555–1612), who both composed large-scale ceremonial works for church and state.

Andrea Gabrieli composed a wide range of sacred and secular pieces, but is particularly noteworthy for using the vast spaces of the Basilica to place different choirs around the building ("cori spezzati"), which would answer each other as an integral feature of these "antiphonal" pieces. His nephew Giovanni continued the

Venetian tradition—in particular Giovanni developed the role of instrumental music to accompany the choirs. His purely instrumental music is among the first to specify the intended instrument(s) and to indicate dynamic markings (loud, soft, etc.)—things we take for granted today.

The vivid and dramatic contrasts of Venetian music at this time heralded the dawn of the Baroque period. The most famous of these composers today is the Italian Claudio Monteverdi (1567–1643). He openly explained that he was composing in a new way—moving from music that dominates the words, to words that dominate the music and shifting from polyphony to *homophony,* where one voice part is dominant, and the others function to provide the harmony. His new style is evident in his *Vespers* of 1610, as well as his opera *Orfeo,* one of the earliest Baroque operas. Both works contain virtuoso solo passages that accentuate the meaning of the text. By this time, it is clear that a desire for music to express the words had become a primary concern[3] (see Chapter 15—*Music and the Soul*).

Baroque (1600–1750 AD)

The German composer Heinrich Schütz (1585–1672) was an important composer of the early Baroque era. Schütz, a pupil of Giovanni Gabrieli and perhaps Monteverdi, took the Italian style back north to Germany. His compositional work focuses mainly on sacred texts, and there is clear evidence of Schütz' personal Christian faith. His earlier works can be more overtly dramatic, while his later style tends to be simpler, including his three unaccompanied settings of the Passion narratives (Luke, John, and Matthew).

Henry Purcell (1659–1695) died young but could fairly be claimed as the most talented composer England has ever produced. (Fans of Elgar or Vaughan Williams may disagree, but they should listen to more Purcell.) Above all, his vocal compositions show great subtlety and expressiveness that exactly reflect the meaning of the text. The aria "When I am Laid in Earth" from his opera *Dido and Aeneas* features a haunting soprano solo set against a chromatic ground bass (repeating bass line). Purcell's many sacred works for choir include a joyful and varied setting of Psalm 96 *O Sing Unto the Lord* and "The Bell Anthem" *Rejoice in the Lord Alway,* which is a sparkling setting of Philippians 4 for soloists and choir.

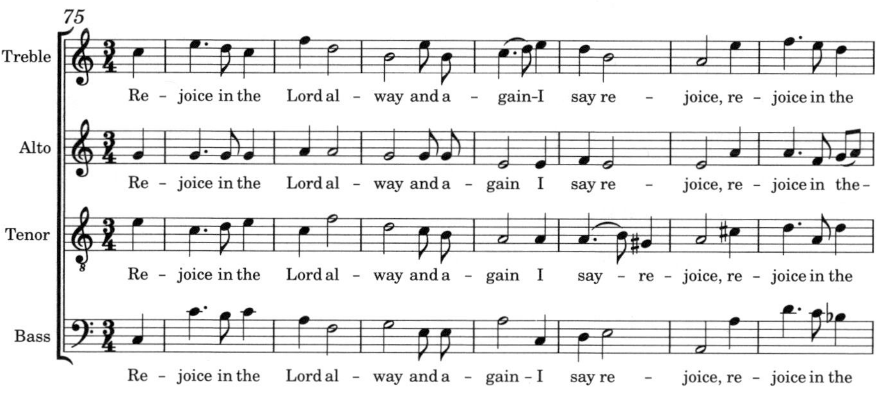

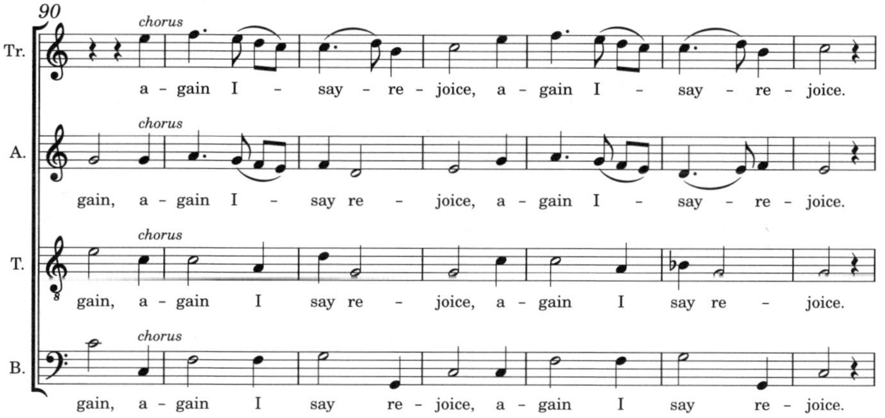

Musical Example 5: Purcell, *Rejoice in the Lord Alway*

Dietrich Buxtehude (c.1637–1707) was of Danish/North German origins and rose to become a famous organist in Lübeck, so famous that J.S. Bach as a young man (in 1705) travelled 260 miles to spend time learning from him. Buxtehude is principally remembered today for his organ music, though he also wrote music for choir and some chamber music.

Purely instrumental music, pieces without singers, blossomed during the Baroque period. As Claude Palisca noted, "More than at any other time in the history of music, the capabilities of instruments and the aspirations of their players were having a deep effect on musical style."[4] Although the violin family of instruments was invented in the early sixteenth century, the subsequent refinement of violins, violas, and violincellos ("cellos" as we usually call them) in the Baroque era brought them center stage and led to the development of recognizably orchestral music.

Jean-Baptiste Lully (1632–1687), a naturalized Frenchman originally from Italy, was conductor of King Louis XIV of France's personal violin orchestra, and Lully composed important operas, music for other stage works, and instrumental dance pieces. In the operas of Jean-Philippe Rameau (1683–1764), his most distinguished successor in France, we hear touches of modern orchestral writing. Rameau wrote a *Treatise on Harmony* (1722) which argued that the triad should be considered the basis of tonality. This was farsighted and accurate.

Venice's powerful influence continued with the music of Antonio Vivaldi (1678–1741). He was the son of a Venetian violinist, who became a fine violinist in his own right. Vivaldi composed hundreds of concerti for orchestra and solo instrument, and he established the concerto's typical fast/slow/fast three-movement form. The best-known of these today are *The Four Seasons* violin concerti, a set of four pieces for solo violin and orchestra that vividly depict the seasons of the year. The first one—*Spring*—has a bright and bustling opening (see overleaf), portraying the singing of birds and flowing streams. The slow movement of the second piece—*Summer*—recreates the stagnant air of a sultry day, moving suddenly into a final movement evoking a thunderstorm and featuring a scintillating violin solo.

Musical Example 6: Vivaldi, *Concerto in E (Spring),* First movement

The third piece—*Autumn*—paints a picture of rural dancing and thanksgiving, followed by a rather stately hunt. The collection ends with a fourth concerto—*Winter*—in which you can at first almost hear people shivering in the freezing cold, but there follows a beautiful slow movement depicting a happy gathering inside round a roaring fire. Vivaldi composed many operas and also pieces of fine sacred vocal music, including his *Gloria,* and at least two settings of Psalm 110 (*Dixit Dominus*).

J.S. Bach was one of many composers to learn from Vivaldi's works, and he transcribed several of them for keyboard. Bach was descended from a long line of German musicians and would rise to become justly recognized as the greatest composer of all time. J.S. Bach's works for voices and instruments demonstrate the heights of musical craftsmanship, and in them he aims for the glory of God. We will return to Bach a little later, but no account of Western music is complete without its greatest genius. Each *Brandenburg Concerto* by Bach is a delight that showcases his talents, often using Baroque dance forms, and wonderfully balancing the instrumental lines.

Musical Example 7: J.S. Bach, *Brandenburg Concerto No. 5,* First movement, BWV 1050

George Frederick Handel (1685–1759) was born in Germany in the same year as J.S. Bach. Handel spent time in Italy as a young adult, which influenced his musical output, but his music began to enjoy most success in England. It was a happy providence for him when his German patron, the Elector of Hanover, became King George I of England in 1714, and Handel settled in those green and pleasant lands, becoming one of its most-loved adopted sons.

Handel wrote forty operas in his career, as well as choral pieces and purely instrumental works. The latter include *Music for the Royal Fireworks*, the *Water Music*, and his concerti grossi for orchestra and harpsichord. Bach's *Brandenburg Concerti* are also in concerto grosso form—where full orchestra alternates with a smaller group of soloists (rather than a single soloist). Handel's *Twelve Grand Concerti* (op. 6) have multiple movements and take inspiration from concerti by the earlier Baroque composer Arcangelo Corelli (1653-1713). Number 11 in A major shows Handel effortlessly mixing elegance, playful imitation, and lively interest.

Handel's anthems for the coronation of King George II alternate pieces of joy and solemnity for choir and orchestral accompaniment, opening with the famous *Zadok the Priest.* Handel weaves harmony and rhythm expertly together in the orchestral introduction, and the tension gradually builds to the choir's triumphal entry singing "Zadok the priest and Nathan the prophet anointed Solomon king" (based on 1 Kings chapter 1). After hearing this resounding and regal piece for the first time, you will understand why it has been performed the coronation of every British monarch since 1727. The other three coronation anthems also use texts from the Old Testament: *My Heart is Inditing* was written for the crowning of Queen Caroline during the ceremony, and has an exhilarating last movement.

Above all, Handel is known today for his oratorio *Messiah,* which premiered in Dublin, Ireland, in 1742. An English oratorio is a large-scale work for vocal soloists, choir, and orchestra on a biblical theme. Handel composed over a dozen of them, including *Israel in Egypt* and *Solomon.* Unlike opera, an oratorio is not a stage drama with costumes etc.; another difference is the prominence of the chorus (full choir) in Handel's oratorios, which shows the influence of the English anthem form dating back to Purcell and earlier. Surely the best known is the "Hallelujah Chorus" from *Messiah.*

51
Trumpet I & II
Timpani
Violin I
Violin II
Viola
Treble
King of Kings, - - - - and Lord of
Alto
King of Kings, - - - - and Lord of
Tenor
for e-ver and e-ver, Ha-lle-lu-jah, Ha-lle - lu-jah,
Bass
for e-ver and e-ver, Ha-lle-lu-jah, Ha-lle - lu-jah,
Cello/Basso continuo

Musical Example 8: Handel, "Hallelujah Chorus", *Messiah*

Messiah sets Bible texts about our Savior Jesus Christ to music in the form of an oratorio. The "Hallelujah Chorus," for example, uses verses from Revelation chapters 11 and 19. One overlooked fact is that the name "Jesus" only features near the end of the work, in the chorus "But Thanks be to God" (1 Cor. 15:57), which must have been deliberate on the part of the librettist Charles Jennens, who compiled the texts for Handel.

The exceptional characteristic of *Messiah* musically is its high quality throughout. A long piece such as this typically has weaker moments, but the beautiful and sublime writing for voices and instruments is consistent from the orchestral overture ("symphony") until the final "Amen Chorus."

It is hard not to see God's providence in the composition of *Messiah,* which Handel accomplished in only three to four weeks. Yet, all musical composition is a gift of God's common grace, so why does this piece in particular occupy such an exalted place in the history of Western music? The answer is likely found in its supreme combination of sublime music with words entirely from the Bible. *Messiah* exclusively uses texts of Holy Scripture, the Word of God which transcends all merely human writing, combined with excellent music composed by a master of the art. Secular authors such as the philosopher Allan Bloom have noted that the greatest works of Western art "were in one way or another responsive to the Bible."[5]

Music has been used to convey truth in song since the days of Eden, and the combination of words and music in singing has been commented on throughout recorded history. Decades before Handel, one of England's greatest poets, John Milton, whose father was a musician, described "Voice and Verse" in his beautiful ode *At a Solemn Music*:

> Blest pair of Sirens, pledges of Heav'n's joy,
> Sphere-born harmonious Sisters, Voice and Verse,
> Wed your divine sounds, and mixt power employ
> Dead things with inbreath'd sense able to pierce,
> And to our high-rais'd fantasy present
> That undisturbed Song of pure concent,
> Ay sung before that saphire-colour'd throne
> To Him that sits thereon

With Saintly shout and solemn Jubilee,
Where the bright Seraphim in burning row
Their loud up-lifted Angel trumpets blow,
And the Cherubic host in thousand choirs
Touch their immortal Harps of golden wires,
With those just Spirits that wear victorious
Palms, Hymns devout and holy Psalms
Singing everlastingly;
That we on Earth with undiscording voice
May rightly answer that melodious noise;
As once we did, till disproportion'd sin
Jarr'd against Nature's chime, and with harsh din
Broke the fair music that all creatures made
To their great Lord, whose love their motion sway'd
In first obedience, and their state of good.
And keep in tune with Heav'n, till God ere long
To His celestial consort us unite,
To live with Him, and sing in endless morn of light.[6]

Classical (1750–1820 AD)

When your friends mention "classical music" today, they are typically thinking of any serious or art music, whenever it was composed. However, in the history of Western music, there is an era known as the Classical period that covers the mid-eighteenth century to the early nineteenth century. As with the earlier musical eras, we cannot be rigid in describing when the Classical period started and ended. For example, the orchestral symphonies by Johann Stamitz (1717–1757), which are vital to the development of music in the Classical era, were composed while Bach and Handel were still alive.

The music of the Classical period reflects a wider cultural concern at the time (seen also in its "neoclassical" architecture) for balance, order, and simplicity inspired by ancient Greece. We also see the continued refinement and establishment of purely instrumental music. Composers developed the "sonata form," which relies on musical themes and their development over a structure with harmonic contrasts. This provides a form, or structure, to compose long instrumental movements in the Classical Symphony. Generally speaking, Classical music is simpler and less ornate than that of the Baroque period.

The two acknowledged masters of the Classical style are Wolfgang Amadeus Mozart (1756–1791) and Franz Joseph Haydn (1732–1809). Mozart was a child prodigy, who started composing at the age of five, and aged seven toured the cultural capitals of Europe with his father and sister. This wide range of musical influences was woven together in his music, which shows great invention and versatility, and which includes dozens of symphonies, concerti, chamber music, and operas.

Mozart and Haydn met, corresponded with each other, and learned from one another's music. This mutual influence is reflected in the set of six string quartets Mozart published in 1785 and dedicated to Haydn. They clearly follow the pattern set by Haydn's 1781 string quartets, which showcase the mature Classical model. Composed for four solo instruments as equal partners (two violins, viola, and cello), these quartets by both composers feature the detailed and comprehensive development of themes, with interchanging moods of drama and finesse. This serious genre of chamber music, contrasting with the more lighthearted chamber music of previous generations, proved lastingly popular with composers.

Drama on a larger scale is found in Mozart's operas, which include all the major types of opera of his day. *The Marriage of Figaro* has a memorable and emphatic overture, which is often performed in symphony orchestra concerts today. Mozart's clarinet concerto is an early masterpiece for this relatively new instrument. He also composed five violin concerti, and four for horn—the jolly final movement of the fourth horn concerto is instantly recognizable. His later symphonies, especially numbers 39–41, are widely recognized for showcasing Mozart's compositional skill. Mozart, as an accomplished pianist, composed and performed in nearly two dozen concerti for piano solo and orchestra. They explored the expressive qualities of the piano, another instrument that came to prominence in the Classical period, and Mozart's compositions contributed to its dominant position during the next century.

Musical Example 9: Mozart, *Piano Concerto No. 23,* Second movement

Franz Joseph Haydn was born in Austria, and his duties as a court musician limited travel until he was in his fifties. Yet the security of his position with aristocratic employers allowed him to compose many pieces and to explore ways of developing the Classical style in music. Haydn was known for his friendly demeanor and optimism, and this is often reflected in his music. He was a prolific composer who wrote in many different genres, ranging from renowned chamber music to large choral works such as his Te Deum No. 2 in C major—a typically bright and boisterous piece that should lift anyone's spirits. Haydn's over 100 symphonies are the most influential of his output: "Through most of his long and full life Haydn gave new dimensions to the symphony; his imagination and inventiveness, his constant desire to experiment, and his amazing productivity affected the development of the symphony more than the contribution of any other composer."[7]

Haydn made his first journey to England in 1791, where he was widely celebrated, and returned a second time in 1794. His last twelve symphonies, the *London Symphonies*, were connected with these visits, and they are still a fixture of symphony orchestra performances today. Audiences soon gave names to some of them, reflecting various unusual musical features: *Surprise* (No. 94), *Miracle* (No. 96), *Clock* (No. 101), and *Drumroll* (No. 103). The final symphony (No. 104) may be the most impressive of them all.

While in London, Haydn attended concerts of Handel oratorios held in Westminster Abbey and these inspired him to write his own masterpiece, *The Creation*, in 1797. *The Creation* is based on texts from Genesis and the Psalms, combined with content from John Milton's epic poem *Paradise Lost*. The drama is evident from the opening instrumental music "The Representation of Chaos." The exuberant chorus declares "Let there be light." From then on the days of creation are described in colorful writing for solo voices, choir, and orchestra. Part One ends with the chorus "The Heavens are Telling the Glory of God", which exudes confidence in the opening words of Psalm 19. Attending a live performance of Haydn's *Creation* will not easily be forgotten.

Flutes
Oboe & Clarinet I
Oboe & Clarinet II
Bassoons
Horns in C
Trumpets in C
Trombone 1
Trombone 2
Trombone 3 & Contrabassoon
Timpani
Violin 1
Violin 2
Viola
Treble
The hea - vens are tell - ing the glo - ry of God,
Alto
The hea - vens are tell - ing the glo - ry of God,
Tenor
The hea - vens are tell - ing the glo - ry of God,
Bass
The hea - vens are tell - ing the glo - ry of God,
Cello/ Double bass

Musical Example 10: Haydn, "The Heavens are Telling the Glory of God", *The Creation*

London also played an important role in this era as the home of Johann Christian Bach (1735–1782), the youngest son of J.S. Bach. The "London Bach" spent time with the young Mozart on the latter's visit to England in 1764 and was an important influence on the young master. J.C. Bach composed a variety of elegant instrumental music and opera, which was shaped by his years living and studying in Italy. His elder brother Carl Philipp Emanuel Bach (1714–1788) was also a notable composer, whose keyboard works in particular, with melodic lines inspired by the human voice, contributed to the molding of the Classical style.

Italy's musical power had begun to wane during these decades, but the Italian Luigi Boccherini (1743–1805) wrote hundreds of pieces and was recognized in his time as not only a great cellist but also influential in the development of chamber music.

In the newly formed United States of America, the Bostonian composer William Billings (1746–1800) became the country's first notable composer. His dramatic choral works on biblical themes, known as anthems and fuging tunes, have an immediacy and vivacity that went on to be preserved in the shape-note tradition of hymn singing in America.

Nineteenth-Century Music

The premier musical genres we are familiar with today were familiar by the end of the Classical period (symphony, string quartet, concerto, opera etc.). Likewise, the orchestra featured the sections (strings, woodwinds, brass, percussion) and most of the instruments that are widely used today. However, the character and scope of music in the West changed dramatically in the early decades of the nineteenth century. This was the era of the Romantic movement in music. There emerged "a strange jumble of trends, toward intimacy, monumentality, and virtuosity."[8]

One man heralds what is known as the Romantic period in music and his name is Ludwig van Beethoven (1770–1827). Born in Germany to a musical family, Beethoven began composing music that was recognizably of the Classical style, yet with some dramatic touches. His first major work is his third symphony, known as the *Eroica,* which is on a larger scale than any earlier symphony (it takes about forty-five minutes to perform). Ultimately Beethoven was to write nine symphonies, including the fifth with its famous four-note opening—this symphony as a whole demonstrates the dominant place of rhythm in his compositions. Beethoven's *Pastoral* (sixth) symphony is quite different in character, portraying scenes from the countryside including joy, contentment, and a violent thunderstorm. His smaller-scale works, e.g. chamber music and songs, are perhaps less familiar. If you are looking for something off the beaten track, you could try listening to his arrangements of Scottish, Irish, and Welsh folksongs!

Beethoven made the emotional life of the composer center stage and in his life elevated the profile and personality of the composer. This became a central feature of the Romantic era in music. However, Beethoven was a complex figure and should not simply be labeled as a "Romantic composer." His later works in particular are unusually dissonant and fragmentary, e.g., the late string quartets; they were not emulated by others until a century later with the advent of atonality (music which rejects tonality in favor of deliberate dissonance). (See Chapter 11—*What Went Wrong?*)

In the early nineteenth century, sacred music and certain forms of opera were acknowledged as serious works of art. But Beethoven pushed for secular music genres such as the symphony or piano sonata to be recognized as art forms equally important to literature and worthy of recognition in their own right. This aspect of his legacy endures down to today.

Beethoven was a virtuoso pianist and the piano plays a central role in his output. His many piano sonatas show his mastery of the instrument, as well as the intensity for which his music is renowned. As a young man, Beethoven studied with Haydn and the early sonatas reflect Haydn's musical influence. Some of Beethoven's piano sonatas acquired names describing their character, such as *Moonlight* (with its brooding first movement), *Tempest*, *Appassionata*, and *Pathétique*. The latter, No. 8 in C minor, drew inspiration from the music of Mozart and J.S. Bach. Beethoven completed five piano concerti and the fifth (*Emperor*) is justly one of his most popular works:

Musical Example 11: Beethoven, *Piano Concerto No. 5 (Emperor)*, Second movement

Although many of the enduring works from the nineteenth century have proved to be purely for instruments (e.g., symphonies and concerti), choral music remained a major part of musical life in the West, whether in performances of J.S. Bach, Handel, or Haydn, and witnessed by Mendelssohn's great oratorios *St. Paul* (composed 1830s) and *Elijah* (composed 1840s). And, of course, opera—whether the works of Rossini, Verdi, or Wagner—maintained a prominent role.

It could be said that the first Romantic composer was the Austrian Franz Schubert (1797–1828), though he employed the genres of the Classical era. His symphonies are still performed often, and his piano works contain some gems. Schubert's song cycles for voice and piano, with their lyrical and subtly expressive melodies, most clearly demonstrate his Romanticism. Schubert's chamber music includes familiar pieces such as *The Trout* Quintet for piano and strings, and the String Quintet in C major, one of his last works.

Musical Example 12: Schubert, *Quintet in A (The Trout)*, Fourth movement

Felix Mendelssohn (1809–1847) came from a distinguished Jewish family in Germany who became Lutherans. There is considerable evidence of Mendelssohn's personal faith in Christ and of his esteem for the Bible, which even religious sceptics who knew him testified to.[9] Mendelssohn set many biblical texts to music, including the oratorio *Elijah* and several psalms, and he took care to quote Scripture in them accurately. His public performance of J.S. Bach's *St. Matthew Passion* in 1829 launched the Bach revival of the nineteenth century. Mendelssohn wove Martin Luther's chorale tune *Ein Feste Burg ("A Mighty Fortress")* into several of his works for piano or orchestra, including the last movement of his fifth symphony *Reformation,* which was written in 1830 to celebrate the three-hundredth anniversary of the Lutheran Augsburg Confession.

Mendelssohn was a child prodigy whose music (in many different genres) was widely performed throughout the nineteenth century. Like Handel before him, he received an enthusiastic reception in Britain—where he met the young Queen Victoria. Mendelssohn's music has a Romantic exuberance that parallels the literature of his day. Some of his major works were inspired by his visits to different countries: the third symphony—*Scottish*; the fourth symphony—*Italian;* both are delightful works. His perfectly crafted *Hebrides* overture evokes the atmosphere of Fingal's Cave on the small island of Staffa, near the western coast of Scotland.

Before his eighteenth birthday, Mendelssohn had composed his Octet for strings (four violins, two violas, and two cellos), which is brimming with energy and adventure, and a concert overture for *A Midsummer Night's Dream.* In later years, he completed incidental music for the latter, including its much-loved wedding march. The piano features prominently in Mendelssohn's output, including many "Songs without words," a genre which he created. His other keyboard works include fine preludes, fugues, and sonatas for organ.

Perhaps Mendelssohn's most performed piece today is his Violin Concerto in E minor—and with good reason since it expertly displays warmth, elegance, and charm. It is no accident that our secular age prefers those Mendelssohn pieces that are not overtly tied to his Christian faith. Even then, there is an innocence and purity in the music itself which led to his works increasingly being sidelined as atheism darkened the West's artistic outlook.

Musical Example 13: Mendelssohn, *Violin Concerto in E minor,* First movement

Frédéric Chopin (1810–1849) was born in Poland but later settled in France. His works for piano are celebrated for their beauty and sensitivity. Many of them use dance forms, such as the Mazurka that draws on many aspects of folk music from the Mazovia region of Poland. In contrast, the compositional approach of J.S. Bach is also felt in Chopin's later music and his twenty-four Preludes continue the tradition begun by Bach's *Well-Tempered Clavier*. (His later Prelude in C-Sharp minor is often published alongside the twenty-four as a suitably captivating encore.) Other piano works by Chopin include Ballades, Études, and Nocturnes with melodies reminiscent of Italian opera. Chopin's two piano concerti are his only large-scale works.

The German composer Robert Schumann (1810-1856) was the same age as Chopin, and he lived only a little longer. As a young man, Schumann heard the virtuoso violinist Nicolò Paganini perform in Frankfurt in 1830. Schumann soon became a composer and music critic; his wife Clara performed internationally as a concert pianist. He wrote much music for piano, and many songs. Schumann's Piano Concerto in A minor inspired Grieg's later work of the same name.

The Hungarian Franz Liszt (1811–1886) was an altogether more flamboyant character. Perhaps the most virtuosic pianist of the century, Liszt toured widely in Europe and was adored by his audiences. His lasting contribution to composition was the symphonic poem, a new musical form he developed from the overture. Liszt's symphonic poems are typically Romantic program music, which seek to express in music a place, story, etc., and they are structured using motivic development—the adapting and connecting of (usually short) musical themes.

The musical significance of opera had waxed and waned over the centuries, even as it retained its prominence in social life in Europe. But the year 1813 saw the birth of two of its most famous composers, whose operas still reverberate around the world today. The Italian Giuseppe Verdi (1813–1901) raised the genre of Romanic opera to new heights. He employed great works of literature (including Shakespeare) in several of his operas (e.g., *Macbeth, Otello,* and *Falstaff*) and was celebrated as a hero in his native Italy. Verdi's operas are masterful combinations of musical flair and the conventional drama of the stage.

Richard Wagner (1813–1883) was born in Leipzig, Germany, and was widely known in his day as a composer, theorist, and polemical author. His early operas utilized the existing form of German Romantic opera, but Wagner developed a vision for music-dramas in which the music was integrated into the plot of vast mythical stories—above all, in his famous *Ring* cycle of four operas (unlike most opera composers, Wagner wrote the words as well as the music). Musically, Wagner's most notable developments were to weave identifiable themes or motifs throughout the tapestry of each work (later known as "leitmotivs") and his increasing use of dissonance (chromaticism) with music of no clear tonal center. His musical influence on his contemporaries and successors was profound and Wagner's disruption of tonality in works such as *Tristan and Isolde* would have lasting consequences for Western music.

Other Romantic composers continued to expand musical horizons yet at the same time restored the symphony to its prominent place. The German Johannes Brahms (1833–1897) was seen by many of his followers as a rival of Wagner. Brahms consciously continued the Classical tradition, while adding a greater emotional intensity to its traditional genres. In his own time, people would talk of the "three Bs"—Bach, Beethoven, and Brahms. This is an indication of Brahms' excellence in compositional technique and the lasting quality of his music. It was many years before he felt able to overcome the shadow of Beethoven in order to write his first symphony, but all four Brahms symphonies are masterpieces. The second symphony is a sunny and tuneful work, with a barnstorming last movement (see overleaf). Brahms composed important chamber music and a variety of piano works—including his characteristic intermezzos, sonatas, studies, and the Hungarian dances.

Apart from the symphonies, Brahms' major orchestral works include two concerti for piano and one for violin. All three works remain firmly established in the concert repertoire. The opening movement of the first piano concerto is powerful and perhaps foreboding. His second piano concerto is more approachable, with an atmospheric and touching slow movement. Brahms' violin concerto was composed for the violinist Joseph Joachim and requires exceptional skill. His last orchestral work was a double concerto for violin and cello—the jaunty theme of its final movement can easily get stuck in your head!

Musical Example 14: Brahms, *Symphony No. 2,* Fourth movement

The music of Antonín Dvořák (1841–1904) is a regular fixture in concerts today, especially his later symphonies. There is a joy and an ease in Dvořák's music, which (like Haydn) reflects the composer's personality, and which should not obscure his skillful musical craftsmanship. Despite the obvious quality of his music, Dvořák was strangely unmentioned on my undergraduate music course. A native of Bohemia (now the Czech Republic), Dvořák's music draws on the folk music tradition of his country.

Later in life, Dvořák came to the USA to direct the newly established music conservatory in New York and travelled to visit a Czech community living in Iowa. He was also introduced to the musical heritage of black Americans by the musician Harry Burleigh (1866–1949). Dvořák's experiences during this time in the States shaped the composition of two of his most performed works: his ninth symphony (*From the New World*) and the *American* String Quartet in F major, Opus 96—both composed in 1893. The poignant slow movement of the ninth symphony unmistakably conveys a longing for home.

Musical Example 15: Dvořák, *Symphony No. 9,* Second movement

There were several important Russian composers of the nineteenth century, but the best known today is Pyotr Tchaikovsky (1840–1893). Like other composers of this era, Tchaikovsky wrote in many different genres, but his most popular works have proved to be his ballet music, six symphonies, three concerti for piano, and one concerto for violin. Tchaikovsky's music has immediate emotional appeal and memorable tunes, enhanced by his skillful employment of the full scope of the modern symphony orchestra.

Edvard Grieg (1843–1907) was a hero in his native land of Norway and his music is intimately connected to its folk traditions. Although best remembered for his Piano Concerto in A minor, he was more naturally at home in smaller forms such as his chamber music and piano music.

French composers exerted an influence on Western music ever since the Notre Dame school of the twelfth century. French keyboard music is one aspect of France's legacy—stretching from the Baroque Couperin family to the organ music of Charles-Marie Widor (1844–1937), who was organist of Saint-Sulpice Church in Paris for an amazing sixty-three years. Widor's contemporary Camille Saint-Saëns (1835–1921) was a child prodigy as a pianist and is known today not only for his famous *Organ* symphony, but also for his piano concerti. It is ironic, and a little sad, that Saint-Saëns' popular and humorous work *The Carnival of the Animals* was not performed in his lifetime.

Modern Era

The dividing line between nineteenth century and modern music is perhaps the hardest to draw of all musical eras. On one hand, many of the lasting trajectories in modern music have their origins in the nineteenth century. On the other, well-known composers born in that century continued writing in the Romantic tradition well into the twentieth century.

German-speaking composers dominated Western music in the nineteenth century. Yet the Frenchman Claude Debussy (1862–1918) found a musical voice of his own. Debussy generally eschews traditional thematic development in favor of sound contrasts; his music is distinctive, and his use of sonorities (especially in his piano works) is memorable. Debussy's harmonic structures include the whole-tone scale, which has six notes and is also used in jazz, and his compositions generally defy the traditional rules of harmony, and instead espouse "modality, suspended tonality, parallelism and unresolved dissonance."[10] It is music as sound for its own sake; not the Romantic model of music as a language of emotional expression.

His fellow countryman Maurice Ravel (1875–1937) was more musically conventional, especially in his deployment of Classical musical forms, yet his harmonies were also enveloped with dissonance that is far removed from the Classical era—featuring unresolved suspensions and a strong modal flavor to the melodies. Ravel's skill at orchestration, how he employed and combined the range of instruments in the symphony orchestra, gave much color to his music.

It would be natural to categorize Gustav Mahler's (1860–1911) output as nineteenth-century music, yet he looks ahead to the modern era. Mahler was born in Bohemia in the Austrian Empire and went on to become a famous conductor in his day, holding significant posts in several European cities and eventually in New York. A key figure in the late Romantic era, Mahler composed vast works for orchestra and voice such as his symphonies and song cycles.

The Adagietto—slow movement—of Mahler's fifth symphony, with its delicate scoring for strings and solo harp, was likely written for his wife Alma, and it is undoubtedly his most prominent piece. Mahler's fourth (in G major), with its own gorgeous slow movement, is perhaps the best symphony for newcomers. His spectacular second symphony—*Resurrection*—requires a huge orchestra with large choir and vocal soloists. It begins with a funeral march, reflects on life's journey in the middle movements, and ends with a stunning last movement which emphatically affirms (in both music and words) the hope of the bodily resurrection.

Mahler's later works are increasingly dissonant and tonally ambiguous. His contemporary Richard Strauss (1864–1949) went further towards atonality, but then returned to more recognizably tonal music, e.g., his final work *Four Last Songs*. Richard Strauss composed many orchestral works, including symphonies and tone poems, and his operas are still performed regularly.

Sir Edward Elgar (1857–1934) became one of England's most notable and versatile composers, despite not receiving formal training in composition. Elgar was a late Romantic who found his own expressive, and somewhat restrained, voice in his Enigma Variations, two symphonies, and cello concerto. Elgar also composed a violin concerto and the attractive three-movement *Serenade for Strings*, which is free-flowing and sounds quintessentially English. His choral works include oratorios and songs. Elgar's *Pomp and Circumstance* marches reflect the imperial character of the Edwardian era in the United Kingdom and showcase several memorable tunes. (It is ironic that the first of these marches has become synonymous in the American Republic with school and college graduations!)

The year 1934 was a sad year for music in England, since it not only saw the death of Elgar, but also two of its other composers: Gustav Holst (1874–1934)—widely known for his orchestral suite *The Planets*—and Frederick Delius (1862–1934), whose *Florida Suite* followed his time living there on a plantation.

Sergei Rachmaninov (1873–1943) was born in Russia and eventually settled in the USA. His works are full-orbed Romantic music and he could be considered the last major Romantic composer. Rachmaninov composed symphonies, piano concerti, chamber music, and solo piano music (including twenty-four Preludes in all the major and minor keys, picking up where Chopin and Bach left off). His flamboyant *Rhapsody on a Theme of Paganini* is really a one-movement piano concerto. The second symphony takes listeners on an epic musical adventure—its slow movement may bring tears to your eyes; the last always brings the audience to its feet.

Rachmaninov was a piano virtuoso who wowed audiences around the world. He is perhaps best known today for his second piano concerto with its unabashed beauty, which combines emotional intensity and soaring melodies with delicate and assured compositional technique.

Maestoso (𝅗𝅥 = 60)
429
Flutes
Oboes
Clarinets in B♭
Bassoons
Horns in F I & II
Horns in F III & IV
Trumpets in B♭
Trombones I & II
Trombone III & Tuba
Timpani
Piano
Violin I
Violin II
Viola
Cello
Double bass
ff
fff
mf
tr
div.

Musical Example 16: Rachmaninov, *Piano Concerto No. 2,* Third movement

The music of Jean Sibelius (1865–1957) is stamped with the mark of his native Finland and has a repertoire of sounds all its own. Sibelius' earlier works are Romantic, with programmatic pieces such as the tone poem *Finlandia,* which proved hugely popular not only in Finland but around the world. He adapted its contemplative central section into the hymn tune that has been used widely. The *Karelia Suite* is another notable symphonic poem and it has a simplicity and directness inspired by Finnish folk music. Sibelius also wrote music for stage works such as his *King Christian II* suite. The *Andante Festivo* for string orchestra and timpani is brief, yet sublime. Although his orchestral works are most acclaimed, Sibelius also composed in other genres such as piano music, songs, and chamber music.

His first symphony opens with a clarinet solo before a dramatic section for full orchestra; the piece's climax blossoms into a rich and melodious ending. As with Brahms, his second symphony has a more optimistic character, and one of the best conclusions of any symphony. The renowned violin concerto, one of the most challenging written for violin, opens with a warm and gentle solo set against shimmering strings. Sibelius expertly balances the roles of soloist and orchestra throughout, creates an exquisite slow movement, and the work culminates in a rollicking last movement.

Sibelius was charting a path which fused a mastery of musical form with carefully worked thematic development, for example in his third symphony. He strayed away from the tonal system in the fourth, but returned to it for the well-known fifth symphony, the final movement of which beautifully depicts the call of a wedge of flying swans. (A good friend of mine compares listening to the fifth symphony with sitting on an iceberg watching the sunrise.) The seventh symphony is an abstract work in one movement which seems to explore a world of colorful orchestral sonorities. Sibelius fell silent as a composer in the 1920s and only sketched fragments remain, leading his many fans to contemplate what could have followed.

Musical Example 17: Sibelius, *Symphony No. 3 in C major,* Op. 52, Third movement

In the early twentieth century, composers in many different countries turned to their folk music traditions for musical inspiration, none more so than the Englishman Ralph Vaughan Williams (1872–1958). Vaughan Williams travelled to gather folksongs, many of which he later arranged with haunting beauty for choir and/or orchestra, but their modal influence is pervasive throughout his prolific output which includes nine symphonies (the seventh derived from a film score), choral works, chamber music, and opera. The polyphony of sixteenth-century Tudor England also interested him and Vaughan Williams' *Fantasia on a Theme by Thomas Tallis* profoundly affected succeeding English composers. Vaughan Williams once said: "The art of music above all arts is the expression of the soul of the nation."

Leoš Janáček (1854–1928) wrote original music which draws on the Czech folk music of his heritage. Born in Moravia, Janáček sought an alternative to German Romanticism by turning to folk music, which he, too, personally collected from his countrymen. This is the musical backdrop to his operas, choral, and instrumental works, which also reflect the inflections of the Czech language.

The USA had begun to attract big-name composers from Europe in the late nineteenth century, such as Dvořák and Mahler, but the twentieth century saw the rise of American composers of international stature. The most famous is George Gershwin (1898–1937), whose natural talent led him to Tin Pan Alley to compose songs, then to Broadway, and on into the world of classical music. Gershwin's first major piece was *Rhapsody in Blue,* which combines jazz harmony and rhythm in an orchestral setting. He went on to write the opera *Porgy and Bess,* film music, and his supremely enjoyable Piano Concerto in F, which belongs firmly in the classical music canon.

Samuel Barber (1910–1981) was born in Pennsylvania and wrote in a very different mold. Most of his pieces are written in the tonal system and a few are widely known such as the *Adagio for Strings* and his violin concerto, with its lightning-fast final movement. His contemporary, Aaron Copland, composed some of the most quintessentially American music of all, such as the patriotic *Fanfare for the Common Man* and his ballet score *Appalachian Spring*. The wide spacing of the orchestral lines reflects the vast geography of the USA and the directness of the melodies relates something of the character of its people. Copland wrote in many genres, including pieces for voices and instrumental works such as a clarinet concerto.

Musical Example 18: Aaron Copland, *Appalachian Spring*

The Englishman Sir William Walton (1902–1983), from my home county of Lancashire, is best remembered today for his coronation marches *Crown Imperial* and *Orb and Sceptre*. He composed a range of instrumental, vocal, and film scores, such as for Laurence Olivier's *Henry V*.

The twentieth century was the era of film music, with several classical composers writing for film. In the early days of Hollywood, Max Steiner (1888–1971) and Erich Korngold (1897–1957), both originally from Europe, made a significant contribution. Korngold's lush, Romantic scores set the tone for many others and are also reflected in his violin concerto.

Perhaps no film composer is better known globally than the American John Williams (1932–). Williams has composed over 100 film scores, including many for the blockbuster movies that are household favorites today. He writes unapologetically in the tonal system, employs the full range of the symphony orchestra, and showcases unforgettable themes. Other well-known film composers include the Englishman John Barry (1933–2011), whose music has an unusual depth in the writing for strings, and the Canadian Howard Shore (1946–).

8

Applying the Principles of Beauty to Music

Several more books would be needed to analyze the works of the composers surveyed above according to the principles of objective beauty. It would be an absolutely fascinating task. The eighteen numbered pieces which feature on the previous pages are, without doubt, objectively beautiful. The fact that these pieces of music have been carefully preserved and regularly performed for generations is evidence enough that many people have recognized them as special.

Music is the organization of sound according to the objective principles of beauty, which are proportion, harmony, simplicity, and complexity. The music that most displays these objective principles is the highest quality and most beautiful music. These compositions resemble the order that is evident throughout God's creation. This understanding is the inheritance of Western civilization. The question is: how should these principles be applied to pieces of music in order to determine which are beautiful? I am not aware of any previous work that has undertaken this analysis. The extent to which a piece of music features these objective principles determines whether it is good-quality or poor-quality music, or whether the work qualifies as music at all.

The assessment of beauty in music must ultimately be decided by listening. Music is an art made in sound ("the mosaic of the air"). Even an experienced musician or listener may need some time to fully absorb a particular piece, that is to hear and understand it.

And those who are most familiar with classical music have a head start in identifying beautiful music. That's because appreciating good music is learned by experience. This can start at the beginning of life—there is no doubt that preborn children hear music when they are in the womb[1]—and should continue from childhood to the end of our days.[2] It is no coincidence that most of the famous composers we have surveyed grew up in musical families and so learned to recognize good music from an early age. It takes time to develop the ability to discern the best music (see Chapter 13—*Taste in Music*).

Thoughtful listening is the first step to recognizing beauty in music. The second is remembering that great things in life are often described as being more than the sum of their parts. There is an elusive aspect to objects of great beauty, such as in music, painting, architecture, or poetry, which means that, though we can break down the various details and methods of production etc., the whole together has a pricelessness that surpasses its constituent parts. In painting, we could look at the use of perspective, individual color selection, use of darkness and lightness etc., in Michelangelo and Rembrandt, Vermeer and Constable, but their greatest works of art may have a distinction that surpasses detailed analysis. Likewise, the most forensic examination of the written music notated in the score, while rewarding and important, may not fully explain the cause of its beauty.

With that in mind, we can turn to think about how music exhibits the principles of objective beauty. Regarding proportion and harmony, the Polish philosopher Wladyslaw Tatarkiewicz (1886–1980) explained, "The general theory of beauty formulated in ancient times declared that beauty consists in the proportions of the parts, more precisely in the proportions and arrangement of the parts, or, still more precisely, in the size, equality, and number of the parts and their interrelationships. This can be illustrated with reference to architecture: thus, it would be said, the beauty of a portico stems from the size, number and arrangement of the columns. And similarly with music, except that there the relations are temporal and not spatial."[3]

Tatarkiewicz described this as "the Great Theory of European aesthetics." What he calls a narrower form of this theory ties proportion directly to number relationships or ratios, which is what put medieval composers in a musical straightjacket until the dawn of the Renaissance (see Chapter 6—*Thinking about Music,* for Pythagoras etc.). However, the broader form of the theory simply recognizes that beauty consists in proportion, harmony, symmetry, or order. Tatarkiewicz wrote: "There have been few theories in any branch of European culture which have endured so long or commanded such widespread recognition, and few which cover the diverse phenomena of beauty quite so comprehensively."[4]

Renowned architect Quinlan Terry provides evidence that these principles of beauty derive originally from the biblical Tabernacle and Temple and were later copied by the surrounding nations. He notes, for example, that the meaning of the Greek word architecture "describes that way of building which is not only great and important but also originated at the beginning of time."[5] Since the God of the Bible is a God of order, and the Old Testament demonstrates his concern for beauty in the design of the tabernacle and temple, this ought not to be surprising.

Proportion

The traditional understanding of beauty often compares music and architecture. We have already considered the parallels between them and noted that in the greatest buildings the small details fit with the overall structure. What could we identify in music that displays a similar *proportion* or balance? Let's consider some questions we could ask of the music we hear.

How does the piece of music as a whole fit together? We could consider the overall structure and whether the different sections complement each other in their character or organization. The short pieces by Lassus, Tallis, and the *Old Hundredth* hymn tune attributed to Bourgeois, (Examples 2–4) are each well formed and balanced in the melodies, harmonies, and rhythms employed.

Thinking of longer works, are there too many, or too few, key changes? Is there too much, or too little, variation of rhythmic patterns? The Great Theory of beauty would suggest that the most beautiful pieces of music are the longest or most varied pieces that nevertheless retain their overall cohesion. A great deal of rewarding consideration could be given to this analysis piece by piece. How does it relate to the movements of a symphony, for example?

Should each one be assessed separately? In most well-known symphonies, the four movements are typically in different keys and have new themes, yet a symphony with one musically weak movement is not generally considered a classic.

The principle of proportion could also extend to the volume of longer pieces—is there a balance of loud and soft sections? A failure here might be simply because of a poor musicianship, which illustrates that the quality of the performance is essential to displaying a beautiful piece of music: "There is a difference between a great performance and a performance of great music. Sometimes there are great performances of great music, other times poor performances of great music, and still other times great performances of bad music."[6]

Another question relating to proportion could be: does the composer's use of form for the piece serve to properly balance the different themes in the work; or, for a piece in sonata form, are they lost or hidden in the development section? The Brahms symphonies showcase his expert deployment of sonata form.

On a more detailed level, do the phrases (the shorter sections of music) in a particular passage balance or correspond to one another? Are the themes properly developed, or are they handled clumsily, or with too much repetition? We could examine whether the voice parts (or instrumental lines) are proportionate, that is, whether there is an overall balance of prominence between them or whether this fails at times—with certain voices dominating while others have a perfunctory role. For example, Palestrina's motet *Super Flumina Babylonis* (Example 1) displays a wonderful balance between the four equally important voice parts, which pass its themes effortlessly from one to another in matching phrases.

Important questions may have to be asked about the use of rhythm in a piece and whether it disproportionately relies on rhythm for its effect or to hold the music together. Pieces which are dominated by the beat or rhythm are not beautiful, though they may be popular. We will return to this later.

It is essential that a piece of music have a sense of closure, of having completed what it set out to say. This relates directly to the need for balance or symmetry in music. With respect to melody or rhythm, good music requires the themes or rhythms to have been fully presented or developed. With respect to harmony, the music must have a recognizable cadence. The final cadence can be considered as the last two chords in music. In the tonal system, music is typically "brought home" by either a V-I or IV-I chord progression—that is, a dominant or subdominant chord followed by the tonic chord of the original key. As Sir Roger Scruton wrote, "It is one of the remarkable features of Western classical music, that it has developed a language in which rhythmic, harmonic, and melodic closure are achieved together, after a venture outwards in which each partner in the enterprise takes its own, often hair-raising, risks."[7]

Harmony

The ancient Greeks viewed musical *harmony* as a foundational example of beauty. Harmony need not only mean whether the notes harmonize, but if a piece is very discordant, it fails this test. Atonal music actively seeks to subvert harmony in favor of dissonance (see Chapter 11—*What Went Wrong?*).

God has written musical harmony into creation, as birdsong indicates. The development of the tonal system allowed for several different voices to sing, or instruments to play, in harmony in works of ever-greater complexity. Pieces in the tonal system are based on a system of harmony, though all the great composers knew how to employ discord and resolution, such as suspensions, to add beauty to their compositions. We could also analyze how they varied the chords used in each key. It would be fascinating to compare movements from Mozart's Piano Concerto No. 23, Beethoven's *Emperor* Concerto, and Rachmaninov's second piano concerto in this way (Examples 9,11, and 16).

Another element to look at is the "harmonic rhythm" in a piece or in sections of it. Harmonic rhythm describes the rate at which the chords change. J.S. Bach usually employs a brisk harmonic rhythm, where the harmony changes quickly. A piece characterized by a slow harmonic rhythm is usually dull—several nineteenth- and twentieth-century hymn tunes suffer from this malady. This is one area in which a greater variety or complexity is needed to create beautiful music.

The principle of harmony could also extend to assessing how other elements of the music combine together. For example, in vocal music, are the notes suitably fitted to the words? Henry Purcell showed brilliantly the art of setting the English language to music (see Example 5). Or take a violin concerto; does the solo part fit with rest of the orchestra so that neither is neglected during the piece? Or, think about tone color—how the composer combines different instrumental sounds together, which is the art of orchestration. (Maurice Ravel was widely recognized as a skilled orchestrator.)

Negatively, if one orchestral sound employed in a symphony (e.g., the brass) dominates the others and obscures them, then we could say that the piece is not exhibiting harmony. Of course, this may not be what the composer wrote in the music; it may be poor musicianship by the conductor or performers. The principle of harmony could especially apply to musical performance, including whether the different orchestral instruments or sections (strings, brass, woodwind, percussion) are in time and in tune with each other.

Simplicity

Perhaps *simplicity* in beautiful music is most easily heard in a good melody, which can be found in various types of music from folk-song to choral works. Explaining in words what constitutes a "good tune," however, is not easy. Obviously, repeating a note eight times does not make a melody, and, at the other extreme, a long and complicated tune is not likely to be pleasant. Typically, the notes of the best tunes mostly move stepwise and avoid large intervals, though this is not always the case. Of the composers highlighted in this book, Antonín Dvořák certainly had an ability to coin a lovely melody—the evocative theme of the second movement of his *New World* symphony (Example 15) is very well known and, notably, its phrases are proportionate.

One feature of Baroque music is an interest in musical ornamentation, with a whole host of different additions to, or tweaks to, melodies. These contribute to the beauty of a piece when handled adroitly by the great composers. However, it is arguable that too much ornamentation can encrust music and obscure the simplicity of its themes. To be clear, simplistic music is not the same as simple music. The latter can be profound, e.g., Bach's Prelude 1 in C major from book I of the *Well-Tempered Clavier* (Example 20).

Pieces which employ highly complex and varied rhythmic patterns are not usually attractive. Some medieval composers went too far down this route, perhaps in part because the rules of harmony at the time were so restrictive and they wanted to explore other aspects of composition. In recent decades, avant-garde composers in the West have released works of bewildering rhythmic intricacy.

Complexity

In considering *complexity* as a principle of beauty, we should remember that it was the invention of tonality and the refinement of modern musical instruments which together allowed composers in the West to write pieces of great complexity. During the Renaissance era, the establishment of tonality brought us polyphony for independent voice parts that harmonized well. So even a four-part chorale must be considered a complex work at one level, such as Lutheran chorales or Genevan hymns, even though more advanced music would come later.

The size and scope of complex works allows them to be more beautiful than small-scale pieces, provided that the overall structure has balance and proportion. As the vast size of St. Paul's Cathedral in London creates a more beautiful space than a small cottage, so a wonderful oratorio or symphony eclipses a folksong. In my view, the most complex beautiful pieces included in this book are J.S. Bach's Mass in B minor, Handel's *Messiah,* and Mendelssohn's oratorio *Elijah,* together with some of the symphonies by Brahms, Dvořák, and Sibelius.

Polyphony, music for independent voices that sound at the same time, is a feature of complex music in the West. (When written for instrumental lines, it is usually described as *contrapuntal* music.) This technique is best exhibited in the great choral works of the Renaissance by men such as Palestrina and Lassus, in instrumental fugues (e.g., for organ) by J.S. Bach and Mendelssohn, and in the great string quartets of Haydn and Mozart. The art of composing polyphonic or contrapuntal music is called counterpoint.

A tendency to abandon polyphony for homophony (a tune with an accompaniment) is a retreat from complexity. Of course, it is not wrong to write pieces comprised simply of a tune with harmonious accompaniment, but historically it has generally represented a reversion to a more basic form of music. This tendency in tonal music can be observed in a significant quantity of music from the Classical era and onwards, and it could be categorized as simplistic. Homophony is a characteristic of "light music," which can be attractive and tuneful on one level without necessarily being beautiful.

An extreme example of overly simplistic music is the repetitive "minimalist" music by modern composers such as Steve Reich (1936–), which repeats musical fragments over and over again. Although it often utilizes complex rhythmic patterns, the almost static use of harmony along with the absence of melody means this conspicuously fails the tests of both complexity and harmony. Such repetitive music may have a hypnotic effect, but it is not beautiful.

Overall, one important way of identifying beauty is to look for *unity in diversity* (see Chapter 5—*Objective Beauty*, for Jonathan Edwards' work *The Nature of True Virtue*). We can see this within the principle of proportion; for example, does the composer's use of form have a balance or symmetry that unites the work as one coherent whole? Or, considering the principle of harmony, does the orchestration of the piece match instruments together well or is the use of different instruments too diverse, scattered, and confusing? Or we can think of unity in diversity as a combination of simplicity and complexity. The most beautiful pieces of music will integrate simplicity and complexity to create unity in diversity—for example, by developing simple themes with varied harmonic and rhythmic treatment, ending with a proper sense of closure. The greater the length and scope of a work, the greater the challenge. No composer mastered it better than J.S. Bach.

9

Bach and Beauty

National Review senior editor Jay Nordlinger wrote in late 2021: "What is the glory of Western civilization? Our political freedom, probably—the rights of individual man. But I would not put music far behind, with Bach leading the way."[1]

Johann Sebastian Bach (1685–1750) is widely considered the greatest composer of all time. Surveying the landscape of classical music, Bach gave us its finest achievements. As we look beyond to the mountain range of great works of art in the West, Bach's music forms the highest peaks, alongside the poetry of Shakespeare and Milton, and the paintings of Michelangelo and Rembrandt.

Why is he so widely recognized as *the* composer of great works? In the life and music of J.S. Bach, technical brilliance, hard work, and flair combined with his devout Christian faith. His works show the full application of the principles of beauty to musical craftsmanship and, in Bach's religious choral works, his music openly proclaims the truth of Jesus Christ.

J.S. Bach was born in Eisenach, Germany, to a family of musicians stretching back centuries, "the most extensive network of practicing musicians in the history of Western music."[2] His father and mother both died while he was around nine years old and so J.S. Bach was raised by one of his older brothers, Johann Christoph. The latter was an organist, who likely gave him his first keyboard lessons, though their late father may have begun teaching Johann Sebastian violin in the preceding years. J.S. Bach clearly liked music from an early age, which is shown by the long journey he made as a young man to experience firsthand the music of Buxtehude in Lübeck in the north of the country. In 1707, he married Maria Barbara, and, after her death, Anna Magdalena in 1721; in total Bach had twenty children, of whom ten lived to adulthood.

As a child, J.S. Bach was baptized in the Georgenkirche in Eisenach and he grew up as a member of the congregation there, linking him with Martin Luther, who preached from its pulpit over 150 years earlier after his return from the Diet of Worms. Bach studied at the same Latin school that Luther had attended generations earlier, sang in the same church, and embraced the same faith in Jesus Christ.

J.S. Bach was a devout Lutheran who was committed to the truths of Holy Scripture and the teachings of his church. He had his own extensive theological library, yet aged fifty-seven he bought a deluxe edition of Martin Luther's complete works in seven volumes, writing a note in his own hand that they were "magnificent writings."[3] Bach's works show the full effects of the theology of the Reformation on music. He actually signed off the manuscripts of his music with the letters "SDG"—abbreviating the Latin *Soli Deo Gloria*: to the glory of God alone. And he went to great lengths to accomplish this in his musical output.

The Japanese Christian Masaaki Suzuki is one of the world's leading conductors of Bach and a member of a reformed church in Japan. He has written:

> . . . The God in whose service Bach laboured and the God I worship today are one and the same. In the sight of the God of Abraham, I believe that the two hundred years separating the time of Bach from my own day can be of little account. This conviction has brought the great composer very much closer to me. We are fellows in faith, and equally foreign in our parentage to the people of Israel, God's people of Biblical times. Who can be said to approach more nearly the spirit of Bach: a European who does not attend church and carries his Christian cultural heritage mostly on the subconscious level, or an Asian who is active in his faith although the influence of Christianity on his national culture is small?[4]

Bach's Music

Bach's specific musical output was largely determined by the jobs he held. After a brief stint in Mülhausen as a church organist (1707–8), he took the post of court organist in Weimar (1708–1717) where he composed in several genres. From there, he became director of music for the court in Cöthen (1717–1723). Since it was a Calvinist court, which sought only simple music in worship, he mainly wrote secular chamber and orchestral music—the set of six *Brandenburg Concerti* (BWV 1046–51)[5] date to this time (see Example 7 above).

The majority of Bach's career was spent as music director (Cantor) of St. Thomas' Church in Leipzig (1723–1750). The Lutheran church has a strong tradition of employing choral and instrumental music in Christian worship and, writing for its services of worship, Bach composed his greatest works. In fact, it seems like he deliberately sought this job in order to have the opportunity to write cantatas openly proclaiming the glory of God and the truth of his Word. At the same time, he was also director of music for the city of Leipzig, which gave him opportunity to compose and perform secular works.

Bach wrote over 1,000 verified pieces during his lifetime, though not all survive, and they cover all the major genres of his day for voice and/or instruments (excluding opera). His duties could be heavy, especially in Leipzig where the church services demanded a significant amount of music—so daily life included composing, writing out the music in parts, taking care of the choir school, leading practices, and conducting/performing his works, as well as being a husband and father.

Solo and Orchestral Works

This was the Baroque period in music and in many ways Bach's music is the culmination of the musical possibilities explored in this era. Indeed, the year of his death (1750) is generally taken to be the end of the Baroque period.

The violin family of instruments, with its clarity, sonority, and range of both volume and expression, had matured by Bach's time to form the core of the orchestra. J.S. Bach was an accomplished violinist, as well as playing several other instruments, and he composed sonatas and partitas for solo violin. The Chaconne from the Partita No. 2 in D minor for solo violin (BWV 1004) may be one of the most profound and moving pieces ever written. It is a demanding movement, which lasts over fifteen minutes. In the hands of a great violinist, the Chaconne sounds like a duet for two violins, such is Bach's writing for the different melodic lines woven into the piece.

Musical Example 19: J.S. Bach, *Chaconne in D minor for Solo Violin,* from BWV 1004

The Prelude from Bach's Cello Suite No. 1 in G major (BWV 1007) for solo cello is only short, but it is one of his best-known works. Its singing melody within a multitude of arpeggios reaches a beautiful climax at the end. The Sarabande movement from the Cello Suite No. 5 in C minor (BWV 1011) is poignant and, unusually for Bach's music for solo members of the violin family, is a single, plaintive melodic line without double stops.[6]

Bach's four orchestral suites highlight the importance of different dance forms in the Baroque era (Gavotte, Sarabande, Bourrée etc.) and they are very enjoyable. You have likely heard the stately Air from the Orchestral Suite No. 3 in D major (BWV 1068), popularly called the *Air on the G string*.

Unlike Vivaldi, Bach is not well known for composing concerti, yet he wrote fine examples including the Concerto for two violins in D minor (BWV 1043), with its lovely slow movement in which the two soloists gently answer one another, as well as many keyboard concerti for harpsichord and strings.

The famous *Brandenburg Concerti* are equal to the best of any Baroque composer. Each one is a concerto grosso, in which the music alternates between the orchestra and a small group of instrumentalists; the six concerti were selected and compiled by Bach at a later date to demonstrate his skills to a potential new aristocratic employer, the Margrave of Brandenburg. The musicologist Claude Palisca observed a keen desire for symmetry in the musical form of these pieces, saying "Bach's perennial quest for fully integrated designs is everywhere in evidence."[7]

Keyboard Music

Bach's *Well-Tempered Clavier* was composed for a keyboard instrument such as a harpsichord, but is equally well suited to the modern piano. It comprises a two-book set, each containing a prelude and a fugue in all of the twelve major and twelve minor keys—so there are forty-eight short pieces in total. The main impetus for this work was to demonstrate that the move to equal temperament opens up musical possibilities in all twenty-four keys (see Chapter 6—*Thinking about Music*). Even these short works show the huge potential of the tonal system and they vary considerably in nature. Book 1 opens with Prelude 1 in C major—whose beautiful simplicity may be unsurpassed by any other piece of music—through Fugue 5 in D major in the dotted-rhythm style of a French overture, the sorrowful Prelude 8 in E-flat minor, and ending with the long chromatic Fugue 24 in B minor.

Musical Example 20: J.S. Bach, *Prelude in C major,* BVW 846

A fugue is a musical form built around a short melody or motif called the subject, for several voices or instrumental lines. Typically, the subject is introduced alone and then combined with the counter-subject, which complements it. From there, the composer introduces the subject in other musical lines or voices successively (a "four-part fugue" has four individual lines of music). He then develops the music, passing through different keys, before returning for the final statement of the subject in the tonic key.

Bach did not invent the fugue, and it has been employed by many composers over the centuries, but he is the greatest exponent of this form. He wrote fugues for instruments and voices across his output, both distinct pieces (e.g., for keyboard or organ) and within longer works.

Fugue has a clear order and symmetry built around the successive statements of the theme and so is a very suitable vehicle for composing beautiful pieces. Bach loved to do so. For example, *The Art of Fugue* (BWV 1080), which was incomplete at the time of his death, contains a series of fugues exploring the musical possibilities of the same, simple subject. (Note that Bach wrote fugues musically, with an ear for all the elements of beauty in music. In the hands of some teachers down the centuries, fugue writing has too often become a barren desert of mechanical, academic study.)

Another seminal work by Bach is his *Goldberg Variations* (BWV 988), a set of thirty variations on a delicate, refined Aria, composed for two-manual harpsichord. It is challenging to perform, requiring great dexterity by the harpsichordist. The music is based on an eight-bar harmonic pattern, which is stated thirty-two times in total—exactly the same musical structure as the Chaconne in D minor for solo violin (Example 19 above), though *Goldberg* takes far longer to perform.[8]

Sadly, the story of this work being played by a young harpsichordist (Johann Goldberg) to lull an insomniac aristocrat to sleep is probably apocryphal. In the original score, Bach wrote that the music was "prepared for the soul's delight of lovers of music."

J.S. Bach was famous in his own day as a virtuoso organist and composer of works for keyboard. He gave us some of the finest pieces ever written for pipe organ, sometimes called "the King of Instruments." There are few things in life as thrilling as listening to one of these works performed on a great organ in an old cathedral, with the power, depth, and intensity of the music filling the cavernous space around you.

The best-known Bach organ work today is his early Toccata and Fugue in D minor (BWV 565), inspired by Buxtehude's music and later promoted by Mendelssohn, but which some scholars doubt was actually composed by Bach. Once you hear the piece's menacing opening, you will not forget it.

Bach's mature organ works are profound and elevating. Many are preludes and fugues and are usually performed in combination, such as the long and noble *St. Anne* Prelude and Fugue in E-flat major (BWV 552), which is one of those rare pieces of music that are equally well-suited to a wedding or a funeral. The Fugue has a three-part structure and three distinct themes, by which Bach may have sought to represent the Trinity. The Fantasia and Fugue in G minor (BWV 542) unites a freewheeling and chromatic Fantasia, with a Fugue on a sprightly dancelike tune—all worked out in masterful counterpoint. Other large-scale works for organ include the *Dorian* Toccata and Fugue in D minor (BWV 538), which lacks a key signature and looks back to the older modal system, and the imposing Passacaglia and Fugue in C minor (BWV 582)—a passacaglia is a Baroque musical form built on a repeating bass line (ground bass), over which the music is developed. The Fantasia in G major (BWV 572) has a florid opening, but its uplifting main section has the quality of almost regal grandeur.

The chorale preludes for organ are smaller-scale works based on a hymn tune and almost certainly used during church services in Bach's day. Dozens of these compositions by Bach survive, and they show as much polish and finesse as his longer works, including the beautiful *Liebster Jesu, Wir Sind Hier* (BWV 730) and *Herzlich Tut Mich Verlangen* (BWV 727). *Durch Adams Fall ist ganz verderbt* (BWV 637), from his *Orgel-Büchlein* collection, vividly illustrates the tragedy of mankind's fall—its use of pervasive chromatic notes symbolizes "the collapse of the harmony between man and his maker."[9]

Musical Example 21: J.S. Bach, *Fugue in E-flat major for Organ (St. Anne),* BWV 552

Choral Music

Dating back to Luther himself, the congregational hymn (chorale) was integral to Lutheran church services and J.S. Bach provided many carefully worked, fresh harmonizations of the famous tunes. His classic setting of Luther's hymn *Ein Feste Berg* is still sung in churches around the world today. Generations of music students have been taught Bach chorales as the supreme examples of composing harmony in the tonal system. His motets are more elaborate and rarely performed, but these are brilliant works; each one sparkles like a diamond.

Bach's church cantatas are on a larger scale, incorporating chorales into longer works for choir and orchestra, and he composed over 200 of them—mainly in Leipzig—to correspond to the liturgical seasons of the church. The cantatas are mainly for solo singers—recitative (descriptive, free-flowing passages) and arias (clearly defined set-pieces, which reflect on the events portrayed) with varying use of chorus and orchestral interludes. Bach went to extraordinary lengths to make the musical figures and choice of instruments reflect the exact meaning of the words. British music journalist Ivan Hewett cited this example:

> In Cantata No 77—tucked away in the Radio 3 schedule at around 11.30pm on December 19—the chorus sings of the law given by Christ to the Pharisee: "Thou shalt love the Lord thy God, and thy one neighbour as thyself." But then the trumpet appears out of the blue with a Lutheran chorale spread over 10 entries, symbolising that this command to love embraces all the 10 commandments. At the same time, the idea of obedience is symbolised by having the melody followed exactly in the bass at half speed. Harmonically, this produces some wonderfully tangy effects, a beautiful illustration of the idea that following God's law makes you free.[10]

Martin Luther had taught that the task of music is to give life, added eloquence, to the biblical texts: "After all, the gift of language combined with the gift of song was only given to man to let him know that he should praise God with both word and music, namely, by proclaiming [the Word of God] through music and by providing sweet melodies with words."[11] J.S. Bach realized his vision in the fullest way. As Sir John Eliot Gardiner has written, Bach's "emphasis on the 'vocal' delivery of Scripture" would "provide his *raison d'être* as a composer of church music."[12] Gardiner led performances of every one of Bach's church cantatas in the year 2000 and described his observations in great detail in his biography of Bach, *Music in the Castle of Heaven*.

Bach also wrote dozens of secular cantatas, for weddings or birthdays of local dignitaries. Though much of this music has now been lost, we know that he sometimes incorporated his existing music into them (e.g., extracts from one of the *Brandenburg Concerti*). His *Coffee Cantata* (BWV 211) is a humorous tale of a father and daughter arguing about her love of coffee!

The crowning glories of J.S. Bach's entire musical output are surely his major works for voice and orchestra: the *St. Matthew Passion* (BWV 244), *St. John Passion* (BWV 245), and the Mass in B minor (BWV 232). The Passions are sacred oratorios composed for church services the week before Easter and they depict the biblical narrative of Jesus Christ's suffering and death on the cross.[13] They continue a long-standing Lutheran musical tradition, which Schütz had contributed to a century earlier, but take it to unprecedented new heights. Both *Passions* resemble Bach's church cantatas—with recitative, aria, and chorus, but on a larger scale—vividly depicting the events leading up to the crucifixion. The works not only intersperse choruses throughout, but the choir also interjects suddenly to participate in the action.

The *St. John Passion* is the earlier work and places center stage the theological emphasis of this Gospel on Christ's deity, opening with a quotation from Psalm 8 on the Lordship of Christ. In the second part, the alto aria *Es ist Vollbracht!* ("It is finished!") proclaims Jesus' last words from the Cross recorded in John's Gospel. It opens in a somber mood, but bursts into joy with the words "See Judah's hero triumphs now, and ends the fight" as the full orchestra joins to triumphantly affirm Christ's victory over sin. A little later the soprano sings a different meditation, the aria *Zerfliesse, mein Herze, in Fluten der Zärhen* ("Dissolve my heart into torrents of weeping"), threading a mournful melody in between flute and oboe lines to create a subtle and captivating musical texture.

The *St. Matthew Passion* is longer, taking two-and-a-half hours to perform. The power of the music and the drama of the biblical text have made a deep impression on generations of listeners. This Passion features exquisite arias such as *Erbarme Dich* for alto, which memorably expresses Peter's tears after his denial of Jesus:

Have mercy,
My God, for my tears' sake;
Look hither,
Heart and eyes weep before thee
Bitterly.

The lovely aria *Aus Leibe* for soprano is a serene reflection of the Christian believer on the love and saving purpose of Christ's death, in which a plaintive flute weaves around the solo singer:

Out of love my Savior is willing to die,
Though he knows nothing of any sin,
So that eternal ruin
And the punishment of judgment
Many not rest upon my soul.

Bach compiled and completed the Mass in B minor near the end of his life, almost as his last will and testament in music. The first two movements (*Kyrie* and *Gloria*) had been composed in the 1730s and Bach added the later movements using preexisting material; the words are from the Lutheran liturgy used in Saxony.[14]

I remember my religious studies teacher in school saying that the angels in heaven are playing Bach's Mass in B minor. At the time, I was doubtful; but, as I got older, I understood that maybe he had a point. This traditional text expresses core Christian doctrines, which are elevated by supremely beautiful music for choir and orchestra (chorus, arias, and duets). The work is a musical Mount Everest, alternating solemnity, joyous celebration, and reverent reflection in music of the finest caliber. The music for the Creed conveys with certainty that these are truths Bach himself believed. Conductor Masaaki Suzuki pointed to one attribute: " 'Eight voices in the Credo!' he says—meaning eight lines of polyphony, unprecedented in any of Bach's cantatas or keyboard fugues."[15]

The holiness of God is portrayed in the *Sanctus* of the Mass in B minor by vibrant and exulting choir and orchestra, as it were surrounded by myriad angels:

Trumpet I in D
Trumpet II in D
Trumpet III in D
Timpani
Oboe I
Oboe II
Oboe III
Violin I
Violin II
Viola
Treble I
San - ctus, san - ctus, san - - ctus, san - - - -
Treble II
San - ctus, san - ctus, san - ctus, san - -
Alto I
San - ctus, san - ctus, san - - ctus, san - - - -
Alto II
San - ctus, san - ctus, san - ctus,
Tenor
San - ctus, san - ctus, san - ctus
Bass
San - ctus, san - ctus, san - ctus,
Cello/Basso continuo

Musical Example 22: J.S. Bach, “Sanctus”, *Mass in B minor,* BWV 232

10

Reflecting on Bach's Music

I first encountered J.S. Bach's music in churches; his monumental organ works and his chorale settings. He would likely have wanted that. Later, I would study the chorale harmonizations, *Brandenburg Concerti*, and *Coffee Cantata* at school (appropriately, since coffee was an integral part of my music studies). I also learned to play some of Bach's keyboard pieces and had opportunities to attend performances of the great choral works at different venues in the North West of England.

Over time, I began to realize that in Bach I was listening to, or participating in, the music of a genius—perhaps it was hearing a performance of the *St. John Passion* in the immense Liverpool Cathedral with friends, or the Fantasia and Fugue in G minor played in a spacious Lutheran church in Germany. Yet, Bach was a humble man who once commented that anyone could compose similar music if he or she worked hard at it: "For him invention was an uncovering of possibilities that are already there, rather than something truly original—hence his view that anyone could do as well, provided they were industrious. God is still the only true creator."[1]

The objective principles of beauty are captured in sound by J.S. Bach. Many people have drawn attention to the proportion and balance throughout Bach's music—from religious cantatas to the concerti and from any of his small-scale fugues to the large-scale overall proportion heard in the *St. Matthew Passion*. The modern-day conductor, Sir John Eliot Gardiner, in his biography of J.S. Bach, noted: "For many people the hallmark of Bach's music lies in the lucidity of its structure and the mathematical satisfaction of its proportions."[2]

As a leading exponent of the tonal system, Bach sought great harmonic variety and invention. The harmonic rhythm of his pieces moves swiftly. His chorale harmonizations are models of how to create a beautiful harmonic texture. As music historian Paul Westermeyer described: "Bach's music is complex, yet it grows out of and affirms the congregation's song."[3]

In his music set to Christian texts for worship, Bach goes to great lengths to accurately, and dramatically, accentuate the meaning of the words. He even incorporates, as we have seen, patterns into the musical structure that usually go unnoticed by hearers. Music professor Calvin Stapert explores Bach's theological and musical craftsmanship in detail in his fascinating book *My Only Comfort: Death, Deliverance, and Discipleship in the Music of Bach*—for example, the multiple ways that the structure and features of the music for the *Credo* from the Mass in B minor represent the theology of the Cross and the Resurrection.[4] Stapert describes how the majestic *Sanctus*, which comes later in the piece, has a "Trinitarian structure" built systematically on the number three. In its overall effect: "Somehow Bach managed, through purely sonic means, to give us some sense of what it is to come into the presence of the holy God."[5] It is a depiction of the vision of Isaiah 6 in music.

Thinking in terms of our broad definition of "harmony," Bach combines the diverse orchestral instruments of his day with expertise, and he matches solo instruments with choir or solo singer in a multitude of different ways. Remember that the organ, like the orchestra, also unites diverse sounds with its range of stops (corresponding to selections of pipes of different sizes and materials).

Bach's music is not perfect and we should not say that Bach always succeeded in over 1,000 works—some pieces may lack simplicity; other pieces may be too long. But everywhere we find unity in diversity on many levels. This is evident in the music he composed across many different genres and for many different combinations of instruments, with or without choir. Bach's use of musical forms in his works gives a unifying framework for rich and intricate writing for voices and/or instruments. And his counterpoint combines complexity with simplicity—a simple theme is worked out and shared between several different voices before coming to a satisfying close, e.g., fugues with simple subjects which are worked out with extraordinary complexity.

In the music of Bach, which is typically contrapuntal, the harmony is divided between equally important voices or instruments. In this, Bach was continuing a musical heritage of counterpoint that dates back to the polyphony of Palestrina and earlier. Yet a change had begun during the early Baroque period, years before J.S. Bach was born, when people also began using "harmony" to describe the musical accompaniment to a solo voice. This deprived music of its complexity (and is epitomized today by guitar chords supporting a vocalist).

But commentators have seen contrapuntal music as reflecting something deeper; how two lives can be different, but harmonious, in marriage or in friendship. John Ahern explains that a biblical view of marriage sees husband and wife as different but equal—two voices in harmony with each other, neither too different ("Both must sacrifice independence for the sake of symmetry") nor the same—he argues that parallel fifths and octaves don't work in counterpoint because they are too similar: "Implicit in the term contrapuntal," says Walter Piston, "is the idea of disagreement. The interplay of agreement and disagreement between the various factors of the musical texture constitutes the contrapuntal element in music."[6]

The Musical Legacy of J.S. Bach

Bach's music lives on today, though like a mountain, most people only view it from a distance. That is sad because there is so much to explore and to enjoy. Yet, even in his own day, Bach did not compose first and foremost for those around him. His religious choral works are almost all in German, so that the congregation could understand the words, but Bach did not make the music easily accessible. It's quite clear that his primary audience was God his Creator. He sought to write beautiful music to the glory of God—when he wrote SDG on the manuscripts, he meant it.

J.S. Bach was a famous organist in his day, but most of his compositions were not widely circulated and some of his cantatas were likely rarely ever performed. At his death, his estate was split up between his family and therefore many of his works remained hidden from view.

Felix Mendelssohn was very important in promoting the music of J.S. Bach in the early nineteenth century. However, it is an exaggeration to say that Bach was forgotten until Mendelssohn revived his reputation with the *St. Matthew Passion* performance of 1829. In the hundred years after Bach's death in 1750, the forty-eight Preludes and Fugues (*The Well-Tempered Clavier*) were used by many teachers, and more than twenty-five editions were published during that time.[7] Both Mozart and Beethoven are known to have played and studied "the 48" as young men, with Mozart transcribing some of its pieces for string ensembles. Later, Chopin's *24 Preludes* pay obvious homage to the great man. The Bach Gesellschaft was a society formed in 1850 to republish all of J.S. Bach's works and, since then, his music has been in no danger of sinking into obscurity.

We can wholeheartedly agree with Calvin Stapert that, "Given Bach's combination of musical prowess, personal devotion, and theological understanding, it is not surprising that his music stands unexcelled among artistic expressions of the Christian faith."[8] But others have gone a little too far in extolling the brilliance of Bach's music. The Swedish theologian and Lutheran archbishop Nathan Söderblom (1866–1931) called Bach's music "the fifth Gospel" and there are Christians who see the performance of Bach's music in itself as a form of evangelism.[9] It is surely music of the highest quality, which lifts up our hearts and points to God because it reflects his glory. Yet only when set to Christian words can it convey the gospel of salvation in Jesus Christ. The same is true of paintings or sculpture, which cannot articulate truth—that is the purpose of words and why God has given mankind the verbal revelation of Holy Scripture.

Aspects of Bach's music were not fashionable at the time of his death, especially as he held to contrapuntal music against the rising lightweight *galant* style, yet his music has proved to be timeless because it epitomizes the objective principles of beauty in sound. His greatest works rank among the greatest works of art of all time.

11

What Went Wrong?

J.S. Bach was born in 1685 into a world shaped by the teachings of the Protestant Reformation. Daily life—its habits, assumptions, and patterns of thinking—were influenced by the biblical worldview. He crafted his music in this atmosphere, as many other leading composers and artists had done before him. However, as the eighteenth and nineteenth centuries wore on, some writers in Europe openly questioned Christian doctrine. Ideas began to circulate suggesting that though God may have created the world, he now stands detached from it (deism), and religious skeptics undermined biblical doctrines. Charles Darwin's theory of evolution proposed that human beings do not have a creator God and relied on the dubious philosophical viewpoint that progress and improvement are inevitable.

As the twentieth century dawned, academic thinking in the West was dominated by a proud, atheistic rejection of the living God. This unbelief was expressed in culture through painting, literature, and, of course, in music. And from there it went on in succeeding decades to influence every aspect of life.

If Bach's music represents the heights of Western classical music, then in the twentieth century this tradition sank to its depths. It is no accident that as intellectuals in the West increasingly rejected the God of truth, goodness, and beauty, its composers did the same and began to write pieces that celebrate ugliness. Some readers may be unaware that leading composers began to deliberately overthrow concepts of beauty in music, including the tonal system, from the early twentieth century onwards. In so doing, they produced works of varying degrees of hideousness.

Francis Schaeffer (1912–1984), the theologian and Christian apologist, drew attention to this shocking trajectory. Comparing J.S. Bach with the Dutch painter Rembrandt from the same era, Schaeffer noted that they had a Christian worldview with the Creator God at its center: "They were both willing to be creatures." But Schaeffer pointed to a turning away from God in classical music, which first surfaced in Beethoven's late works (for example, his late string quartets: see Chapter 7—*Surveying Composers*). He relates this to the teaching of the apostle Paul in Romans 1, in which men exchange what God has revealed in creation for idols, and uses Arnold Schoenberg's music to demonstrate what went wrong.[1]

Atonality and Serialism

Arnold Schoenberg (1874–1951) was born in Vienna, Austria, and began his musical career writing in the late-Romantic tradition, including very large orchestral works. But, in the first decade of the twentieth century, Schoenberg decided that he had no further use for the tonal system and began looking for ways to overthrow it. What he settled on became known as "atonality" and it marked a new phase of modernism in music. Schoenberg cast aside the tonal system of organized harmony and replaced it with a system of organized dissonance. Instead of writing music based on a traditional (diatonic) scale, from the 1920s onwards he composed using a random arrangement of the twelve semitones of the chromatic scale. This "row" is then repeated in different patterns—the practice is often referred to as the twelve-tone method. It was later called serialism.

Atonal music is often described as "music without a tonal center," but that is somewhat of an evasion, because the concept is systematically built on discord. In fact, Schoenberg went to great lengths to avoid any harmony in his atonal works. What he called the "emancipation of dissonance" from tonal implications[2] was actually the tyranny of dissonance. Schoenberg was engaged in the modern quest for autonomy—in his case, the autonomy of composers.

One of Schoenberg's first pieces to employ atonality was *Erwartung* (Expectation), Op. 17—a work for soprano and orchestra, which radiates despair. It is directly connected to the distorted and dark Expressionist school in art, and reflects the anti-Christian beliefs of psychoanalyst Sigmund Freud, who "regarded religion as a human construct grounded in ignorance, fear, fantasy and guilt."[3] Later works by Schoenberg demonstrating his twelve-tone method include his Variations for Orchestra Op. 31 and Third and Fourth String Quartets Opp. 30 and 37.

Other early atonal composers include Anton Webern (1883–1945) and Alban Berg (1885–1935). Both were from Vienna and studied under Schoenberg, hence they are collectively referred to as "the Second Viennese School."[4] Berg allowed harmony to surface at times, even in his twelve-tone works such as the *Lyric Suite* for string quartet and his Violin Concerto, whereas Webern was more absolutist and focused on very abstract and concentrated atonal music. This was an outcome of his philosophical belief that the twelve-tone method represented "progress" in music, described by one commentator as "the inevitable result of music's evolution."[5] Here is an explicit connection of Darwin's theory with the debasement of music. Webern's religious outlook was pantheistic and he even labeled twelve-tone music as in some sense "salvation."[6]

Sadly, Schoenberg's modernist work was very influential on composers throughout the twentieth century. My secular undergraduate music degree presented him as the natural continuation of the line of composers from Bach to Beethoven to Wagner. Today, hidden from public view, Schoenberg and his successors continue to be venerated in the academy. Other, better, composers such as Dvořák, Sibelius, and Elgar, were never named in my history of Western music class.

The great works of classical music, such as those surveyed earlier, all use discord and resolution within a system of tonal harmony. No one is arguing for bland, colorless music. The atonal movement did not begin because there was anything essentially wrong with the classical tradition. The modernists rejected tonality because they wanted to. The Second Viennese School retained traditional musical forms and gestures from the classical tradition; nevertheless the ugliness of the unrelenting discord they composed is obvious.

Atonal works are inherently disturbing and have never found widespread acceptance by general audiences. It is not hard to understand why. Harmony has been recognized as one of the core principles of beauty since at least the days of ancient Greece. Even the birds in their songs testify that God has placed musical harmony in his creation. In fact, it is very difficult to write music that is constantly discordant because so many different combinations of notes suggest harmony—and that fact alone indicates that atonal compositions are a rebellion against the created order. It is no exaggeration to say that these works represent atheism in music; composers, "professing themselves to be wise. . .became fools" (Rom. 1:22).

The philosopher Sir Roger Scruton firmly rejected the atonal movement, pointing out that it is "the attempt to *avoid* something"—namely harmony. He observed that Schoenberg's output renders "into audible forms the complex and harrowing emotions that arose with the collapse of spiritual order in Central Europe. . ." and added: "It is as though anxiety were programmed into this music and can never be wholly eliminated."[7] Scruton convincingly argued that hearers inevitably hear atonal music against a background of tonality. This is not surprising, since however sinful human beings become, we can never totally overthrow God's created order, and the tonal system is an organization of the harmony in sound which God has set in this world.

In atonal works, the dissonance is never permitted to resolve. This perpetual lack of resolution in atonal compositions denies them the convincing overall structure and proportion made possible by tonality. The composer George Rochberg (1918–2005), rebelled against his twelve-tone education and later adopted traditional harmonic composition because in his view "only tonality (with its power of forecasting and delaying cadences) gave music the dynamic momentum that made possible the genuinely coherent and expressively meaningful articulation of long temporal spans."[8]

Alternatives

Modernists have advocated atonality as the progressive development of Wagner's extreme chromaticism. But, rather than the way forward, it is actually a dead end—as the history of avant-garde twentieth-century music demonstrates (see below). Composers such as Debussy and Ravel sought alternative harmonic structures.

English composers such as Vaughan Williams sought inspiration from centuries-old folk music. All three, to varying degrees, drew on the modal system to develop a different harmonic language. In fact, Brahms had earlier done the same, for example, in his fourth symphony.

It is certainly not the case that only Christians continued to write classical music based in harmony. For example, Vaughan Williams was not a Christian believer (though he set many Christian texts to music) and he wrote some attractive music of lasting quality. The obvious beauty of this tradition in music is still employed by those willing to embrace it in many different countries, including film composers to the present day (see the *Modern Era* in Chapter 7—*Surveying Composers*). It is undoubtedly true that over the last hundred years many tonal pieces of classical music have been written that are worthy of exploration and which deserve a much wider audience.

However, composers since Schoenberg's time have studied atonal music and many have been influenced by his methods. Men who wrote some beautiful pieces in the tonal system, such as Aaron Copland and Samuel Barber, both also composed atonal pieces which stand quite apart from their famous works. Composers for the past century have often experimented with very different styles—you cannot simply try listening to an unfamiliar piece by a familiar name and assume it will be good.

Igor Stravinsky (1882–1971) was "arguably the most important composer of his time."[9] Stravinsky wrote a wide range of works and employed dissonance in his music, but is better known for his subversion of rhythm by mixing different meters and countering rhythmic expectations by use of accents and rests. Born in Russia, Stravinsky created his own sound by utilizing elements of the country's musical traditions, including characteristic blocks of sound repeating a short pattern (ostinato) and lack of development.

His early works, such as the ballet scores for *The Firebird* and *Petrushka,* are fairly accessible, but in his infamous score for *The Rite of Spring*—a ballet set to a horrifying plot—Stravinsky developed his rhythmic irregularity and musical dissonance to a heightened level. This work also demonstrates his preference for a more sparing, "dry" orchestration, in contrast to the rich sounds of the Romantic era.

In his "neoclassical" period that followed, Stravinsky went on to apply his idiomatic methods to the musical forms of classical music in pieces such as his Symphony in C and the Octet for Wind Instruments. Although this music usually has a tonal center of reference, it is in fact "neotonal" because it does not follow the rules of traditional harmony, [10] and the level of chromaticism usually makes his music quite dissonant.

Composers of this era had begun to take Arnold Schoenberg's structural principles used in atonality, especially the serial repetition of a pattern, and apply them to other areas such as rhythm, so that the movement became known as "serialism." Late in his career, Stravinsky also utilized serialism in works such as *In Memoriam Dylan Thomas*.

What should we make of Stravinsky's music? His employment of continually shifting rhythm runs counter to the principle of proportion or symmetry in music. This practice has no regularity or order in the rhythm. And he frequently rejects harmony in favor of dissonance. Like Schoenberg, there is plenty of evidence that Stravinsky sought to subvert the objective principles of beauty in music.

One successor, Frenchman Olivier Messiaen (1908–1992), followed a similar path. His work could be characterized as post-tonal, relying on dissonance and rhythmic complexity for its effect. It is frequently bewildering, so the label "contemplative"—attributed by his fans to Messiaen's works—is seriously misplaced.

Avant-Garde Experiments

Other followers of Schoenberg and Stravinsky went to even greater lengths to employ barbaric practices in sound. Straining to overthrow beauty and to shock their hearers, composers such as Edgar Varese (1883–1965) and Karlheinz Stockhausen (1928–2007) replaced music with chaotic or grotesque noise, often employing electronic means to produce masses of sound that are repulsive and incomprehensible. Pierre Boulez (1925–2016) extended the principles of serialism to produce instrumental works that are exceptionally difficult to play and offensive to the ear. Iannis Xenakis (1922–2001), a European architect and composer, sought to produce works in both sound and architecture that model randomness (see Chapter 5—*Objective Beauty*).

The avant-garde descended into ever more confusion in the output of John Cage (1912–1992). Cage, influenced by Buddhism (as was Stockhausen), gloried in chance, pure noise, and "blurring of boundaries between music, art, and life."[11] He experimented with shoving objects inside a piano to create different sounds, and his best-known piece—4' 33" (*Four Minutes, Thirty-Three Seconds*)—requires the performer(s) to sit silently and play nothing for the duration of the piece. Ridiculously, Cage's instructions claim there are three parts to the work! I was subjected to a "performance" of this at university and decided that reviewing some previous lecture notes was a better use of my time.

How did the classical music tradition succumb to such utter nonsense? On one level, the rise of state funding for artists and composers in the West allows them to ignore public displeasure. Many avant-garde composers have been insulated from the need for any wider appeal by the certainty of a university salary. In God's common grace, the products of their work continue to be rejected by most people around them. But the intellectual elites have secured taxpayer funding for their tastes. In mid-twentieth-century Germany, the Darmstadt summer courses for "new music" were state sponsored (at first by the US authorities after World War II) and became a breeding ground for the works of Stockhausen and Boulez among others.[12]

Like pagan Athenians in ancient Greece, these twentieth century composers constantly sought "to hear some new thing" (Acts 17:21). La Monte Young (1935–), a leading founder of minimalism in the avant-garde movement (paring music back to primitive and simplistic fragments of sound), once said: "Often I hear somebody say that the most important thing about a work of art is not that it be new but that it be good, but I am not interested in good; I am interested in new—even if this includes the possibility of its being evil."[13]

Various social or political theories have been advanced to explain the modernist and avant-garde movements and that is not an irrelevant discussion. Yet ultimately the cause must be traced back to people's worldview. Since the so-called Enlightenment, men began to reject biblical revelation and turn inside themselves, becoming vain in their imaginations, and their foolish hearts were darkened (Rom. 1:21). Until the early twentieth century, Western composers continued to work within a musical tradition founded on the Christian worldview, even if they were not practicing Christians. But Schoenberg and his successors rebelled and, instead, promoted sheer, unpleasant noise.

The works of these composers so defy the objective principles of beauty that they cannot properly be called music. John Cage even proposed replacing the word "music" with "organized sound." The musicologist Richard Taruskin wittily remarked: "Where Schoenberg had "emancipated the dissonance," in other words, Cage now proposed to complete the job and emancipate noise."[14]

R.C. Sproul exposed the philosophy of avant-garde artists such as John Cage: "Some modern musicians have attempted to create chaos, although it's an impossible task because you cannot intentionally be unintentional. You can't intentionally create ultimate chaos. There is still a pattern to this pretended chaos. They're trying to communicate through a very loose kind of form, whether it's in painting or in music, a statement against harmony and order and rationality, all of which have theological implications. It's part of the secular mood of despair that says there is no ultimate coherency."[15]

The descent into atonal and avant-garde expressions of ugliness painfully illustrates the darkness that envelops men's hearts when they turn their backs defiantly against the God of beauty. Avant-garde music captures the atheist spirit of despair.

12

Music as Mass Entertainment

Western music in the twentieth century saw two different, but related, developments taking place. As elite composers promoted increasingly avant-garde expressions of barbarism in sound, their works were incomprehensible or repulsive to those beyond their ivory towers. At the same time, the widespread availability of recorded sound saw popular music descend into whatever most immediately entranced the largest number of people. Commercial success was (and remains) its goal.

Mankind has been making music since the dawn of time—to accompany joyous or solemn occasions, or simply for fun, to express sadness, or to reflect on life. The human voice is the universally available instrument, but only those songs passed down through oral tradition or written down in notation survive today. Our God-given capacity for invention and industry has also enabled people to make a dizzying variety of musical instruments from wood, metal, animal bones, horns, or skins, etc. Archaeological remains of musical instruments dating back thousands of years have been found across the world.

In a general sense, then, we can say that folk music has always existed in human culture—especially songs. Many oral cultures around the world have preserved and passed on their epic histories, stories or myths in song to aid memorization. By folk music, I mean traditional forms of music connected to a particular community or place—music which may be vocal and/or instrumental and which groups of people often join together to perform. A folk song in Great Britain or North America is typically strophic—for example, a ballad has a single tune set to a poem of several verses, each with the same metrical (syllabic) pattern.

There were revivals of some forms of folk music in the nineteenth and twentieth centuries led by interested performers, musicologists, or national governments. The American twentieth century folk music revival combined traditional instruments with distinctly modern songs (often with a political message). Folk music has certainly influenced popular music at times over the last few generations in the West, but, when we talk today about "pop," we generally mean something else.

The modern concept of pop music is inseparable from mass entertainment and the advance of technology over the past 150 years or so, including—since the 1960s—electronically-generated sound. Pop music is recorded using microphones and distributed by media widely to people of many social backgrounds. Video portrayal of the performers on screen has become essential for them to gain recognition and a fan base. Unlike folk music, pop music is presented to others; it's not usually music that people gather to perform. And it typically has an urban background—not rural origins like folk music.

Country music, which developed from the folk traditions of rural America, is a modern genre that is a distinct form of pop music. Initially featuring a vocalist, guitars, and other strings, country music has expanded since the mid-twentieth century to feature other instruments such as drums and has seen its own offshoots such as Bluegrass. Media distribution (by radio, followed by newer technologies) has been important in disseminating country music.

The nineteenth-century roots of pop music are found in the music halls in England and vaudeville entertainment shows in the USA, and, more specifically, in the popular songs of Stephen Foster and Tin Pan Alley. In the twentieth century, ragtime piano music, then jazz, paved the way for early rhythm and blues, leading to rock music, and the whole panoply of Western pop music available today.

How does this music measure up against the objective principles of beauty? Since God has given us the gift of music in his creation, the music we listen to should seek God's glory by being beautiful. This is something that few people apply their minds to, even though it is absolutely necessary if we are to love God with all our minds (Matt. 22:37; 1 Cor. 14:15). The task is made more difficult because pop music in the West has become like universal sonic wallpaper which is present wherever we go. It is hard to think critically about something you do not notice.

It would be foolish and simply wrong to dismiss all popular or folk music as ugly. A good tune, well performed, has a beauty all of its own. Yet there are degrees of beauty; a simple solo song does not have the proportions or complexity of a symphony. Returning to the analogy of architecture, a much-loved piece of country music corresponds well to the evocative log cabin of the American West, but any of the symphonies discussed earlier has the far larger dimensions—and greater beauty—of an historic cathedral.

Yet something went wrong in the mid-twentieth century, when popular music became corrupted by a beat that dominates and overpowers the music. The source was rock music, starting in the 1950s, and its prominent beat spread, via related genres such as disco, into the rest of pop music. The beat is celebrated by pop enthusiasts and secular authors such as Bob Stanley, who draw attention to "the rock-solid beat" at the start of "rock 'n' roll" in the 1950s: "Everything was now permissible as long as it created the most stupidly, gloriously distorted noise."[1]

Rock Music

Bill Haley and the Comets were catapulted to fame with *Rock Around the Clock* in 1955. Elvis Presley was already recording, and reached worldwide prominence the following year. Other big names followed, including the Beatles and the Rolling Stones in the 1960s, and rock 'n' roll morphed into rock music generally.

Without doubt, "the big beat" is at the core of rock music. It's even in the name of perhaps the most famous band of all time: the *Beat*les. But we need not single out one band or performer in particular. No one seeks to deny that the beat lies at the heart of rock music's propulsive power.[2]

What's the problem here? All music has a beat or underlying

pulse that gives it rhythmic structure. This is like the regular "left, right, left, right" of soldiers on parade, or the steady pulse of a beating heart. Likewise, the beat or pulse of music holds everything together, allowing the music to move together in and through time. As we have noted, rhythm is one of the four basic elements of music.

Some pieces of music composed down the centuries have relied more on rhythm than others. It is evident in much of Beethoven's music, some works by Sir William Walton, or in the sound of marching bands. The immediate precursors of rock music—ragtime, jazz, and early rhythm and blues—clearly rely on rhythm as an important part of their identity.

But the big beat exploded into Western culture with rock music. It is generated by the drums in conjunction with the electric bass guitar, which elevates the beat and also provides the grounding for the harmony.[3] Electric amplification allowed a small number of instruments to form bands in which each performer can be clearly heard. Both the drum kit and the bass guitar were twentieth-century innovations, the latter replacing the double bass, which was deemed too quiet for those who wanted something altogether new and earth-shattering.

The dominating power of the beat in rock music is clearly disproportionate. Even if a particular song may have a catchy tune, the beat overwhelms the rest of the music and so violates the objective principles of beauty. And the big beat has a powerful effect on the human body, which has its own natural rhythms (pulse, breathing, walking etc.). The physical impact on people is not well understood, but there is a growing body of medical evidence showing that heavy metal music, for example, has potentially harmful effects on the heart and nervous systems of healthy people and on those who are ill.[4] One study found that listening to heavy metal after heart surgery "can lead to stress and/or life-threatening arrhythmias."[5] Some commentators on music have suggested that repeated listening to rock has an addictive effect, comparable to alcoholism or drug use.[6]

The sheer loudness of rock music is another of its defining characteristics. The volume grips people and often mesmerizes them. A leading avant-garde composer, Luciano Berio (1925–2003), noted with admiration: "Microphones, amplifiers and loudspeakers become not only extensions of the voices and instruments but become instruments themselves, overwhelming at times the original acoustic qualities of the sound source."[7] It is surely irrefutable that listening at rock's loudest decibels can damage human hearing.[8] Christian authors John Blanchard and Dan Lucarini observed: "It is meant to blast the emotions and the mind—not to reflect truth, honesty, integrity or beauty, nor to encourage a discerning response or produce any beneficial result."[9]

A dominating beat is now everywhere, across all forms of popular music. This is why it is so important that you think about music. This is not to say that every piece with drums is ugly; no, some have all the musical elements in better proportion; with a good tune, harmony, and rhythm. Every piece of music—popular and classical—must be evaluated by the same objective principles. It is likely that the powerful drums that open the first movement of Brahms' first symphony are disproportionate, though this is not a feature of other works by Brahms. Ask yourself about such music: if the overpowerful beat was removed, would the rest of the music still make sense without it? Or is there not much music left? If a piece doesn't cohere without its big beat, then something is intrinsically wrong with it—disproportion is woven into its fabric.

From the start of rock 'n' roll, the vocalists enjoyed calling out, shouting, and making other decidedly non-musical sounds. As the output quickly turned towards aggressive noise, the instruments in later variants of rock used deliberately distorted sounds (usually by electronic means) and singers would only approximate to singing a tune.

Rock went on to spawn rap, which has no harmony and often vicious words; it is a form of rhythmic speech which is entirely dependent on the big beat. Arising in America in the late 1970s and closely related to hip hop music, its lyrics frequently revel in violence and profanity. Yet, even if this medium were set to better words, the ugliness of the sound would remain. As the distinguished American mezzo-soprano Marilyn Horne was known to remark, "It may be rhythm. It may be rhyme. But it ain't music."[10]

There are other features of rock music culture that are obviously contrary to biblical teaching. Take the words, which constantly celebrate sexual immorality, impurity, and blasphemy, and the onstage seductive behavior of the performers. This is so pervasive it is impossible to refute.[11] Read any history of rock music and it is intertwined with references to illicit drug use in songs and in the personal lives of the stars. We could cite almost any famous group. Bob Stanley commented: "Every stage of the Beatles' career had a complementary drug: speed (their Hamburg and Merseybeat period), cannabis (the sleepy *Rubber Soul*), acid [LSD] (*Revolver* and *Sgt. Pepper*) and heroin (Lennon's crack-up on *The White Album*)."[12] The drug-taking history of the Rolling Stones is notorious. While some famous composers of classical music lived immoral lives, for which they will have to give an account to God, their sinful personal behavior was not paraded as a virtue for multitudes to emulate.

There is an argument that certain classical musical genres have been connected with decadence; certainly, the plots of some operas are mired in immorality, and Christians measuring them against the Bible will find that these works fall far short. Yet these works have not pervasively changed the general culture as rock music has, and, despite the lyrics, objectively beautiful music has been composed for many operas. The opposite is the case for rock music.

Cultural Impact

Some may argue that it is possible to listen to rock in complete isolation from the culture associated with it. That argument is not persuasive since the lyrics themselves are flawed. But even if the music could be clinically isolated from its context, the music is still disproportionate. And we cannot ignore the widespread cultural impact of this movement, which validates and promotes immoral attitudes and behaviors among vast numbers of people.

From its beginning in the 1950s, rock music has allowed shrewd businesses and top performers to generate immense profits from sales by targeting children. This is exploitative. With mass media providing music to young people apart from their parents and community, it has grabbed their attention, promoted rebellion against authority, and shaped their tastes for a lifetime. As commentators have noted, "The independent identity of teenagers, and their economic and cultural freedom, were proclaimed most effectively by the clothing and entertainment markets that most powerfully manipulated and exploited them."[13]

Rock music has played a big part in mainstreaming celebrity culture, even if a fascination with celebrities came a little earlier in the modern era. Today, the latest big-name star is treated as an idol, who is often in effect worshipped. Simply observe their adoring fans (or worshippers) at a live event. This is a religious act which is often overlooked in our secular age.

These matters need to be addressed plainly and honestly because they have been ignored or evaded for so long. There is clear evidence that rock music can not only be physically harmful, but also harmful to a person's soul (see Chapter 16—*Bringing Disorder to the Soul*). The impact of rock on the lives of individuals and society as a whole is deeply serious, especially since the big beat now permeates pop music generally. Proponents of popular music have said of the Beatles, "Their appearance on *The Ed Sullivan Show* on February 9, 1964, was possibly the most significant cultural event in postwar America. Their rise, the scale of it and their impact on society, was completely unprecedented."[14] We should note the importance of mass media—here, TV—in generating the widespread impact. While the cultural messaging of rock music (a rebellious obsession with opposing moral and lawful authorities) has been destructive, this book's focus is on the nature and effects of the music itself.

The philosopher Allan Bloom (1930–1992), in his unlikely bestseller about the decline of higher education—*The Closing of the American Mind*—identified rock as a profoundly negative influence on the desires and aspirations of students. Bloom was scathing, direct, and uncompromising; he rejected rock music because of its reliance on the beat (while also referencing Maurice Ravel's *Bolero* for the same fault). Bloom wrote, "Rock music has one appeal only, a barbaric appeal, to sexual desire. . ." and warned that "Rock music provides a premature ecstasy and, in this respect, is like the drugs with which it is allied."[15]

Bloom lamented that such music is especially marketed to children: "It is of historic proportions that a society's best young and their best energies should be so occupied. People of future civilizations will wonder at this and find it as incomprehensible as we do the caste system, witch-burning, harems, cannibalism and gladiatorial combats. It may well be that a society's greatest madness seems normal to itself."[16] It is very sobering that he, as a secular commentator, wrote: "The family spiritual void has left the field open to rock music."[17]

Worldview on Display

American musicologist Charles Hamm wrote that popular music in the USA has almost always been "music for entertainment, leisure listening, dancing; mass entertainment, pitched in a style making it easily accessible to millions of listeners."[18] People are not on their guard when they are being entertained. This has allowed the influence of rock music to be uncritically absorbed by so many. So many people never think about the music they are listening to.

As you drive round any city in the West, you will see ugly, modernist buildings erected over the past century. Houses, office blocks, libraries, theatres—there are examples all around us of architecture that is functional, but distasteful. There is no complexity, or where there is complexity there is no proportion or symmetry. This is the frozen music of our day. Our eyes see the anti-God attitudes expressed in architecture; our ears hear this same rebellion in atonal and rock-permeated popular music.[19]

The influence of rock completely dwarfs that of atonal music—because rock music is in the Western air we breathe. But both atonal music and rock music belong to the same pagan culture: atonal compositions reject the goal of beauty in music; the big beat in rock abuses music by twisting it to pander to people's sensual desires. God's creation is full of good things, but the Bible warns us against abusing them by our sinfulness and emphasizes the need for self-control (e.g., 1 Cor. 7:31; Acts 24:25). The fact that the Western world is now drenched in rock-inspired pop music is clear evidence that God is giving our culture over to sinful works of darkness (Rom. 1:28) as men turn their backs on him.

In light of this, I cannot agree with author and music academic Harold Best that "art and especially music. . .are essentially neutral in their ability to express belief, creed, moral and ethical exactitudes, or even worldview" or that "we are free to assume that all music possesses its own kind of worth."[20] These false premises lead to an uncritical acceptance of popular music and a failure to see that some types of music are an abuse of organized sound by sinful men. It is not truly loving people to endorse degraded forms of music; the way of love is to lift people's horizons to better music. In so doing, we would obey Micah 6:8 ("to do justly, and to love mercy, and to walk humbly with thy God") and bring all things, including music, *coram Deo*—before the face of God.

13

Taste in Music

We need to think about the music we hear—to consider its quality and what effect it is having on us. Yet many people do not. This is not a new problem. Augustine wrote centuries ago: "Like the birds, vulgar performers can get their notes right and vulgar audiences can approve, but they cannot give any reasoned explanation."[1]

What is new today is that technology allows people to access almost unlimited amounts of music of every conceivable type. It is a part of our lives, consciously or not, in our homes and in all kinds of public places. John Blanchard and Dan Lucarini wrote: "Music's penetration into our modern society is nothing short of a phenomenon, something that has a profoundly significant impact on the lives of millions of people around the world."[2] The invention of recorded music, like any other form of media, has proved both a blessing and a curse. We can enjoy so much, but popular music has often been cheapened and degraded to appeal to our worst instincts.

At the same time, classical music, which bequeathed so much beautiful music to mankind, plummeted in the twentieth century into a nadir of noise, which remains influential in elite musical circles today. The academic world is also in the grip of a rigidly applied relativist worldview that tries to pretend that all types of music are equal—that John Cage's *Four Minutes, Thirty-Three Seconds* of silence is of equal worth to Handel's *Messiah*. University professors teach with all seriousness that ugly chants and banging noises from a culture steeped in spiritism are to be esteemed equally with the mesmerizing choral polyphony of Palestrina. This is as absurd as pretending that a mud hut is as beautiful as a king's palace. The problem is not limited to the arena of music. There is a political crusade in the West to overthrow all great works of art because they are allegedly the product of a repressive cultural elite.[3] Such prejudice is rife on college campuses, with students sadly indoctrinated to hate their heritage rather than taught to prize what is good about Western civilization.

From at least the time of ancient Greece, it has been uncontroversial to believe on rational grounds that some music is better than other music. But, in the world of the twenty-first century, merely stating that not all works of art are equal risks bringing charges of elitism or, at worst, cultural supremacy. Perhaps this is tangled up with some wrong thinking about living in a democracy, where decisions are made by majority vote. Sir Roger Scruton noted accurately: "In a democratic culture people are inclined to believe that it is presumptuous to claim to have better taste than your neighbour."[4] Allan Bloom expanded on the same theme: "Although every man in a democracy thinks himself individually the equal of every other man, this makes it difficult to resist the collectivity of equal men. If all opinions are equal, then the majority of opinions, on the psychological analogy of politics, should hold sway."[5] So, the thinking goes, if many people around me enjoy rock music, who am I to object? And yet, the cultural elite that rules today is contemptuous when most people reject modern art. We are left in an irrational situation—popular music must be accepted as entirely good because it is popular, yet when most people find the avant-garde movement distasteful, its works must be celebrated anyway!

We can be thankful that there are objective standards of beauty, even if it is not fashionable to say this today. The fact is, there is good-quality music and poor-quality music. And there are pieces that abuse God's good gift of music and pieces that use it well. Some compositions are more beautiful than others, depending on the extent to which they exhibit the objective principles of beauty. A piece which demonstrates these in a more fitting combination—or at greater length—is more beautiful than a piece that does not achieve it as well, or much at all.

Different kinds of beauty are appreciated by different people, and even at different stages in life and learning. Some may have better discernment in assessing paintings, others in listening to music; some may excel at appreciating architecture, others are more judicious in their enjoyment of poetry. No one is equally capable in every area.[6]

Yet it is disappointing that so many people today like pieces of music that are flimsy, insubstantial, and musically inadequate. As we have seen, there are objective ways of analyzing a song, or a symphony, or a ballet score, to assess whether it is worthy or poor. Gene Edward Veith clarifies: "In every dimension of our lives, including the arts, we need to be able to discern between good and evil, truth and falsehood. Art calls also for another level of discernment—between the aesthetically good and the aesthetically bad."[7] He explains that "Developing 'good taste' means learning to like what is 'good'. Taking pleasure (subjectively) in what is excellent (objectively) is the definition of good taste."[8] It could be said that developing good taste in the arts is a matter of growing in wisdom.

Developing Good Taste

Let's consider a helpful parallel between music and food, since we are consumers of both. There is plenty of food available in twenty-first century Western countries, but by no means all of it is good for you. You may have a favorite dish, which has a delicious flavor, and order it often when you go out to eat. But just because it tastes nice does not mean it is healthy. Too much sugar, trans fats, or too much fast food, will eventually harm your body. In a similar way, there is plenty of music on offer, but is it all healthy? Could some of it, in fact, be bad for you?

Karen DeMol, in her short book, *Sound Stewardship: How Shall Christians Think About Music?*,[9] compares a good musician to a good dietician, whose work gives us a healthy diet. Her suggestion can be developed further. A good musical guide can lead you to music which will do good to your soul. The best, the most beautiful music brings glory to God and will do you good. Lesser quality music is not in the same league.

Ugly music, which is out of proportion (e.g., with an overpowering beat) can only harm the soul. The same goes for atonal music, which is deliberately built on discords. This is not a matter of taste, but of understanding right and wrong. Surveying rock music, Allan Bloom saw "nothing noble, sublime, profound, delicate, tasteful or even decent. . . . There is room only for the intense, changing, crude, and immediate. . ."[10] It is fascinating that the same research that highlights the dangers of playing heavy metal to patients recovering from heart surgery found that classical music had positive effects on the patients.[11]

Plenty of food consumed in the West today is bad for you. But God, in his common grace, provides so many different types of food that are healthy and nutritious: vegetables, eggs, meat, fish, etc. There is plenty of room for people to like different things. You may prefer salmon and I may choose cod. So, in a world full of audio recordings, there is plenty of high-quality music available, and different people have different favorites. I may prefer Sibelius; you may go for Mendelssohn instead.

The key point is that you should seek to develop a taste for worthy music that does you good, music that most displays the objective principles of beauty. The music that brings God glory is that which is beautiful. An extensive menu is found in the classical music canon, given to us by the providence of God—works for voice and/or combinations of instruments, of different characters and moods, and in a range of styles stretching back for centuries. This book has surveyed only a handful of examples; there is a vast and varied library to explore.

To be clear, no one should argue that all classical music is good and worthy of our attention. Many pieces of classical music composed down the years have been of poor quality, dull or repetitive, static or self-indulgent, and these have been rightly forgotten. They may be of historical interest, but they do not deserve the attention of a general audience. Generally speaking, the most well-known works in the classical canon continue to be performed and cherished because they are the best.

Yet popular music parades a lot of poor-quality music, and it is often lacking in substance. Even if a particular pop song has an attractive tune, the quality of the performance itself is usually woefully inadequate, with singers unable to accurately sing the notes. The emphasis is not on performing good-quality music; instead, the goal of pop music is pleasing fans. It is time for Christians, in particular, to develop a healthier musical palate. We need to listen to music with discernment. The implications of this may include abandoning some familiar pieces that we have grown up with and enjoyed.

Another problem in music is "kitsch," a type of bad art which cheapens or sentimentalizes what it portrays, such as a souvenir that has no real artistic value, but may recall fond memories—plaster figures in a garden, or generic, trite love songs. As Harold Best explained, "It is intemperance and overstatement, based on a desire to imitate something really good, to work within a style but without the eye or ear for the subtle relationships among detail, nuance, and overall shape."[12]

We can compare kitsch to cotton candy (or candy floss), which has zero nutritional benefit. It may look or sound "cute," but detracts our minds and affections from things of more lasting value. Much popular music (and some classical music) is written for its emotional effect, rather than because the music has objective value. Gene Edward Veith elaborates on the problem: "Art that has no other purpose than popular appeal. . .will seek to gratify its audience's desires but in doing so will offer them nothing of real value. By pandering to the lowest common denominator and appealing to the simplest emotions, the art of popular culture—whether television dramas, romance novels, or kitsch—restricts rather than enlarges its audience's experience."[13]

Take Your Time

Consider another aspect of the parallel between music and food. Some foods are an acquired taste. Perhaps olives, Brussels sprouts, or dark chocolate? Only some people develop an appreciation for them, and then only over time. This is true for the most complex classical music, for example the longest works of Bach, Brahms, or Elgar. That is not usually the wisest place to start for a newcomer to classical music. Shorter works, perhaps with familiar words, or with clear musical themes (such as pieces by Haydn or Mendelssohn) may be a better place to begin. Start discovering what you prefer in classical music by finding a selection or playlist of fifty or so "favorite classics" and listening to them regularly. Your local classical music radio station may be a great place to start, though beware that some have a tendency to promote obscure and less beautiful pieces to cater to fashionable, elite opinion.

It is vital that Christians think about the music they are consuming, as one aspect of being transformed by the renewing of the mind (Rom. 12:2). There is one important difference between using our mouths to taste food and using our ears to savor music—we have to engage our minds to evaluate music. This sets musical understanding on a higher level than eating food. We need to reflect on the music we hear and why we like it (or otherwise). Like many things in life, including crafts and sports, musical understanding has to be learned. This should not be controversial. It takes time and care to learn how to carve wood or to sew a dress. A non-American cannot be expected to visit a baseball game and immediately comprehend everything that's going on. He or she needs to learn the rules, the personalities, the wider rivalries, etc. And yet, the immediate impact of popular music and its easy availability leads people to yearn for it; they do not stop to think. The pop music industry has a strong commercial incentive to promote music that mesmerizes people in this way—it brings more sales and more money.

Learning to appreciate music takes time. Taste in music can be improved by listening to good-quality classical music with focused attention, and by hearing people discuss it in detail. Seek out podcasts, books, magazines, or broadcasts where experienced music commentators talk about the main aspects of great pieces—such as the use of harmony, musical form or structure, choice of instruments, or how the music conveys the words. The development or interaction of themes or motifs is integral to the best classical music. Yet a casual, unthinking listener can miss this completely. There are many ways in which music can be heard incorrectly, for example "by grouping or dividing tones wrongly, by misplacing accent and emphasis, by hearing an up-beat as a down-beat, a background as a foreground, a figure as a theme."[14]

Any appreciation for beauty comes by contemplating things that are beautiful. You may need to listen to a piece of classical music several times to learn it, to begin to grasp its overall direction and its many twists and turns. The musical examples in this book are given as a starting point for appreciating fine music. There are other areas of life, far beyond the scope of this book, where our individual tastes may need significant improvement. Many of us need to learn to better appreciate what is lovely in art, poetry, architecture, clothing, gardening, and home furnishings. The objective principles of beauty are equally applicable to these noble, God-given pursuits which equally call for thoughtful, discerning appreciation. This is far superior to following the whimsical dictates of fashion, to which so many enslave themselves.

14

The Bible and the Soul

Music influences the soul of man in profound and sometimes mysterious ways. But the existence of the soul is largely ignored today, which is hiding the true impact of music on us. Christian theologians throughout history have affirmed the reality of the soul, which is so plainly taught in the Bible. But for the past century it seems that the relationship of music to the soul has been largely forgotten. It is surely time to explore it again.

Perhaps the best known statement by J.S. Bach is: "The ultimate end or final purpose of all music. . . is nothing other than the praise of God and the recreation [or refreshment] of the soul." The rest of the quote is less well known: "Where this is not taken into account, then there is no true music, only a devilish bawling and droning."[1] Bach recognized the effect of music on the soul, something that was often discussed during the Baroque era. But the soul has a supernatural origin, and so, with the rise of atheism and secularism over past 150 years, anti-Christian intellectuals have sought to redefine it out of existence. The language of modern psychology talks about "the self," not the soul.[2]

Yet there have been rare modern-day authors who have reached back into the past and uncovered this recent deceit. The philosopher Allan Bloom came from a secular Jewish background and was not a practicing Christian, but he was a distinguished classicist who was well acquainted with the philosophy of the ancient Greeks and their writings about the soul. The central theme of his book *The Closing of the American Mind* is that the West now denies the reality of man's immortal soul and so there is no inquiry into ultimate truth: "We cannot even agree on a name for this irreducible bit of man that is not body. Somehow this fugitive thing or aspect is the cause of science and society and culture and politics and economics and poetry and music."[3]

R.C. Sproul taught about music that "The sounds we hear have a powerful ability to affect the heart and the soul. . ."[4] Sir Roger Scruton wrote that "the ordering of sound as music is an ordering of the soul" and that music somehow reflects "the movements of the human soul."[5] And even modern music critics occasionally reference the soul, such as Ivan Hewett writing for *The Daily Telegraph* in the United Kingdom: "That's the beauty of music. We think we are simply listening to wonderful melodies, but all the while, unnoticed, it provides an education for the soul."[6]

Biblical Teaching on Body and Soul

What does the Bible actually teach about the soul of man, and how can Christians explain its interaction with music?

The opening pages of Scripture reveal that mankind was created male and female in the image of God (Gen. 1:26–27; Gen. 2:7, 22–23). From the beginning, the Bible explains that man is a spiritual and physical being. As a human being, I do not have a body and a soul; I *am* body and soul. The Bible uses a variety of words to express the spiritual aspects of man's nature, such as "soul," "spirit," "heart," "reins" (kidneys), and "mind."

In the New Testament, Christ teaches the twofold nature of man as body and soul: "And fear not them which kill the body, but are not able to kill the soul: but rather fear him which is able to destroy both soul and body in hell" (Matt. 10:28). J. Gresham Machen remarked on this verse that Jesus "is only making explicit what really underlies all the teaching of the Word of God."[7] Our Lord Jesus outlines the same body/soul dichotomy in his teaching that evil thoughts and actions originate from the heart of man (Mark 7:14–23) and several of the apostle Paul's letters echo the same basic distinction (e.g., Rom. 8:10; 2 Cor. 7:1; Phil. 1:22–24).

The Westminster Confession of Faith (4:2) summarizes the biblical teaching: "After God had made all other creatures, he created man, male and female, with reasonable and immortal souls, endued with knowledge, righteousness, and true holiness, after his own image. . ." We know that Christ is truly God and truly man, yet without sin—John 1:14; Hebrews 2:17, 4:15. The Chalcedonian creed of the Christian Church (AD 451) affirms the "reasonable soul and body" of our Lord Jesus Christ.[8]

The theological concept of body and soul is known as dichotomy and has been widely accepted in the church down the centuries. However, a few theologians (including some of the early church fathers) have taught a trichotomy of body, soul, and spirit; citing 1 Thessalonians 5:23 ("I pray God your whole spirit and soul and body be preserved blameless unto the coming of our Lord Jesus Christ") and Hebrews 4:12 ("For the word of God is quick, and powerful. . . piercing even to the dividing asunder of soul and spirit. . ."). However, the evidence of Scripture obviously favors dichotomy. As the twentieth-century theologian Louis Berkhof stated about this issue, "It is a sound rule in exegesis that exceptional statements should be interpreted in the light of the *analogia Scriptura,* the usual representation of Scripture."[9]

The Bible teaches that body and soul are a functional unity. Indeed, Scripture sometimes uses the word "soul" to represent the whole person (Gen. 2:7); it also refers to "body" at times in a similar way (Rom. 12:1; James 3:2, 6). Jesus' words in Matthew 10:28 indicate that both soul and body are subject to the fall and that man as a unitary being will face God's judgment. This emphasizes our obligation to live holy lives in every aspect of our being (1 Cor. 6:20).[10]

Body and soul are intimately and closely connected—they are only divided at a person's death, and then only temporarily until the resurrection of the body (Eccles. 12:7; Rev. 6:9; John 5:28–29). This biblical teaching tells us that the soul is important and that it is immortal, but not in the same way as ancient Greeks held. It contradicts the philosophy of Plato which viewed the soul as superior to the body—a fragment of deity in a "prison house" of human flesh. And Scripture denies Plato's idea that a man's soul is immortal in the sense that it preexisted his body and will be reincarnated.[11] J. Gresham Machen said that the Bible "teaches very plainly that the connection between body and soul is the normal and desirable thing and that a disembodied state is a state of nakedness from which the Christian desires to be delivered. Thus the Christian doctrine of the resurrection of the body is very different from the Greek doctrine of the immortality of the soul."[12] Every Christian will rise by the power of God—body and soul—to live forever with the Lord in the new creation.

But what exactly is the soul? This is not easy to explain, even though its existence is self-evident. John Calvin wrote that the soul of man is "an immortal yet created essence, which is his nobler part." While recognizing that the whole of man is made in the image of God, Calvin taught that "the proper seat of his image is in the soul."[13] The seventeenth-century Puritan John Flavel put it this way: "The soul of man is a vital, spiritual, and immortal substance, endowed with an understanding, will, and various affections; created with an inclination to the body, and infused thereinto by the Lord."[14]

The soul is a spiritual, not a material, substance—but we must admit that its nature is inscrutable to us, like the spiritual nature of angels. Yet we can say that the soul is simple, in that it is pure and not made up of different parts.[15] Without doubt, the soul is the center of human personality and we can describe what it does. Although a spiritual substance, our souls interact with the physical world as our bodies sense and respond to external stimuli and information.[16]

The Bible teaches that animals have a soul in the sense that they are living creatures (e.g., Prov. 12:10), but not of the same kind as human beings. Christians must seek to exercise good and careful dominion over the animals. However, the modern West is steeped in evolutionary confusion, so we must be clear that animals are fundamentally different from mankind—they are not made in the image of God and are incapable of reasoning. Their souls are of a different nature from the soul of man. Although God has given birds the gift of song, they do not perceive beauty in music because they do not have the capacity for intelligent perception.

Augustine on the Soul and Music

Augustine of Hippo, the early church theologian, knew from experience the power music can exert over people and was determined to avoid the sensual misuse of it. As we have seen, he compared "vulgar performers" of music to birds, who do not understand what they are doing. His six-volume treatise *De Musica,* written in the late AD 380s, addresses the nature and proper use of music. Augustine's principal thoughts are set out in the sixth volume, where he urges mankind to look beyond the created gift of music to God his Creator.[17]

In *De Musica,* Augustine primarily addresses rhythm in music (he never got round to writing the later books on melody he had planned) and he fully incorporates the Pythagoreans' narrow, mathematical view of music into his thinking (see Chapter 6—*Thinking About Music*). But Augustine also sets music in the context of a biblical worldview, in which we obey God through an "ordered love":

> Now, do you think that I should speak at length about this, when the holy Scriptures in so many volumes and with such authority and sanctity tell us nothing but this, that we shall love our God and Lord with all our heart and with all our soul and with all our mind and love our neighbor as ourselves [Luke 10:27]? Thus, if we direct all these movements and rhythms [*motus numerosque*] of our human activity to this end, we will undoubtedly be purified.[18]

Augustine clearly teaches an interaction between man's soul and music. He recognizes that man's pride can divert him to enjoy unwholesome pleasure in music, even to the point of enslavement to it. In contrast, he stressed that morally good music is perceived first in the soul of man, rather than by his bodily senses.[19] It is not necessary to accept Augustine's philosophy here (which saw music as governed by numerical patterns) to share his concern about the power of music to do harm. A key part of his argument is that the soul perceives and responds to good music before the other senses do, but that morally degraded music stirs up sensual pleasure instead. The man that turns his back on God becomes proud, "which causes the soul to fall from the contemplation of truth to a lower state of distraction. At this lower level it focuses its attention on bodily pleasure."[20]

Augustine is arguing that the soul which has turned away from God embraces morally degraded music. Even though good-quality music is a common grace gift of God to all people, it can be rejected as he is rejected. This is evident in our own times in the ugly music all around us.

The Faculties of the Soul

Augustine, and also John Calvin, were influenced by Plato's teaching which emphasized the separateness of soul and body—though these two great Christian theologians had the Bible as their primary frame of reference and opposed Plato's idea of the preexistence of man's soul. One consequence of this Platonic strand of thought was to downplay the interaction of body and soul.

In contrast, most Reformed theologians in the Puritan era followed Thomas Aquinas (1225–1274) and other medieval scholastic theologians in seeing a close union of body and soul. Aquinas lived at a time when the works of the Greek philosopher Aristotle had been rediscovered in the West and he incorporated many aspects of Aristotle's teachings and observations in his own theological writings. It could be said that Aquinas Christianized Aristotle, adding, for example, the resurrection of the body, which was unknown to ancient Greece.[21]

Aquinas followed Aristotle in stressing a close relationship between body and soul, teaching that "the soul is the form of the body." In this view, the soul has a far broader role than in Platonic thought and includes animating the body. Aristotle also wrote about the "faculties" (or powers) of the soul and Aquinas expertly applied this idea using Christian concepts. Protestant scholars later developed the teaching in greater detail. As the contemporary Christian philosopher Paul Helm has explained, "The Reformed may be said to use pagan faculty psychology as a framework, or structure, providing a way or ways in which the unsystematic biblical anthropology may be presented."[22]

The Bible describes many aspects of man's soul or spiritual nature, often using the word "heart." As the Puritan John Owen (1616–1683) wrote, "The *heart* in the Scripture is variously used; sometimes for the *mind and understanding*, sometimes for the *will*, sometimes for the *affections*, sometimes for the *conscience*, sometimes for the *whole soul*. Generally, it denotes *the whole soul of man* and all the faculties of it, not absolutely, but as they are all one principle of moral operations, as they all concur in our doing good or evil."[23]

What the Scripture teaches about the soul is not set out systematically, so faculty psychology provides a helpful classification of what man's soul can do. According to Girolamo Zanchi (1516–1590):

"All potencies of the soul are called faculties, i.e., *dynameis* [powers]. And they are called *facultates,* because by them those things happen easily (*facile*) to which they are destined by the Creator."[24]

Faculties describe what the soul is capable of. To be clear, faculties should not be understood as separate parts of the soul like the wheels or headlights on a car. A better analogy would be that the "faculties" of a car are its abilities to drive forward, pull a trailer, or turn a corner.

Most Reformed orthodox theologians have distinguished two basic faculties of the soul—the understanding and the will. "Understanding" describes the rational or intellectual capacities of the mind; "the will" man's power to make choices or decisions. Some, like John Flavel, regarded "affections" as a third category, though it has been more common to see affections as an activity of the will, inclining towards what it desires or away from what it does not. Sometimes theologians have written elaborately about the faculties, but we should note that each faculty is not a "subsoul" with a personality of its own—the soul is an indivisible unity.[25]

Joel Beeke and Paul Smalley draw attention to the Bible's frequent language of the human heart and its ability to love, which involves both a person's will and his emotions: "The greatest duty and delight for which God created our souls is to know and love the Lord (Deut. 4:35, 39; 6:4–5). We might tentatively propose that the soul's faculties can be best summarized in the capacities to know and to love."[26]

It is important to remember that, in this fallen world, the movements of man's soul are not neutral. Our faculties can be disposed towards good or towards evil actions. Our mind, will, passions, and emotions, often act in sinful ways that are directly contrary to God's moral law. Scholars describe the tendency of the soul as its "habit," that shapes what we think and do.[27]

The New Testament frequently ties changes between moral goodness or evil to our affections. Seen in this way, virtues and vices are powers of the soul.[28] In Scripture, we are taught that virtues are the fruit of the Holy Spirit's regenerating work in believers through union with Christ:

> Be kindly affectioned one to another with brotherly love; in honour preferring one another." (Rom. 12:10)

> "If there be therefore any consolation in Christ, if any comfort of love, if any fellowship of the Spirit, if any bowels and mercies, fulfil ye my joy, that ye be likeminded, having the same love, being of one accord, of one mind." (Phil. 2:1–2)

Such verses indicate the renewed soul's capacity to love others; we have seen that the power to love is a primary faculty of the soul. John Owen wrote about how sanctification changes our affections/passions:

> This mortification of our affections toward these things, our love, desire and delight, will produce a moderation of passions about them, as fear, anger, sorrow and the like; such will men be stirred up unto in these changes, losses, crosses, which these things are subject unto. . . . When the mind is weaned from the world, and the things of it, it will be sedate, quiet, composed, not easily moved with the occurrences and occasions of life: it is dead unto them, and in a great measure unconcerned in them. This is that "moderation" of mind wherein the apostle would have us excel.[29]

While recognizing man's conscience as a fact, which Aristotle did not, Christian scholars have debated how to describe it in terms of faculty psychology. What is sure is that our conscience tells us we are sinners who have broken God's law (Rom. 2:14–15).

Theologians have written a great deal down the centuries about the faculties of the soul, especially in relation to man's state of corruption after the fall and our need for salvation in Christ. The Scriptures teach that our souls need to be made new by the work of God's Spirit (Ezek. 36:26; Titus 3:5). As our Lord Jesus said, every one of us must be born again (John 3:7).

15

Music and the Soul

How does the soul respond to music? Exploring the faculties of the soul will shed great light on this. In what ways are the mind, the will, the affections, and the heart affected by music? Some striking conclusions can be drawn from these observations, as long as we remember to be careful—we are dealing with soul actions that are real but nevertheless mysterious.

You may find the first thing we can say surprising. It is the soul that hears music through the ear. As Herman Bavinck explained: "It is not the ear which hears but the spirit of man which hears through the ear."[1] This analysis has a long pedigree—the Huguenot Philippe de Mornay (1549–1623) located the perception of music in the soul rather than the body.[2] Of course, using our ears means that the body as well as the soul participates in the appreciation of music (see Chapter 2—*Music in Creation* on the precision design of the human ear). Obviously, our bodies are essential for hearing, composing, and performing music.

Beauty, whether visually or in sound, is perceived by the mind. This has been widely recognized.[3] So we can say that man is intended to consider music with his mind, and then the affections or emotions follow. John Calvin, commenting on psalm singing, wrote, "The unique gift of man is to sing knowing that which he sings. After the intelligence must follow the heart and the affection, a thing which is unable to be except if we have the hymn imprinted on our memory, in order never to cease from singing."[4]

Most people perceive music as either pleasurable or not, even if they hardly notice the sound. It is well known that some music brings evident happiness; other music causes solemn reflection, or may stir up grief or even anger. This is how music is constantly used in movies and drama—changing in mood, volume, or style, as the action develops on screen. From the classical music canon, Elgar's string miniature *Sospiri* Op. 70 may bring a tear to your eye; Tchaikovsky's *1812 Overture* could very well rouse you to action; traditional wedding music is often chosen for its joyfulness, such as Jeremiah Clarke's *Trumpet Voluntary*. Memories or associations play their part as well—"Happy Birthday" has a jolly tune, but likely stirs good feelings more because of its familiar context than for any musical qualities.

Affections

Most Puritan and Reformed writers have seen the affections as an activity of man's will, rather than a faculty in their own right—taken together, they are the arena of our desires. The language of "affections" usually addresses human emotions, though today the word "affection" is also used for a milder regard for something ("he had affectionate memories of his childhood toys"). In the Puritan era, there were thought to be four main states of emotion: joy, fear, hope, and grief.[5] Often today, we talk about our feelings but "feeling" is an ambiguous word because our feelings can be caused by our body or our soul—we feel the sea breeze on our face; we feel the roughness of sandpaper; we feel joy at a wedding; we feel apprehension before an interview.

Many of the Puritans used "affections" and "passions" interchangeably. I have already quoted John Flavel on the centrality of the soul to our emotions: "All the affections and passions of hope, desire, love, delight, fear, sorrow, and the rest, are all rooted in it, and springing out of it; and for habits, arts and sciences, it is the soul in which they are lodged and seated."[6] As time went by, though, "passions" increasingly came to represent stronger expressions of emotion and this is now the general use of the word.[7] We talk about loving someone *passionately* or seeking something with intense passion. It usually indicates a desire that takes over the whole person, at least for a time.

The Bible constantly connects music with our minds, above all directing that we should worship God by singing what is true. Note its focus on the mind in two historical examples of contrasting people—bad King Saul (1 Sam. 16:23) and the godly prophet Elisha (2 Kings 3:15). In both cases, the playing of the lyre (presumably with song) restrained the harmful tendencies of the mind to agitation or distraction. Music could be called medicine for the mind. Matthew Henry the Puritan pastor, commenting on the former passage, wrote: "Music has a natural tendency to compose and exhilarate the mind, when it is disturbed and saddened. . . . On some it has a greater influence than on others. . ."[8]

In times past, many others have commented on music's influence on the soul. Martin Luther wrote, "We have so many hymns and Psalms where message and music join to move the listener's soul. . ."[9] He called music

> . . . a mistress and governess of those human emotions—to pass over the animals—which as masters govern men or more often overwhelm them. No greater commendation than this can be found—at least not by us. For whether you wish to comfort the sad, to terrify the happy, to encourage the despairing, to humble the proud, to calm the passionate, or to appease those full of hate—and who could number all these masters of the human heart, namely, the emotions, inclinations, and affections that impel men to evil or good?—what more effective means than music could you find?[10]

The anonymous Christian author of the treatise *The Praise of Musicke* (1586) argued that music helps us think clearly about who we are: "Musicke. . . hath a certaine divine influence into the soules of men, whereby our cogitations and thoughts . . . are brought into a celestiall acknowledging of their natures."[11]

The Anglican theologian Richard Hooker wrote at length in 1597 about the moral influence of music (and we will return to the wider context of his debate with Puritan theologians about the Church of England's liturgical use of music):

> Touching musical harmony whether by instrument or by voice, it being but of high and low in sounds a due proportionable disposition such notwithstanding is the force thereof, and so pleasing effects it hath in that very part of man which is most divine, that some have been thereby induced to think that the soul itself by nature is or hath in it harmony. A thing which delighteth all ages, and beseemeth

> all states; a thing as seasonable in grief as in joy; as decent being added unto actions of greatest weight, and solemnity, as being used when men most sequester themselves from action.

Hooker goes on to describe in detail the effect music has on the soul. Once more, the mind is central:

> The reason hereof is an admirable facility which music hath to express and represent to the mind, more inwardly than any other sensible mean, the very standing, rising, and falling, the steps and inflections every way, the turns and varieties of all passions whereunto the mind is subject. . . . In harmony the very image and character even of virtue and vice is perceived, the mind delighted with their resemblances, and brought by them often iterated into a love of the things themselves. So that although we lay altogether aside the consideration of ditty or matter, the very harmony of sounds being framed in due sort and carried from the ear to the spiritual faculties of our souls, is by a native puissance [power] and efficacy greatly available to bring to a perfect temper whatsoever is there troubled, apt as well to quicken the spirits as to allay that which is too eager, sovereign against melancholy and despair, forcible to draw forth tears of devotion if the mind be such as can yield them, able both to move and to moderate all affections.[12]

Music is almost universally understood to touch the emotions. For example, Quintilian, the first century AD Roman educator and author of the *Institutes of Oratory,* wrote: "Music . . . by means of the tone and modulation of the voice, expresses sublime thoughts with grandeur, pleasant ones with sweetness, and ordinary ones with calmness, and sympathizes in its whole art with the feelings attendant on what is expressed."[13] Author Brian Vickers noted: "*The Institutes* also helped to transmit some of those famous stories of the power of music over human behaviour. Praising the ancient music, which celebrated heroes and gods, Quintilian scorns its decadence in the Roman theatre, and appeals: 'Give me the knowledge of the principles of music, which have power to excite or assuage the emotions of mankind'."[14]

In 1547, the Swiss humanist Glareanus praised the composer Josquin des Prez by saying: "No one has more effectively expressed the passions of the soul in music than this symphonist."[15] He went on to compare Josquin's effectiveness in music to the power of the works of Virgil, the classical Roman poet.

Rhetoric

This highlights the importance of *rhetoric* during the Renaissance and Baroque eras, applied both to words and to music, in the tradition of Quintilian.

> *Grammar, logic, and rhetoric constituted the Trivium, which was promoted by humanist educators from the fifteenth century onwards.*[16] *This revival of the Trivium, and rhetoric in particular, helped turn music away from the purely mathematical conception of it that dominated academia in the medieval period [this was important to the development of tonality. See Chapter 6—Thinking about Music].*[17]

Renaissance classes in rhetoric taught pupils the works of great classical orators and authors. The goal was for students to learn how to speak with persuasive power and to sway the emotions of their hearers. It has been noted that "rhetoric in the sixteenth and seventeenth centuries went into the psychology of the passions in extraordinary detail, devoting hundreds of pages to what it called *pathologia,*"[18] so it was natural to apply this intellectual framework to music as well.

The concept of rhetorical expression in music was applied with vigor by composers from the renaissance onwards, and music's effect on the emotions became a central consideration in the seventeenth and eighteenth centuries.[19] This is seen throughout the music of the Baroque era. Over time, it was developed into an elaborate system by some German music theorists. (Secular authors today refer to this as the "Doctrine of the Affections.") These treatises sought to map specified emotions to particular genres of music, extending even to the shape of melodies.[20] Many have argued since that this was overly speculative. Authors such as Johann Mattheson (1681–1764) relied on the Enlightenment philosophy of Descartes and therefore saw music as animating passions in the body, rather than immediately affecting the soul as had been accepted historically.[21]

The eighteenth century saw a gradual rejection of biblical revelation in favor of rationalism ("the Enlightenment") and therefore the soul, the spiritual aspect of our nature, became less of a focus for reflection and study. Nevertheless, the Christian church—in its creeds, confessions, and preaching—continued to assert that mankind is made in God's image, body and soul.

16

Bringing Disorder to the Soul

Music has a peculiar power to affect the soul. It can shape, or even overpower, our thoughts and our emotions. However, the normal order is that our mind perceives and contemplates beauty in music (or the absence of beauty), then the emotions follow. That is why it is desperately important to think about and reflect on the music you hear. Decades ago, Harry Blamires warned in *The Christian Mind* that even within the church "the mind of modern man is neglected and forgotten."[1]

Our souls are affected constantly by what happens moment by moment and we sometimes respond in obvious ways (with thankfulness or regret; anxiety or anger) and sometimes in ways we can't comprehend. It is evidently not only music that interacts with our souls. People, places, events, memories, all play their part in our lives day by day. Herman Bavinck wrote: "Everything can potentially enrich or harm the soul and can impact the soul from the vantage point of good or evil."[2]

What more can we say about the interaction of our mind and emotions? The Puritans applied a Christian perspective to the eudaimonistic teaching of Aristotle, relating to the goal of happiness or the good life, in many aspects of their writings. John Owen wrote that happiness is supremely found in communion with God. In the context of ethics, the Puritans taught that our affections should be moderated by reason.[3] Noting that the Puritans unanimously rejected Stoicism's suppression of the emotions, Paul Helm summarizes the Reformed teaching: "The objective of the reason is to modulate such feelings [joy, fear, hope, and grief] in line with Christian virtues and to make the virtues more achievable. This involves the making of the expression of feelings or emotions fitting and proportionate to the states of affairs that generate them, to prevent them reaching such a pitch that they cloud the judgment or affect the states of the body. The objective is not only controlling those that are excessive, however, but of expressing fully those that are sluggish."[4]

By "reason," in this context, Reformed theologians mean the "practical reason"—ability to distinguish good from evil, right from wrong.[5] Edward Reynolds (1599–1676), a member of the Westminster Assembly and later Bishop of Norwich, wrote about disciplining the emotions: "So the agitations of the passions, so long as they serve only to drive forward, but not to drown virtue,—as long as they keep their dependence on reason, and run in that channel wherewith they are bounded,—are of excellent service in all the travel of man's life; and such as without which the growth, success, and despatch of virtue would be much impaired."[6]

Only a soul made new by regeneration can exercise his or her emotions in ways that are holy. This is the fruit of the Holy Spirit (Gal. 5:22–25). Yet non-Christians are still capable of exercising control of their emotions and channeling them properly. Even though totally depraved in the sight of God, mankind is capable of doing morally right things (telling the truth, helping others, administering justice, for example). The Canons of Dort state that, even after the fall, mankind can recognize "the difference between what is moral and immoral, and demonstrates a certain eagerness for virtue and for good outward behavior," though this can never bring someone to a saving knowledge of God[7] (see Chapter 2—*Music in Creation* for more on the doctrine of common grace).

Herman Bavinck considered our wills and emotions as "the faculty of desiring" and he wrote movingly about our enjoyment of beautiful things: "The beautiful has that nature that its viewing gives delight. As beautiful, it is not an object of our desiring, so that we would want to possess it, but its uniqueness is such that seeing it, observing it, knowing it, delights us, provides us pleasure and enjoyment. And that enjoying of the beautiful, that resting in it and being blissful in its presence, are an expression of that power of the soul that is ordinarily, but in far too narrow a sense, called the faculty of desiring."[8]

Music which is objectively beautiful can stir the emotions so that they "run in their channel" (as Edward Reynolds said)—this is God's design. It is easy to see how beautiful music can help us think clearly or calm our emotions (as it did for the prophet Elisha in 2 Kings 3:15). This is using music as God intended. But at times music can cause the emotions to overflow and sweep away our reason. This is a danger we must be alert to. It could be the misuse of good music or the effect of bad music. In theory, any type of music—opera, symphony, or song—can be overindulged by sinful people, as a banquet of either healthy or unhealthy food can become an occasion for gluttony. Let's be clear that even the best music can be misused by sinful men to try to mask the pangs of conscience. As Matthew Henry commented about King Saul's use of music, "Many whose consciences are convinced and startled are for ever ruined by such methods as these, which drown all care of the soul in the delights of sense."[9] Later in Israel's history, the prophet Isaiah (Isa. 5:12) indicted those who were using music for partying and not turning to God: "And the harp, and the viol, the tabret, and pipe, and wine, are in their feasts: but they regard not the work of the Lord, neither consider the operation of his hands."[10]

The triune God created us to love him with all our heart, mind, soul, and strength and our neighbor as ourselves (Matt. 22:37–39). But we are fallen. As the prophet Jeremiah proclaimed: "The heart is deceitful above all things, and desperately wicked: who can know it?" (Jer. 17:9). John Owen wrote that the fickle and deceitful nature of our hearts "is the disorder that is brought upon all its faculties by sin."[11] The combined working of our corrupt hearts and Satan's temptations "inflames all the affections, and puts the whole soul into disorder."[12]

The Scriptures warn us not to abuse what we have: "And they that use this world, as not abusing it: for the fashion of this world passeth away" (1 Cor. 7:31). We should be on our guard against this temptation.[13] The best music can sometimes be prized too highly. Humans are capable of idolizing anything, good or bad, and substituting it in place of God. Some evidence of this could be that those people who most appreciate the arts in the secular West have often lived decadent lives. Perhaps they are treating the fine arts as idols which bring them pleasure, rather than thanking God for these good gifts. As John Calvin famously cautioned, man's nature is "a perpetual factory of idols."[14]

Poor-quality music can also shape our souls in unhealthy ways. Music that is kitsch, written simply to stir the emotions and which has no objective merit, provokes people's emotions without reference to beauty. Many pieces composed for casual entertainment over the past couple of centuries have fallen into this category. Such poor-quality music simply needs to be swapped for better quality music—and that is a process of discovery at different rates for different people, applying the objective principles of beauty. Yet we live in an entertainment culture that actively encourages us not to consider such things, but simply to mindlessly enjoy ourselves. The twenty-first century world of screens is obsessed with visual imagery which rapidly moves from one thing to the next, without any logical connection and little encouragement to sober reflection.

The Soul and Ugly Music

When something is made to be ugly, or when something good is abused, it says something about God's creation—and therefore about God—which is not true. Although God certainly is separate from his creation, yet he made it all to "speak" of his glory. But the tide of music in the twentieth century turned in an entirely contrary direction. Composers started to promote ugliness, discord, disproportion, and even chaos in music. Since truth, goodness, and beauty belong together, then the opposites—lies, corruption, and ugliness—also belong together; what is ugly is linked in some way to what is morally bad.

Consider atonal music. Our minds were given above all to love God, who is the author of everything that is true, good, and beautiful. Our thoughts, then, should not rejoice in what is plainly ugly. It is sad to observe that the composers of atonal music, by their love of discord, show evidence that their thinking has become futile and corrupted (Rom. 1:21).

God built symmetry and order into his creation, even in his design of the human body, and this applies no less to the soul. When the different actions of our souls take their proper place, then this is orderly.

But disproportion is ugly. John Milton's poem *At a Solemn Music* describes how "disproportioned sin" broke the perfection of the garden of Eden (see Chapter 7—*Surveying Composers*). Milton, like many others, relates sin to disorder and disproportion.[15] Adam and Eve allowed their desire for the forbidden fruit to overcome what their minds knew to be wrong. Author Scott Aniol helpfully summarizes the biblical teaching: "Sin brought ugliness into the world. Because of sin we now have *dis*-order, *dis*-proportion, and dullness."[16]

Disproportion in music is most apparent today in the "big beat" of rock-inspired pop. What can be said about its effect on people as body and soul? It seems most likely that its primary impact is on the body, and harmful consequences for the soul flow from this. Remember that the body and soul are a functional unity and intimately connected, responding to and influencing each other deeply.[17] Nevertheless, God has not revealed to us how this interaction of body and soul works. It is quite mysterious, but we know intuitively that it is true. When we are happy, we smile. When faced with danger, our hearts race. When we are grieving, we cry. A broken heart has obvious physical effects.

The dominating beat of rock music is pleasurable to the body, perhaps because it mimics physical rhythms such as the heartbeat or breathing that are integral to our bodies. The big beat uses this physical effect to bypass the mind and causes people to love its disproportionate music, which is ugly.[18] Because it bypasses the mind, this music also very easily stirs emotions to overflow in unhealthy ways—simply look at the irrational behavior of crowds at many pop music concerts.

I do not say that it is wrong for music to have a physical effect on people. It has always been understood that the changing tempo of a piece of music can stir the emotions. Music for dance needs a clear pulse or beat so that we can dance to it. There is nothing wrong with tapping your foot to a familiar march.

But the disproportionate beat in rock music excites people's emotions without engaging the mind, bringing disorder to their souls. It is possible that after prolonged exposure to rock music, the soul loses its capacity to discern beauty in music, and perhaps more widely. This is unhealthy for the soul.

The fact that there can be a physical response to music is supported by evidence that animals interact with music, even though they do not have intellects to perceive beauty.[19] Given the integration of our body with our soul, physical actions affect the soul and can stir emotional responses—such as pleasure in running, or embracing loved ones. It should be no surprise that music, aiming primarily for a physical response, should also incite an emotional response.

Governing our Emotions

Puritan theologians warned that sinful emotions can overcome the mind, overriding its abilities to distinguish what is pleasurable from what is right. Francis Rous wrote that "carnall pleasures have this venom ordinarily in them, that their height groweth or continueth, by the diminishing or suppression of the reasonable soule."[20] Similarly, Richard Baxter "frequently urged his readers to employ their intellectual capacities in a manner that will curtail emotional waywardness and elicit appropriate affections for objects of true worth."[21] It is dangerous when our emotions run wild. Herman Bavinck unequivocally taught: "Emotions and passions play a far greater role in the lives of individuals and in the history of nations than healthy intellect. They are the weightiest factors and strongest powers that we know in the world of human beings."[22]

Given the power of music to sway the emotions, using music contrary to God's design has great potential to disorder the soul. Much as junk food harms the body when one consumes what is bad for it, we can say that a diet of ugly music harms the soul. It desensitizes a person's soul, as does enjoying trashy novels, brutalist architecture, and immoral films. A lifestyle of enjoying ugly things will have lasting effects in all areas of life.

I do not say that loving lesser quality music, or being totally unappreciative of music, is sinful. But we have reviewed modern musical genres that are defiantly ugly. Is it sinful to take pleasure in something because it is ugly—could it be a sin of ignorance (c.f. Leviticus 5)? That is a question worth pondering. Certainly, we should learn to love the good, the true, and the beautiful. When we do that, we are imitating God (Eph. 5:1). The opposite is also true—people imitate their idols and become like what they worship. If we devote ourselves to what is ugly, we ought to consider the effect it will have on us, as in the psalmist's warning about idolatry: "They that make them are like unto them; so is every one that trusteth in them" (Ps. 115:8).

Reflecting on these somber truths, and the implications for Western culture which is reveling in ugliness, should bring home to us important lessons. In all aspects of life, Christians must be transformed by the renewing of their minds if we are to live lives of obedience to God (Rom. 12:2). Everything in our lives should be brought under the searching light of Scripture, however uncomfortable it may make us.

17

Music and Character

Music has no power to bring salvation. It belongs to the realm of common grace. But music has potent effects on mankind and can help assuage or channel people's emotions in healthy ways. It was long thought in Western culture that music can shape a person's character for good or ill.

Theologians and philosophers throughout the centuries have acknowledged the power music has to influence people. John Calvin taught, ". . . there is scarcely in the world anything which is more able to turn or bend this way and that the morals of men, as Plato prudently considered it. And in fact, we find by experience that it has a sacred and almost incredible power to move hearts in one way or another." He continued: "It is true that every bad word (as St. Paul has said) perverts good manner [behavior], but when the melody is with it, it pierces the heart much more strongly, and enters into it; in a like manner as through a funnel, the wine is poured into the vessel; so also the venom and the corruption is distilled to the depths of the heart by the melody."[1]

Elsewhere, in his commentary on 1 Corinthians, Calvin wrote regarding chapter 14:7–9, "We all know from experience how great power music has for moving men's feelings, so that Plato teaches, quite rightly, that in one way or another music is of the greatest value in shaping the moral tone of the state." He later noted more generally (with reference to 1 Corinthians 15:33) that even pagan Greeks recognized the corrupting influence of bad moral examples on a person's mind and heart.[2]

Calvin and the Reformers could be scathing at times about the failings of the pagan philosophers of Greece and Rome. Yet here

Calvin commends Plato's teaching about the moral influence of music. The philosophers of ancient Greece, including Plato and Aristotle, wrote plainly about objective beauty and believed that learning to appreciate it was essential to forming a good character in young people. Yet Plato's beliefs about the influence of music in particular are frequently mocked today by those who have not studied them.

In his work *The Republic,* Plato discusses the moral impact of music on those who hear it.[3] He recommends excluding certain Greek musical modes from the ideal republic because they encourage degenerate behavior. Although scoffed at by casual readers today, Plato's argument was that music composed in certain modes was associated with action, e.g., either honorable marching, or wild, disreputable dancing. According to Allan Bloom, Plato was aiming for music to serve higher ideals in education: "Plato teaches that, in order to take the spiritual temperature of an individual or society, one must 'mark the music'."[4]

Other thoughtful philosophers—down to our own times—have commended Plato's insight that music shapes character. Sir Roger Scruton drew attention to music and dance, inviting us to contrast dancing to a Baroque Gavotte with the gyrations (and sometimes brutality) of the crowd in a live performance of heavy metal. The descent of dance illustrates, and goes hand in hand with, the descent of morality: "The transition from the Viennese waltz, to ballroom dancing, to ragtime, to the Charleston and Tango, to swing, to rock, and on to all the successors of rock, tells us much about the moral transformation of modernity. Love, sex, and the body are perceived differently now; courtesy and courtship have disappeared from dancing just as they have disappeared from life."[5]

Scruton criticized heavy metal and similar forms of rock music as idolatrous, and lamented that the rhythm (or beat) destroys the music. In contrast, good music has wholesome effects: "Through melody, harmony, and rhythm, we enter a world where others exist besides the self, a world that is full of feeling but also ordered, disciplined but free. That is why music is a character-forming force, and the decline of musical taste a decline in morals."[6]

Martin Luther, centuries before, called music "a mistress and governess. . . of the emotions, inclinations, and affections that impel men to evil or good" and asked "what more effective means than music could you find?"[7] The Anglican theologian Richard Hooker likewise alluded to good music promoting good character, arguing that there is something in music itself which reflects virtue and vice, and leads the soul to love what is virtuous: "In harmony the very image and character even of virtue and vice is perceived, the mind delighted with their resemblances, and brought by them often iterated into a love of the things themselves."[8]

These theologians and philosophers believed that music can have beneficial effects on the soul—the mind and emotions—which help shape an orderly and good character. We can suggest from the ground covered so far that the best music is most likely to direct people towards good conduct. It is surprising that so little is said about the influence of music in our own day. Perhaps among Christians, it is a result of the neglect of the doctrine of common grace?

Conscience is a common grace gift, which guides people towards what is right and away from what is wrong (Rom. 2:15). It can be suppressed or ignored by sinners, but not all the time. Sir Roger Scruton argued that condemning degraded art involves someone rightly using his conscience: "The person with good taste turns instinctively away from certain things, since they 'contaminate' his conscience, and tempt him towards sympathies that he should not have."[9] The conscience can evaluate right and wrong in every aspect of our lives. But it may be difficult today to educate the conscience to reject ugly music, since pervasive rock-inspired popular music has deafened or muffled this aspect of the conscience in many people.

The apostle Paul sought the growth of the church in Corinth into spiritual maturity in Christ: "In understanding be men" (1 Cor. 14:20). In a similar way, Christians should aim for maturity, growth in wisdom, when assessing the culture all around them. We should lead the way in discerning between what is noble and what is base, and we should not shrink back from talking about it. Martin Luther was not a man to shy away from controversy. Thankfully, he never experienced the worst of modern music, but his warning from 500 years ago against degraded music is surely applicable: "Take special care to shun perverted minds who prostitute this lovely gift of nature and of art with their erotic rantings, and be quite assured that none but the devil goads them on to defy their very nature which would and should praise God its Maker with this gift. . ."[10]

Christians should affirm "rational self-government of the soul" not only to produce good outward conduct, but also for a right ordering within ourselves of our minds and desires. We should aim to please God with both our body and our soul.[11] But is moderation in music—appreciating beautiful music and rejecting ugly music—a matter of sanctification for Christians? The Bible's call to pursue holiness (Heb. 12:14) surely has consequences for every area of our lives, including discerning what is good, true, and beautiful. Christians may differ on how to apply this, but we surely cannot ignore it.

We should turn away from anything that brings disorder to our souls, including music, and in so doing seek to be salt and light in this dark world (Matt. 5:13–16). Francis Schaeffer once said: "The Christian's life ought to be a work of art. . . . Our lives can be ugly or they can be beautiful, as well as dealing with truth and untruth. . . . There ought to be a beauty of life that stands in continuity with the message which the Christian gives."[12]

Learning to Appreciate Music

Since the music you listen to can be healthy or unhealthy for your soul, it matters a lot. Developing good taste in music is a wholesome and enjoyable pastime. We have compared some music to a log cabin—it is homely, but limited. Seek to expand your horizons to music on a larger scale, with more unity in diversity. It is more exciting and fulfilling to explore a palace than a log cabin.

As R.C. Sproul movingly expressed, "The reason that classical music is called classical is that it has endured the test of time. That music has a richness, a depth of content that continues to awaken the stirring of the soul as these elements of beauty become more and more recognizable in our experience."[13] Learning to appreciate classical music takes time, something else that is alien to an era like ours that demands instant rewards. It is best to start becoming familiar with good music in childhood—so start young children early on listening to the best music (yes, even before they are born). Parents can make music together with their family (not least in family worship), and outside the home allow their children to learn an instrument and join a choir. Encourage them to put the hard work in and learn to perform with excellence. In times past, music making was considered a noble art: "a skill worthy of the knowledge and exercise of the greatest Prince" (Henry Peacham's *Compleat Gentleman,* 1622).[14] Those who develop a particular aptitude for music can be encouraged to study music at college or university. I enjoyed many aspects of my music degree, despite its fashionable regard for avant-garde and atonal works. It would greatly benefit the twenty-first-century church to have more people trained in how to analyze and appreciate good music.

There is no exhaustive manual to appreciating music any more than there is to appreciating poetry or painting. But there are clear and objective principles which will guide us. The greatest works in the classical music canon are those which most clearly exhibit proportion, harmony, complexity, and simplicity. Time spent listening to and becoming familiar with some of the pieces referenced earlier will pay rich dividends and can be a blessing to your soul. This especially applies to those pieces that set good and true words to music. Of course, the greatest words that can be set to music are the words of Scripture since they are divinely inspired.

Christians should lead the way not only in appreciating classical music, but in performing and composing beautiful pieces of new music in the tonal system. After all, classical music was the development of the Christian worldview, and it was made possible by the universal human capacity for music. Therefore, although it arose in the West, it should not be restricted to only select people or places. Witness the popularity of Bach in Japan in recent years[15] and the fact that classical music is both performed and enjoyed in diverse countries globally by people of all ethnic backgrounds. It is important to understand, in this era of radical Marxist agendas, that great classical music is not bound by Western culture but in fact transcends it.

When someone hears and appreciates a beautiful piece of music, he mirrors his Creator who beheld his creation and pronounced it very good (Gen. 1:31). While properly enjoying beautiful music (or literature, architecture, etc.,) brings satisfaction or consolation to the soul, it cannot in itself bring salvation. Enjoying the arts is a common grace blessing; it does not bring redemption from sin. Nevertheless, beautiful music does point to the God of beauty, and the Lord may, in his mysterious providence, use a person's interest in any of the fine arts as one step on the road to introducing him or her to the gospel of Jesus Christ.

18

Three Questions

There is a vast selection of music available to us today—from symphonies to banal melodies to senseless noise. We could perhaps characterize it as the good, the bad, and the ugly. Never before has it been easier to access beautiful music, but many people do not choose to listen to it. As people in the West have increasingly rejected the God of truth, goodness, and beauty, they have increasingly lost the capacity to appreciate beauty themselves.

But Christians should pursue a better path. We have the Word of God and the illumination of the Holy Spirit to guide our steps (Ps. 119:105). Herman Bavinck wrote that "The Christian, who sees everything in the light of the Word of God. . .[has] the means at his disposal by which he can recognize the true and the good and the beautiful and separate them from the false and sinful alloys of men."[1]

We have been reviewing a biblical perspective on music relating to objective beauty and common grace, but how can we apply this practically to make right judgments about music? The principles we have reviewed should lead us to ask three essential questions:

- 1. Is there anything intrinsically wrong with this piece of music?
- 2. Is it good, average, or poor-quality music?
- 3. Is the music suitable for Christian worship?

1. Is There Anything Intrinsically Wrong with this Piece of Music?

The Bible warns clearly that mankind should use the good things of God's creation without abusing them (1 Cor. 7:31). This has a wide application to our lives because, as sinners, we are prone to misusing what God gives us. When it comes to listening to or performing music, ask yourself: Does this piece use or abuse God's good gift of music?

Two modern trends blatantly reject the objective principles of beauty in sound—a delight in discord and the disproportion of a dominating beat. The former is usually found in avant-garde modernism, the latter most often in popular music. But that is not always the case—some modern jazz composers toyed with atonality, and some pieces of classical music (e.g., Ravel's *Bolero*) are overly dependent on a powerful rhythm. Discordant music is a rebellion against the God of beauty, whether it is Beethoven's late string quartets or the cacophony of Stockhausen. Igor Stravinsky's *Symphony of Psalms* is a very dissonant work for choir and orchestra, which uses the words of Psalms 39, 40, and 150. However, using biblical texts cannot cover up the ugliness of the music—the combination of Scripture with persistent discord is dishonoring to God. Whatever words may be attached, even a psalm or the most poetic hymn, the fundamental problem with the sound remains.

Rhythm is integral to music and a subtle use or development of rhythm is one of its glories. But the "big beat" of much popular music today is an abuse of rhythm. If you are not sure whether a particular piece is overly reliant on its beat, then try listening to (or playing) the piece without the heavy beat and ask yourself if it "works"? Would the piece hold together? Is the tune singable and memorable on its own?

It is past time for someone to sound an alarm, especially when the dominating beat of a band is now entrenched in most evangelical churches. I was once in the balcony of a large evangelical church for a worship service and saw everyone in the pews below swaying collectively in time to a strong beat from the electric bass guitar and drum kit. I don't think any of them realized that the music had gripped them in this way. It is likely that these Christians were not singing with understanding of the music or the words, contrary to the Bible's clear command (1 Cor. 14:15).

We need to soberly admit that a dominating drumbeat is characteristic of the music of pagan societies, where it can be used to induce a form of trance.[2] Famous rock stars have openly talked about what they used their music for. Mickey Hart, drummer in the rock band the *Grateful Dead,* wrote in his book on the history of percussion that "Drumming is made for trance and for ecstatic states." Jimi Hendrix, one of the biggest names in the history of rock music, once said: "Atmospheres are going to come through music, because the music is a spiritual thing of its own. You can hypnotize people with the music and when you get them at their weakest point you can preach into the sub-conscious what you want to say." Mick Jagger of the *Rolling Stones* said back in the 1960s, "We're moving after the minds and so are most of the new groups. . . music is the key to it all because music opens the door to everybody's mind."[3]

The big beat has an addictive effect that makes it popular and commercially successful. It elicits a physical response without conscious use of the mind, but, even so, the words sung are absorbed by the hearers. How awful this is when the words in rock music are so often crude, violent, and bitterly opposed to God. Various intensely anti-Christian themes have been promoted in popular music over the past few decades, including satanism and the occult. The Beatles were by no means alone in promoting the teachings of eastern religions.[4] The corrupting influence is intrinsic to both the music and its unwholesome lyrics.

There are, of course, other ways that people find to misuse music. The minimalism of Steve Reich or Philip Glass is overly simplistic, and its incessant repetition of musical fragments can also have a hypnotic effect. In a different vein, the following comments on Wagner's music by distinguished musicologists give pause for thought, because it is able ". . .by its sheer and overwhelming power to suggest or arouse or create in its hearers that all-embracing state of ecstasy, at once sensuous and mystical."[5]

Music is not neutral. There is abundant and convincing evidence that it has power to shape our souls for good or to bring disorder to them. Where music is deformed by ugliness, it will surely not be pleasing to the living God, who delights in beauty.

2. Is It Good, Average, or Poor-Quality Music?

Compositions that use the gift of music properly will pass the first test (above), but we cannot say that they are all equally good or worthy of our attention. There are poor-quality pieces that do not use the gift of music very well. There are average pieces that do not excel. And there are good-quality pieces that clearly exhibit the objective principles of beauty.

Such judgments should be made about music of any type, whatever its origins or style. We should weigh every piece as we hear, sing, or perform it. Does it show proportion in its melody and musical form? Do the voices and/or instruments harmonize? Is it overly complicated, or too simplistic? Is the harmony varied or dull? Are the different elements of the piece integrated—that is, do they fit together? (See Chapter 8—*Applying the Principles of Beauty to Music.*)

These are not questions of how the music makes us feel or how familiar we are with it. This book argues that the classical music canon contains the finest and most objectively beautiful music. By its nature, folk music is not as complex, but some simpler music still has value even though it is not the highest-quality music. Lovely folk song is enjoyable. There are compelling reasons to object to pop music today; not every piece has the overpowering beat that makes it ugly, but none of it is high-quality music according to the objective principles of beauty—it is too basic and lacks variety or musical interest.

There is, no doubt, an element of taste or aesthetic sense in discerning between good-quality and bad-quality music. One person may dislike a particular folk song; another may love it. Like taste for food, taste in music can take time to develop. I could never eat olives. But now, over a few years, I have developed a liking for them. Yet, remember that developing taste in music—like any other of the arts—must involve reasoning using our minds, which goes far beyond using our taste buds only for pleasure. As Sir Roger Scruton wrote, "The judgement of taste in music is in the end no different from the judgement of taste in poetry. We can recognize the precise way in which our sympathies are being enlisted by a piece of music, and condone or recoil from it accordingly."[6]

We must also be mindful—across every style and genre of music—of the allurement of empty kitsch. Music can manipulate our emotions by an excess of sweetness in harmony, melody, or lush orchestration. It is the equivalent of the cute garden statuettes or sentimental trinkets of undiscerning homeowners.[7] Christians should encourage one another to be more careful about their choices and pleasures. Consider this warning from Roger Scruton, which applies both to kitsch and to rock music: "Without the conscious pursuit of beauty we risk falling into a world of addictive pleasures and routine desecration, a world in which the worthwhileness of human life is no longer clearly perceivable. . . . We seem to be caught between two forms of sacrilege, the one dealing in sugary dreams, the other in savage fantasies."[8]

Even when we judge the music to be good quality, we must still ask the question: Are the words high quality—does the poetry match the words? Poetry is one of the arts and a whole subject for study in its own right. The most beautiful music belongs with the most beautiful words; John Milton described Voice and Verse as "harmonious sisters." There is always something special about the human voice that makes it preeminent because it was made by God, and it can convey words of truth and life. Martin Luther marveled at the wisdom of God's design in mankind's ability to sing.[9] The greatest works of music in Western civilization are those which combine the best music with the best words, supremely texts from Holy Scripture.

Sadly, sometimes beautiful pieces of music have been set to words that are unwholesome or unbiblical. Christians should pay attention to what is being sung in secular pieces (from songs to madrigals to opera), since words can have sinful themes. Calvin's warning about the power of music to drive immoral words into our hearts deserves to be remembered.[10] It is all too easy to get carried away and not realize what we are singing. Likewise, we should be alert to music written for Roman Catholic worship (often with Latin texts), since some pieces are settings of prayers to the Virgin Mary or prayers for the dead, both of which are contrary to Scripture. Bible-believing Christians come to different conclusions about whether they can, in good conscience, enjoy recordings of such pieces simply for their musical quality.

Thinking about music and listening for objective beauty will inevitably lead you to reject some famous and popular pieces of music. It takes effort to walk down a crowded street when many people are headed towards you in the opposite direction. But Christians should always be prepared to stand out from the crowd. We need to remember that music may be popular for all the wrong reasons, perhaps because it is linked to a certain celebrity or has such sentimental emotional impact that it makes a lot of money for the artist/producers. On what basis do we decide what is good quality and what is poor quality? The best way to know is by taking time to become familiar with the highest-quality music.

There are beautiful songs and stirring serenades to be found in the music of cultures across the world. However, no culture has been influenced by the light of biblical Christianity as much as Western culture. Bible-believing Christians should not be surprised that the greatest artistic works on record are the products of the Western tradition over the past 1,000 years. In particular, the Protestant Reformation taught the real, biblical, perspective on this universe and mankind's true place in it as God's image-bearer.

It should be no surprise, then, that the impact of the Reformation spread to music, government, art, technology, and every area of life. Western culture advanced in wealth, science and technology, and this ultimately brought everything from modern medicine to the space program. In classical music, the impact of the Reformation reached its height in the works of Johann Sebastian Bach, whose music excels at forming unity in diversity, proportion and harmony in sound. Imagine how much he would have enjoyed performances of his works on the advanced musical instruments available today—Bach never got to hear his keyboard works played on a grand piano! As Gene Edward Veith rightly said, "His music is both intricate and patterned, passionate and intellectual, attaining the perfect balance of form and freedom."[11]

3. Is the Music Suitable for Christian Worship?

Music's highest purpose is the worship of God. That is the primary reason God gave us the gift of music. The principles examined so far are integral to a right understanding of music in worship. And yet there is much more to be said—above all we must consider our theology of worship. The triune God created mankind to worship him, and Christians should gather together in local congregations on the Lord's Day every week to do so (Ps. 111:1; Heb. 10:25; 1 Cor. 14:25). What should be the role of music in our worship services?

It has often been said that the Puritans were enemies of music, but this is simply not true. Leading English Puritans such as Oliver Cromwell, John Milton, and John Bunyan loved music. An orchestra about 100-strong played for the wedding of Cromwell's daughter Frances during his time as Lord Protector.[12] References to music abound in the works of both Milton (e.g., *Paradise Lost*) and Bunyan (e.g., *The Pilgrim's Progress*). Instrumental music flourished during the Commonwealth when Puritans ruled England and Wales (1649–1660), and it was during this era that the violin came to prominence in Great Britain.

The Puritans did strongly disagree with the Anglican (Church of England) view that instrumental music should be used in church worship, so they set their sights on the removal or silencing of organs. Richard Hooker was a leading figure in defense of the Anglican view of music in worship.[13] But the Puritans followed John Calvin's teaching that singing in Christian worship should be simple and unaccompanied (see Chapter 20—*Calvin and Corporate Worship*).

The Puritans were emphatically not against music as a whole. The early and influential Puritan theologian William Perkins (1558–1602) endorsed music as a recreation, alongside shooting, running, wrestling, fencing, chess, and draughts: "all of this kind, wherein the industry of the mind & body hath the chiefest stroke, are very commendable, and not to be disliked." While rejecting other entertainments, Perkins gave this rule: "Our recreations must be profitable to ourselves, and others; and they must tend also to the glory of God."[14]

The musicologist Percy Scholes, in his engaging book *The Puritans and Music* written in 1934, rediscovered the truth and identified certain eighteenth-century Anglican enemies of the Puritans as the source of the calumnies against them. Scholes himself was not a Calvinist, but he quoted extensively from primary sources to demonstrate that the Puritans on both sides of the Atlantic enjoyed musical performances and knew the blessing and benefits of music. While psalm-singing in corporate worship was *a cappella* in Puritan New England, *accompanied* psalm-singing and music generally were permitted at home.[15] Increase Mather, one of the most influential ministers in Massachusetts, wrote in 1684: "Indeed the sweetness and delightfulness of music has a natural power to lenifie [soften] melancholly passions."[16]

Puritan governments did not ban music, either in New England or Old England. On the contrary, the first orchestral concerts that we know of occurred under Puritan rule in both Britain (1657) and New England (1731)—the Commonwealth government under Cromwell went as far as to establish a Committee for the Advancement of Music.[17] This was very different from their convictions about theatres, which they closed in England because plays were thought to promote immorality—an opinion shared by many non-Puritan figures of the era as well.

It was in fact Quakers in the seventeenth century, led by George Fox, who vigorously opposed all forms of music. Puritans were more broadminded. John Bunyan did not only weave references to music into his writings; he enjoyed playing himself. Bunyan may have fashioned a flute out of chair leg, and he certainly owned a violin made out of metal, both of which survive to this day. John Owen, often referred to as the Prince of Puritans, also played the flute.[18]

Modern misconceptions about the Puritans and music may have been colored by the attitudes of some evangelicals in Britain and America during the nineteenth and twentieth centuries. This later opposition to secular music, especially secular songs, reflected a desire to separate from such music and other "worldly amusements."[19] The key theological influence behind this was pietism that sought holiness, at least in part, by simply separating from common practices in the surrounding culture. Even though separation from worldliness is a biblical command (2 Cor. 6:17; 1 John 2:15–17), this sort of pietism can become legalistic—identifying sanctification with conformity to man-made rules rather than heartfelt obedience to God's moral law.

This all goes to show that we cannot determine if music is suitable for church worship by looking merely at what music Christians in general have liked or rejected. It is a church's theological convictions that determine its worship practices. While the circumstances will vary in different times and cultural contexts, the worship of God must be governed by the Word of God. Everything we have examined so far indicates that God expects the highest quality music in worship, but the form that this takes will be guided by our theology.

19

Music in Church History

Music has a varied history in the worship of the Christian church. Yet, wherever the gospel has advanced around the world, our worship has featured song. Singing has always been the main (and at times the only) type of music used in Christian worship. There are many commands throughout the Bible to sing praise to God, such as Psalm 100 which exhorts all people to "come before his presence with singing" (v. 2). Sung praise should be our response to who God is: "Sing unto the LORD, O ye saints of his, and give thanks at the remembrance of his holiness" (Ps. 30:4). Psalm 47:6 has an emphatic fourfold repetition: "Sing praises to God, sing praises: sing praises unto our King, sing praises". Take up the book of Psalms, spend a few minutes looking through it, and you will find many references to song.

In Old Testament times, King David introduced organized singing in worship, together with instruments (1 Chronicles chapters 15, 16, 23, and 25)—in preparation for worship in the temple that his son Solomon would build. David appointed 4,000 Levites to worship with music, who were led by 288 key musicians from the tribe of Levi (1 Chron. 23:5; 25:7). We read in 1 Chronicles 15 that Chenaniah was music director (vv. 22, 27) and Heman, Asaph, and Ethan had leading roles (vv. 17, 19). They participate in worship as planned when King Solomon dedicates the Temple (2 Chron. 5:12–13).

Later, Jesus and his apostles sang psalms together (Matt. 26:30). Elsewhere in the New Testament, the book of James encourages Christians to sing psalms in times of rejoicing (5:13). Revelation says that those who are redeemed by God sing the song of Moses and the Lamb (15:2–4; cf. Ex. 15). The key New Testament texts about singing in worship are similar passages in Ephesians and Colossians:

> Ephesians 5:19: "Speaking to yourselves in psalms and hymns and spiritual songs, singing and making melody in your heart to the Lord."
>
> Colossians 3:16: "Let the word of Christ dwell in you richly in all wisdom; teaching and admonishing one another in psalms and hymns and spiritual songs, singing with grace in your hearts to the Lord."

All the evidence points to the fact that from the days of the apostles, the church was obedient to this command to sing. Paul and Silas even sang praises during times of imprisonment (Acts 16:25). The following century, in a letter to the Emperor Trajan in about AD 112, Roman governor Pliny the Younger noted that Christians sang hymns to Christ as God before daylight.[1]

Divergent Views and Practices

Over the past two thousand years, the Western church has adopted different musical practices and styles at different times. Most Christians are unfamiliar with this history, but it provides an illuminating and essential backdrop to the contemporary debates about music in church. When I reflect on my own childhood years in northern England, how did it come to pass that music with a band was offered at my home evangelical church, whereas the music in cathedrals was for choir and organ? Later, as an adult, I have been a member of a Presbyterian church with *a cappella* singing and another in which a pianist accompanies the hymns and psalms.

Most Western churchgoers today will probably be shocked to hear that, for the first thousand years of the Christian era, the church banned musical instruments entirely in worship. From its beginning, the only music in worship services was unaccompanied singing in unison.[2] Certainly, the New Testament commands Christians to sing, and this continued the musical tradition of the Jewish synagogue. The human voice is uniquely able to convey propositional truth in words lifted up by song to God. Clement of Rome (fl. c. AD 96) and Ignatius of Antioch (c. 35–c. AD 107) both emphasized that singing or chanting in worship with "one voice" in unison "was an image of the unity and harmony of all Christians."[3] The early church sang psalms, and there is evidence that they also sang hymns centered on the Bible and the person of Jesus Christ—one of which may have been the hymn *Very Flesh, Yet Spirit Too* by Ignatius of Antioch.[4] Bible commentators have drawn attention to hymnlike passages within the New Testament epistles (e.g., Phil. 2:6–11; 1 Tim. 1:17).

A clear reason for the prohibition on instruments in the early church was to absolutely distinguish Christianity from immoral pagan festivals which used them (the apostle Paul may be alluding to the latter in 1 Corinthians 13:1.) It was only sometime between AD 1000 and AD 1300 that organs, and later other instruments, began to feature in church worship. It seems that the organ was deemed appropriate for a number of reasons, including its lack of association with pagan rituals.[5] However, to the present day, the Eastern Orthodox churches only permit unaccompanied singing in their worship services. This is also true of Reformed churches adhering to Calvin's practice.

Music historian Paul Westermeyer has identified three approaches to music in worship in church history:[6]

- *Encouraged* (Ambrose / Luther)
- *Allowed with restrictions* (Augustine / Calvin)
- *Against* (Pambo / Zwingli)

Ambrose (c. AD 340–397), Bishop of Milan, was a firm advocate of sung music, and he composed hymns, perhaps including the *Te Deum*. He highlighted the centrality of biblical psalms to Christian worship, calling them the "voice of the church."[7] Augustine (AD 354–430) was baptized by Ambrose in Milan and sat under his preaching, but he was more restrained in his approach to music. In his *Confessions*, Augustine recounts the powerful effect of music on people's emotions and only accepts singing in worship where it does not detract from the words.[8] The obscure figure Pambo, who perhaps lived in Egypt in the fourth century AD, is said to have opposed all singing in worship. This has been a rare view in church history.[9]

During the medieval period, singing in church became increasingly elaborate—first with Gregorian chant in the ninth century, advancing gradually to polyphony (see Chapter 6—*Thinking about Music*). Polyphonic music could only be performed by trained choirs, and it came to dominate all the sung elements of worship. The congregation was gradually silenced. This was a significant departure not only from church history, but also from the clear biblical teaching about congregational singing.[10] There were opponents. Ethelred, Abbot of Rievaulx Abbey in Yorkshire (c. 1109–1166), decried the complex sung music, which he compared to horses neighing and "the agonies of a dying man." Later, the well-known churchman and scholar Erasmus (1466–1536) lamented, "Modern church music is so constructed that the congregation cannot hear one distinct word," and said that people "go to church to listen to worse noises than were ever heard in Greek or Roman theatre."[11]

The Protestant Reformation

The recovery of the Bible was at the heart of the Protestant Reformation. The Word of God was restored to its rightful place in the life, government, and worship of the church. This had immediate implications for the place of music in worship. The magisterial Reformers revived congregational singing in the local language and sought to make the meaning of texts clear throughout worship services, in preaching and in song. They swept out of churches overly-complicated choral music and replaced it with the singing of psalms and, in some countries, hymns.

Martin Luther often affirmed that "music is next to theology." He was an accomplished musician (see Chapter 3—*Christians and Music*), and one author has commented: "Luther's theological understanding of music began with his personal involvement in and attachment to music."[12] Luther believed that biblical texts combined with music have great power to affect our souls: "The fathers and prophets wanted nothing else to be associated with the Word of God as music. Therefore we have so many hymns and Psalms where message and music join to move the listener's soul."[13]

This is the origin of the Lutheran tradition of using psalms and hymns in worship, together with instrumental accompaniment, since, for Luther, "voices and instruments sounding together are a theological opportunity, the sound of joy of the redeemed as they glorify the God of grace."[14] Luther resisted producing a German liturgy until he was sure he had chants that fitted the German words well, allowing the words to be clearly heard, and music that elevated rather than obscured their meaning. He composed his own chants and modified existing ones so that they were singable for congregations, rather than merely soloists.[15] Contrary to what is sometimes claimed, Luther did not use the popular tunes of his day in his output for worship.[16] The later composer Lucas Osiander (1534–1604) set an enduring precedent in giving the chorale melody to the soprano, rather than the tenor as had been done previously.[17] The Lutheran heritage would culminate two centuries later in the music of J.S. Bach.

The consensus of Christians throughout the ages has been that we should sing to God in worship. However, the early Swiss Reformer Ulrich Zwingli (1484–1531) rejected all music in worship services including singing—there was preaching, prayer, and the Bible was read responsively during services. He said that the New Testament command to sing "in our hearts" did not mean physical singing using our voices.[18] But Zwingli was perhaps the most accomplished musician of the Reformers. Knowing the power of music to distract from the Word, and overly influenced by Platonic philosophy, he reacted strongly against its use in worship.[19] Zwingli's view was unusual (as was Pambo's) and perhaps driven by the early zeal of the Reformation against the corruptions of the medieval church.

Events in England

The Church of England was established in the 1530s after King Henry VIII broke with Rome. Its *Book of Common Prayer* written by Thomas Cranmer (1489–1556), Archbishop of Canterbury and martyr, excluded all but a couple of hymns (e.g., the *Te Deum*). Instead, the *Book of Common Prayer* featured saying—or chanting—through the entire book of Psalms each month during the course of morning and evening prayer services. Cranmer held the Reformation emphasis on understanding the words and was against polyphony in church worship, instead insisting "for every syllable a note." A modern biographer of Cranmer noted: "He wanted a plainsong which would be functional, comprehensible to and even performable by any persevering member of a congregation."[20]

Metrical psalms in English were first published in the Sternhold and Hopkins "Old Version" in 1562. The Old Version translated the psalms into rhyming English in Common Meter—verses of four lines, with alternating lines of eight and six syllables (8.6.8.6.). Some were arranged in Double Common Meter (8.6.8.6. twice). Over the next two centuries, English-speaking Protestants produced many different editions of metrical psalms, including the *Bay Psalm Book* in Massachusetts in 1640 (the first newly printed book in British North America), the *Scottish Psalter* of 1650, and the "New Version" of Tate and Brady in 1696. The tune *Dundee* was one of twelve "common tunes" for the earlier 1615 Scottish Psalter.[21]

The Church of England later developed the more complex Anglican chant, still performed in cathedrals today. Cranmer's emphasis on music that carries the words with clarity was maintained even when polyphonic music was reintroduced by later generations. This is evident in the music Henry Purcell and others composed for the Chapel Royal in seventeenth-century England. However, by the next century John Wesley was criticizing as "direct mockery of God" church anthems and similar pieces which set different words to be sung simultaneously.[22] Instrumental music was allowed in Anglican churches, usually the organ in most parish churches, though the Puritans strongly objected to this. Later, instrumental ensembles also emerged in the mid-eighteenth century ("West Gallery Music").

The Baptist pastor Benjamin Keach (1640–1704) seems to have been the first Protestant to introduce hymn singing in England, but the cause was significantly advanced by the advocacy and hymn-writing ability of the Congregationalist Isaac Watts (1674–1748). Watts' famous hymns include *When I Survey the Wondrous Cross* and *Joy to the World*. The eighteenth century was the era of classic English hymnody, with other figures including Charles Wesley (brother of John), John Newton, and William Cowper. Charles Wesley wrote thousands of hymns, such as *O, For a Thousand Tongues to Sing* and *Love Divine, All Loves Excelling*. Newton and Cowper were friends and neighbors who initially composed hymns for midweek church meetings and published them as *Olney Hymns,* named after the Parish where Newton pastored. The Moravians in continental Europe also sang hymns—Count von Zinzendorf's hymn *Jesus, Thy Blood and Righteousness* was translated into English by John Wesley.

20

Calvin and Corporate Worship

The Word of God was central to John Calvin's theology and to the Protestant Reformation, so it should come as no surprise that Calvin believed music in congregational worship should be governed by the Bible. His approach was more cautious than that of Luther, but, unlike Zwingli, he believed that there is an important role for music in church worship. As R.C. Sproul explained, "Calvin sought to reform the church's life and worship by driving out of the church all negative worldly influences of art that would obscure the Word of God."[1]

Calvin saw singing in worship as one form of prayer; the other was spoken prayer. He strongly commended both, "provided they are associated with the heart's affection," and said we should use our tongue for God's glory, "for it was peculiarly to tell and proclaim the praise of God."[2] Yet, like Cranmer, he insisted on the primacy of understanding the words when singing, writing in the *Institutes*, "We should be very careful that our ears be not more attentive to the melody than our minds to the spiritual meaning of the words."[3]

Psalm singing had given voice to the French Reformation from early in the sixteenth century, as the Huguenot movement swept across France.[4] This influence was also felt in Geneva, where metrical psalms were at the core of worship during Calvin's ministry, and the songs of the New Testament were also used (e.g., those of Mary and Simeon in Luke chapters 1 and 2).[5] Tunes for the Genevan Psalter in French were provided by Louis Bourgeois (see Example 4 for the tune *Old Hundredth* in Chapter 7—*Surveying Composers*) and other composers. This was published in its final form in 1562 with 125 tunes and 110 different meters—much more varied than the English "Old Version" of the same year.[6]

Calvin sought to return to the simplicity of musical practice in the early church. He insisted on congregational singing, with one note per syllable, sung in unison, and entirely unaccompanied. Regarding the latter, he taught that instrumental music in worship belonged to the ceremonial law in the Old Testament that was abrogated by the coming of Jesus Christ. Commenting on Psalm 33, Calvin wrote that in the church's worship, "Musical instruments in celebrating the praises of God would be no more suitable than the burning of incense, the lighting up of lamps, and the restoration of the other shadows of the Law." Calvin also cited the apostle Paul in 1 Corinthians 14 that worship should be in a known tongue, which is only possible by the human voice, and therefore excludes instrumental music.[7]

More generally, Calvin commended the potential for music to promote moral behavior (see Chapter 17—*Music and Character*) and he permitted a broader range of music outside congregational worship, including singing in parts and playing instruments. For example, he wrote in the preface to the Genevan Psalter:

> And in truth we know by experience that singing has great force and vigor to move and inflame the hearts of men to invoke and praise God with a more vehement and ardent zeal. Care must always be taken that the song be neither light nor frivolous; but that it have weight and majesty (as St. Augustine says), and also, *there is a great difference between music which one makes to entertain men at table and in their houses, and the Psalms which are sung in the Church in the presence of God and his angels.* [emphasis added][8]

Calvin set the pattern for exclusive *a cappella* psalm singing in Reformed church worship in other countries beyond Switzerland, including France, Scotland, Germany, and the Netherlands (because of the influence of the Dutch government, organs remained in the churches there, but at first the church did not permit them to be played during services[9]). The Genevan tradition was carried to New England by the Puritans. Cotton Mather in his history of the New

England colonies (*Magnalia Christi Americana,* published 1702) reechoes the theological view that musical instruments belonged to the abolished ceremonial law: "Now, there is not one word of institution in the *New* Testament for instrumental musick in the worship of God. And because the holy God rejects all he does not command in his worship, he now therefore in effect says unto us, 'I will not hear the melody of thy organs.' "[10] In the nineteenth century, C.H. Spurgeon (1834–1892) shared those sentiments. Congregational worship at Spurgeon's Metropolitan Tabernacle in London was unaccompanied, though he continued the Baptist tradition of singing both psalms and hymns.[11]

The Regulative Principle

The conflict in seventeenth-century Britain between the Puritans and the Anglican hierarchy (including King Charles I) in large part revolved around requirements for church worship. The theological questions were carefully deliberated by the Westminster Assembly, which gathered gospel ministers from around the country between 1643 and 1652, and formulated the Westminster Confession of Faith—often seen as the culmination of the Protestant church confessions. The Assembly sponsored a metrical edition of the Psalter (the basis of the *Scottish Psalter* of 1650)[12] and its *Directory for Public Worship* (1644) said: "It is the duty of Christians to praise God publicly by singing of Psalms together in the Congregation, and also privately in the Family. In singing of Psalms, the voice is to be tunably and gravely ordered: but the chief care must be, to sing with understanding, and with Grace in the heart, making melody unto the Lord."[13]

Chapter 21:1 of the Westminster Confession sets out what is known as the regulative principle of worship: "But the acceptable way of worshipping the true God is instituted by himself, and so limited by his own revealed will, that he may not be worshipped according to the imaginations and devices of men, or the suggestions of Satan, under any visible representation, or any other way not prescribed in the holy Scripture." Its proof texts include Deuteronomy 12:32; Matthew 15:9, the Second Commandment (Ex. 20:4–6), and Colossians 2:18–23.[14] The Westminster Confession also recognized that the cultural "circumstances" vary by different times and places: “There are some circumstances concerning the worship of God, and government of the Church, common to human actions and societies, which are to be ordered by the light of nature and Christian prudence, according to the general rules of the Word, which are always to be observed.”[15]

The regulative principle goes far beyond music and applies to every aspect of the church’s worship.

As theologian Derek Thomas has explained, “Put simply, the regulative principle of worship states that the corporate worship of God is to be founded on specific directives of Scripture. Put another way, it states that nothing ought to be introduced into gathered worship unless there is a specific warrant of Scripture.”[16] My late pastor, Brian Norton, emphasized that “the underlying principle in this is that any approach to the Father is in and through Christ.” The fact that worship must be exclusively through Jesus Christ “necessitates biblical commands in order to guard it.”[17]

With the understanding that temple worship and the ceremonial law were abolished by the coming of Christ, the Puritans followed Calvin in sweeping away all elaborate ceremonies and seeking instead a simple, spiritual worship. In the realm of music, they eliminated instrumental accompaniment because it is not specifically endorsed in the New Testament and they practiced exclusive psalmody because the psalms are directly from Scripture. Defenders of this view have argued that “psalms, hymns, and spiritual songs” in Ephesians 5 and Colossians 3 refer to titles of psalms used in the Greek Septuagint translation of the Old Testament, and they dispute evidence that the early church used hymns, affirming in any case that Scripture has the highest authority.[18]

Other Protestant Christians have held to a different theological principle—that, as long as the Word of God governs worship, what is not forbidden by the Bible could be allowed by the church. They cite, for example, the lack in the New Testament of any detailed equivalent of the book of Leviticus to govern corporate worship. This is the historic position of Lutherans and Anglicans—worship should be based on biblical principles, and musical instruments may be used, provided they contribute to excellence in worship and do not become a distraction. Beauty was, after all, integral to Old Testament tabernacle and temple worship—the priests’ garments were made "for glory and for beauty" (Ex. 28: 2, 40). A classic formulation of this theological perspective is given by Article 20 of the Church of England's Thirty-nine Articles of Religion, its Reformation-era confessional standard: "The Church hath power to decree Rites or Ceremonies, and authority in Controversies of Faith: And yet it is not lawful for the Church to ordain any thing that is contrary to God's Word written, neither may it so expound one place of Scripture, that it be repugnant to another."

Many Reformed churches holding to the regulative principle have permitted the singing of hymns and instrumental accompaniment in worship—arguing that we should explicitly name Jesus Christ and reference the Trinity in our sung praise, and that the psalms themselves promote the use of instruments, so that neither hymns nor instruments are unscriptural. Such churches testify that good accompaniment helps congregational singing; even very experienced singers can easily drift out of tune and out of time when unaccompanied. Looking back over church history as a whole, it is evident that hymns have usually featured in worship alongside psalms and other biblical material. (The Eastern Orthodox church, for example, has a long history of singing hymns, though it has resisted instruments in worship.[19])

Ultimately, the application of these theological principles is a matter of conscience. The Presbyterian W.S. Plumer commented on Psalm 33: "Those who decline or refuse the use of instrumental music themselves, ought not to judge their brethren who think it profitable. 'Who art thou that judgest another man's servant?' [Rom. 14:4]. Brethren who wish to have instrumental music, ought not to use their liberty maliciously. It is not right to make a schism in the body of Christ on such points."[20] Derek Thomas draws on chapter 20.2 of the Westminster Confession of Faith, concluding: "To insist on a certain action in worship that Scripture does not expressly command is to violate freedom of conscience."[21]

21

Worship or Entertainment?

Churches have sung God's praise since New Testament times and there have been many debates over the centuries about the form this should take. But how should we apply to worship all that we have considered so far about the nature and purpose of music? What place does beautiful music have in the worship of God? Before considering that question, we need to consider the theology of worship itself.

Throughout church history, whatever the time or place or denomination, Christians have believed that worship should be focused on God. As the theologian R.B. Kuiper wrote succinctly: "Worship originates with God, not with man."[1] It is the duty and joy of man as a creature to worship his Creator. While it is true that God is omnipresent, in corporate worship the church comes into his holy presence to meet with the God who has entered into covenant with us. This should have implications for every aspect of a Christian worship service. Presbyterian pastor John Keddie has written, "The truth is that the great priority of the Christian Church in the broadest sense is the worship of God. What could be more important?"[2]

In his majestic book *Gospel Worship*, the Puritan minister Jeremiah Burroughs described worship as "a special coming before God" in three specific ways: first, to offer the homage due to God our Creator; second, in receiving the means of grace God communicates his glorious mercies to his people; and third, we come before him actively in faith—it is "required in every duty of worship that you should stir up the faculties of your souls and all the graces of the Spirit of God, and you should act them upon God. . ."[3]

We come in worship as sinners, but as those who are reconciled by the work of our Savior Jesus Christ, who even now intercedes for his people as their High Priest (Heb. 7:25–26; 10:19–22). We come before God in heaven, who views what we do in worship, as do the angels (1 Cor. 11:10; Rev. 22:16). We come on the Lord's Day, as God has appointed (Ex. 20:8; Acts 20:7; Rev. 1:10). Therefore, as the preacher warns in Ecclesiastes 5:1–2: "Keep thy foot when thou goest to the house of God, and be more ready to hear, than to give the sacrifice of fools: for they consider not that they do evil. Be not rash with thy mouth, and let not thine heart be hasty to utter any thing before God: for God is in heaven, and thou upon earth: therefore let thy words be few."

Our worship should be serious. Christian worship must be governed by the revealed will of God in Scripture and shaped by the holy character of God. Leviticus chapter 10 relates how God struck dead Nadab and Abihu, sons of Aaron the High Priest, when they offered "strange fire" before him in worship, which the LORD had not commanded. After this shattering blow, God speaks in verse 3, saying: "I will be sanctified in them that come nigh [near] me, and before all the people I will be glorified." Expounding this verse, R.C. Sproul wrote: "The most important ingredient of worship is that the holiness of God is made manifest. We are to honor our holy God and to acknowledge and give glory to His majesty and His transcendent greatness. There should be an atmosphere of fear and trembling in our worship."[4] Writing about the same verse, Jeremiah Burroughs considered God to be saying: "This is the glory that I stand upon above all other things, that My name may appear to be holy, that I may appear to be a holy God."[5]

Authors D.G. Hart and John Muether have affirmed unreservedly that God despises false worship, and point to the fact that the first four of the Ten Commandments relate directly to worship.[6] They reject the common idea that sincerity and informality are the best guide to good worship, noting the modern claim that "we are more sincere when we are spontaneous and liberated from restraint" is building on the shifting sands of human emotions, and therefore can be completely out of step with the character of God.[7] Some advocates of contemporary worship practices have explicitly linked liberal ideas about the nature of God with the desire to remove traditional ways of worship from church: "The whole mindset of traditional worship did not fit those exploring the boundaries of new theologies, including some of the fundamental presumptions about the divine-human relationship."[8] This is another way of saying that theological liberals do not want to worship a holy God.

The Worship Service

Worship is a distinct, conscious act of bowing down before God. It has been argued in recent decades that the whole of life is worship, implying that there is nothing particularly special about congregational worship. However, that is a false understanding which confuses 'worship' and 'service': "Service is what we owe to our covenant God in *all* that we do (Romans 12:1–2). But worship is a particular act of service in which we offer more conscious adoration."[9] The distinction between these concepts is evident in the words of our Lord Jesus in Matthew 4:10, where he cites the second commandment: "Thou shalt worship the Lord thy God, and him only shalt thou serve." There is a parallel here with prayer. The Bible commands us to "pray without ceasing" (1 Thess. 5:17), but also describes specific times of prayer (Matt. 6:6).

The different aspects of a worship service can be classified as elements, circumstances, and forms. New Testament *elements* of worship are the Word (read and preached), prayer, song, sacraments, and a collection (Acts 2:42, Col. 3:16, and 1 Cor. 16:1–2). The *circumstances* of worship—when and where the congregation gathers, for example—will vary by the cultural context (see Westminster Confession of Faith 1:6). Our theology expresses itself in practice in the *forms* of worship: what is prayed, read, and what is sung—psalms, hymns etc.[10] The modern "worship wars" usually center on the forms that we sing, but should first be set within the broader context—worship must never be man-centered, and the whole service is an act of worship, including the preaching and the prayers, not only the music. The cultural context for Christian worship may guide its *circumstances*, but should not be used to twist the *elements* or *forms* in an unbiblical direction, for example by allowing lengthy singing to dominate the other elements of worship, or skew the fundamental orientation of worship away from God to man.

Jeremiah Burroughs taught that "the worship of God must be suitable to His greatness" and "the more we sanctify His name, the more we shall be in love with worship."[11] Our worship must look up by faith to God and give him glory. At the same time, he works through the worship service to strengthen our faith and to build us up by the Holy Spirit. We gather together with fellow Christian believers to edify and encourage one another—we don't come simply as individuals for our own private benefit (Col. 3:16; Heb. 10:25).

The Reformers taught that the marks of a true church are the preaching of the Word, administration of the sacraments, and church discipline. D.G. Hart and John Muether highlight that corporate worship is a key part of the church's mission of discipleship: "Instead of dumbing it down, we need to have our worship wise up. Through worship God disciples his people."[12] They also argue convincingly that the current crisis in Reformed worship is inextricably connected to the increasing rejection of Sabbath observance by Christians in the West.[13] Two services are better than one. Worship is the best way to spend time on the Lord's Day.

Entertainment Everywhere

The Anglican Bishop J.C. Ryle explained that, first of all, true public worship must be directed to the right object, namely the triune God.[14] At different times in church history, worship has been misdirected towards angels, saints, or the Virgin Mary. In the modern era, we have focused worship on ourselves. The individual preferences and pleasures of sinful people are prioritized in Western culture today, so churches have now adopted a new attitude to worship—not one that first asks, "What does God want?", but instead, "What do people want?" This would be dangerous at any time, but in the early twenty-first century it has led to rock-inspired pop that gives people entertainment. The band with singers on stage is now ubiquitous in evangelical churches. The performers will typically be church members, and most of the congregation likely enjoy the music played. But we must step back and see that this represents a subversion of the whole concept of Christian worship. The focus is no longer on seeking what God requires in worship but on doing something we find pleasurable.

God has called the church out of the world to be a holy people: "But ye *are* a chosen generation, a royal priesthood, an holy nation, a peculiar people; that ye should shew forth the praises of him who hath called you out of darkness into his marvellous light." We are strangers and pilgrims on this earth (1 Peter 2:9, 11). As Christians come before the holy God in worship, we should not expect to use music that is indistinguishable from the pagan culture around us. The early church categorically rejected that approach.

Yet worship today has become man-centered. Evangelicals are making mankind's felt needs the primary focus of worship services "through therapeutic forms of positive reinforcement that orient worship more toward self-fulfillment than to self-denial."[15] Worse still, the pop-style music they are bringing before him is poor-quality at best or ugly at worst. This may sound stark, but it is the truth, and we should lament it. As Gene Edward Veith states emphatically, "Entertainment is not the purpose of going to church. Indulging ourselves in aesthetic pleasure is not the same as worshiping. . . . The Bible calls us to repentance, faith, service, and self-denial—qualities utterly opposed to the entertainment mentality. In Christian worship, the congregation is not the audience; God is the audience."[16]

The introduction of bands and pop music into Christian gatherings started in the 1960s, not long after the rise of rock music, with the "Jesus People" in California.[17] By the 1990s, what is known as contemporary Christian music was being widely adopted across the denominations. Academics Lester Ruth and Lim Swee Hong, who are advocates of this music, trace parallel developments in the charismatic movement and in a broader pragmatic approach, which converged by the mid-1990s: "In an increasing number of Pentecostal, evangelical, and mainline congregations, worshipers engaged in practices that half a century earlier were largely unknown. These included informality, hands lifted in the air, projected lyrics, bands, drama and other arts, and times of congregational singing of choruses."[18]

This revolutionary tide has now widely influenced many churches, spearheaded by the church growth movement which advocates "seeker-sensitive" worship services. The church growth strategy springs from the deep well of pragmatism in evangelicalism. Though the motivation may be a well-meaning desire to evangelize, there is a fundamental problem with the seeker-sensitive model of worship—an unregenerate person is not naturally attracted to worshipping the holy God. When churches adopt this strategy, God is denied worship focused on him and, instead, sinners are given the entertaining music they like. Another baleful consequence of this movement has been to displace the pastor from leading the act of worship, with a musician becoming the worship leader.[19] While this has roots in a modern charismatic theology of temple worship, it aligns well with the practices of pop music, and wrests control from God's ordained servant of the Word. Hymn books—a good practical source of discipleship and theology—have been jettisoned in favor of projecting the words onto screens to allow people to move around informally and to dance during services.[20]

The sequencing of different types of music in contemporary worship is carefully planned; an obvious method is the repetition of choruses to stir people's emotions at the start of the service. Eliciting such feelings by the power of music is often confused with the work of the Holy Spirit. While it is important to seek the Holy Spirit's help in our worship, emotional manipulation is the wrong way to do so. Using the power of music to create emotional "spiritual" moods should have no place in Christian worship.

Lester Ruth and Lim Swee Hong celebrate the "liturgical iconoclasm" of contemporary worship: "Suspicion of liturgical inheritances has given it a predilection for novelty and a presumption that accessibility, relevance, and, above all, effective impact are the measures of worship faithful to God."[21] This is undoubtedly the outlook of most evangelicals today, but these worshippers should stop and consider this sober warning from R.C. Sproul: "When we begin to pander to the 'audience' rather than to God, we are in serious trouble. The Old Testament worship service where the people were the most enthusiastic and energetic consisted of the singing of praise songs by an overflow congregation while dancing around a golden calf (Ex. 32:17–19). Worship is not an arena for open experimentation. If we 'worship' by doing what we enjoy, rather than by doing what is pleasing to God, our worship will gravitate toward idolatry. It is our duty, as much as possible, to learn what true worship is supposed to be like."[22]

The modern-day composer and author Paul S. Jones, in *Singing and Making Music,* advocates a more Bible-based approach to church worship, emphasizing the need for psalms and hymns that are God-centered and excellent. Yet, surveying today's church, he concludes that its value systems "reflect society's primary philosophy (what 'works'—*pragmatism*), its objects of attention (ourselves—*narcissism*), its occupation (our own amusement or pleasure—*hedonism*), and its basis of belief (our opinions—*relativism*). . . A 'me-focused' age, though, is hardly one that should inform and define our approach to God."[23]

Failing the Test

Too many people assume that the music they like most is suitable for worshipping God. I earlier suggested three questions to consider for any piece of music: first, is there anything intrinsically wrong with this piece of music?; second, is it good, average, or poor-quality music?; and third, is the music suitable for Christian worship? The rock-like music used in much church worship today depends on the big beat, so it fails the first test. This ugly music brings disorder to people's souls, bypassing their minds and causing their emotions to overflow. Such people are not worshipping with understanding (see Chapter 16—*Bringing Disorder to the Soul*). Christians should be wary of any religious event that produces "gentle animal excitement" rather than true worship.[24]

In fact, much pop-style music used in evangelical churches today also fails the second test—by objective standards it is poor-quality music which is simplistic and banal. It is therefore unsuitable music to bring to the God of beauty in worship, no matter what words are being sung: "shoddy, shallow, poorly written music should be avoided . . . only what is quality, well written music is worthy of an offering to God."[25] Moreover, contemporary church music is often composed for solo singers—with angular tunes and syncopated (off beat) rhythms—which makes it hard for congregations to sing. If the singers on the stage were to stop, little sound would be heard from the rest of the church.

The music of popular entertainment carries with it assumptions which consumers bring with them into church services. If music in church is presented as something prepackaged that simply requires passive listening, this discourages the congregation from seeing it as an activity they should participate in. Moreover, pop fans easily identify the solo singer on stage as someone who is representing the expression of their own individual thoughts. This leads famous musicians to be idolized—inside or outside church worship services.

Both Augustine and Calvin taught that the church's music must be compatible with the sober worship of God. D.G. Hart and John Muether have reflected, "Godly fear should characterize our song, in both words and melody. We need to ask whether a given hymn or praise song can cultivate the sensibilities of reverence, along with self-control, discipline, and moderation."[26] In the character of the music, its shape and mood, rock-inspired pop is inconsistent with reverent worship. There is also the related question of whether the massive, profit-driven music industry should be driving what Christians do in the worship of God.

Author Harold Best, who is sympathetic to contemporary Christian music, nevertheless warns conservative evangelical churches: "It has turned out that many evangelists and church growth leaders scout out culture, identifying what works, borrowing this, imitating that, and, in the process, dragging in numerous artistic and musical associations from the very culture that they then turn around and condemn in their preaching."[27]

Advocates of contemporary Christian music sometimes point to Old Testament instrumental worship as justification for rock music in church. But they should note that only four instruments were specifically authorized for corporate worship by King David (harp, lyre, cymbal and horn/trumpet: 1 Chronicles 15:16–24; 16:4–6; 25:2–6 and 2 Chronicles 29:25–30), which therefore excluded the percussive beat of drums.[28] Likewise, there was no emphasis on rhythm in the music of the early church, which was comprised only of singing.[29] The Old Testament references additional instruments, which were used for other events outside of worship (e.g., the procession of the ark recorded in 1 Chronicles 13 and Psalm 150). King David's institution of the musical elements and forms of worship in the Temple was carefully regulated and far from the casual policy of so many churches today.

The elevation of contemporary music practices in a church usually reveals a theology that gives the worship of God a low place. I do not say that singing hymns and psalms (*a cappella* or with instrumental accompaniment) is inherently virtuous or always good music. Not at all. People in any church context can come with cold hearts, and not worship in spirit and in truth as Christ commanded (John 4:24). But traditional Protestant worship practices, combining good theological content with engaged hearts and minds, point us away from ourselves to our Creator and Redeemer.

Beyond music, a good deal of other dubious practices are taking place in church services today, which are evidently more about putting on a show than a sober act of worship—such as fog machines, party-tricks, high-wire performances, and more. In contrast, one result of the regulative principle is that it protects congregational worship. "It is important to realize that the regulative principle as applied to public worship frees the church from acts of impropriety and idiocy—we are not free, for example, to advertise that performing clowns will mime the Bible lesson at next week's Sunday service."[30]

22

Reforming Church Music

In his treatise *The Necessity of Reforming the Church* (1543), John Calvin set out the two principal goals of the Protestant Reformation: first, the restoration of the right worship of God, and second, declaring the biblical doctrine of salvation. The Christian church in the twenty-first century also desperately needs a reformation of its worship, realizing that God is its audience, not man. This has implications for every aspect of a worship service, including biblical preaching, prayer, and confession of sin, since ". . . the service is a holy conversation between heaven and earth. It cannot be repackaged as a form of entertainment or congregational meeting."[1] When it comes to music, this should reflect God's "glory, beauty, holiness, and order, and should direct men to him and to his ways."[2]

Worship is a matter of theology. The third of our three questions asked: "Is the music suitable for Christian worship?" It will only be suitable if a biblical theology of worship governs both the music and sung texts. We can conclude from the Bible and church history that music in worship should be distinctively Christian, prioritize congregational singing, and be unmistakably directed towards God. Church leaders will make the practical decisions about how to apply these principles in their own time and place. Churches must carefully evaluate their worship practices based on the Bible and not uncritically baptize the music of the surrounding culture. Much of the debate inevitably revolves around what is sung in worship—Brian Norton gave three key reasons why it is very important to consider this: "i) A great deal of the theology people have is derived from what they sing; ii) It is a God-appointed means of stirring up and involving our emotions but it does so through our minds and keeping us together; iii) Precisely because singing has been given a wrong place and one which has engendered a great deal of passion and division."[3]

Those churches which practice hymn singing should also practice *inclusive* psalmody. The commands of Ephesians 5:19 and Colossians 3:16 mean we cannot exclusively sing hymns. Ambrose, the fourth-century bishop of Milan, called the Psalms "the voice of the church." They are inspired by God, reveal his character, and point forward to the coming Messiah. The Psalms are ideally suited to use in worship, since the 150 psalms cover praise, proclamation, and prayer. Calvin cited three main purposes of Christians singing psalms in worship: praising God for his mercy and grace, the edification of believers, and reflecting on the work of God in our lives.[4] Remember that various psalms convey emotions that are not typically found in hymns, e.g., grief and lament. Bible commentator Derek Kidner wrote: "The poetry of the psalms has a broad simplicity of rhythm and imagery which survives transplanting into almost any soil. Above all, the fact that its parallelisms are those of sense rather than of sound allows it to reproduce its chief effects with very little loss of either force or beauty. It is well fitted by God's providence to invite 'all the earth' to 'sing the glory of His name'."[5]

Tunes for Psalms and Hymns

Since Christians know that God is the author of beauty, we should bring beautiful music to him in worship. The hymn and psalm tunes of the Reformed tradition were composed for congregational worship. They are not an old-fashioned genre; rather they are the ideal musical genre for group singing in any era—whether in congregational or in family worship. As the principles of Classical architecture can be applied in every generation to make a new building, so we can apply the timeless objective principles of beauty in music to compose new tunes for God's people.

Like any other type of music, we should seek for hymn tunes that are the highest quality. In the twenty-first century, this means selecting the best of the old and the best of the new. There is no inherent virtue in either antiquity or modernity when it comes to music or poetry. Good elements for congregational singing have been composed at least since the time of the Reformation down to the present day.

The best music combined with the best verse is memorable throughout our lives and will prove a real blessing to the souls of the congregation. Scott Aniol explains, "As Christians consider truth and righteousness, they should respond with their affections. . . . Our emotions must be connected to biblical truth."[6] Luther commented on Psalm 4 that "it is the function of music to arouse the sad, sluggish, and dull spirit. . ." and when the words of a psalm "are sung to artistic music, they kindle the mind more intensely and sharply."[7] Paul S. Jones, writing in the twenty-first century, picks up the same theme: "Music clothes the Word of God with sound and also reinforces its message with meaning beyond the realm of words. It communicates with our souls as a metaphysical force."[8]

Those tunes that have endured have a memorable melody, harmonic variety, a regular rhythm, and a coherent internal layout. These are the four main characteristics of a good hymn tune, rightly identified by author Armin Haeussler: 1) a singable tune; 2) well-harmonized; 3) proper rhythm; and 4) "sturdy architecture" which in all its aspects are "closely-knit, balanced, and logical." Haeussler gave some fine examples from different countries, including: *Old Hundredth* (see Example 4), *Tallis' Canon, St. Flavian, Dundee, Forest Green, Leoni, Rhuddlan, Veni Emmanuel, Lobe Den Herren, Ein Feste Burg,* and *Nun Danket Alle Gott.*[9] The choice of tunes sung by congregations will vary from culture to culture. In my experience, Americans gravitate towards music which has directness and immediacy, whereas Englishmen have a tradition of more restrained music. Welsh hymn tunes have a marked range of emotional intensity: compare *Rhuddlan* and *Cwm Rhondda* with *Aberystwyth* and *Bryn Calfaria,* or *Godre'r Coed* and *Llwynbedw.*

Good-quality music is not sappy, sentimental music that merely sways the emotions and is lightweight and repetitive. Regrettably, this too often characterizes compositions for Christian gatherings from the past two hundred years. Many traditional hymn tunes used in churches today have little harmonic variety and an instantly forgettable tune. Poor-quality music cannot be justified in worship simply by calling it "Christian music," even if it sounds different from "worldly music" and talks of Jesus Christ. We should heed John Calvin's warning: "Such songs as have been composed only for sweetness and delight of the ear are unbecoming to the majesty of the church and cannot but displease God in the highest degree."[10]

Of course, the same tune can be used for different hymns or psalms. As long as it is a fine-quality tune, this will greatly help the congregation because it is familiar. But when a particular hymn has become married to one tune—such as for *Amazing Grace*—then there should be strong grounds for changing it.[11] (People new to transatlantic travel will be surprised to find their favorite hymn married to an unfamiliar tune on the other side of the ocean—*Rock of Ages, When I Survey the Wondrous Cross, O Little Town of Bethlehem,* etc.) Whatever country you are worshipping in, it is very important that the mood of the tune matches the mood or character of the words. There is a great difference between words of triumphant proclamation and lamentation, and they require obviously different music—a military march is not suitable for a lullaby.

As well as choosing the finest tunes, churches should also seek excellence in their singing. Learning to sing well requires training and effort, and many people today—including Christians—have little musical education, so there is much work to do. Everyone in the congregation should be encouraged to sing, and churches would be wise to arrange times outside of worship services to improve singing and to learn new tunes. John Wesley's *Rules for Methodist singers* are a good guide, in which he recommended singing together, lustily, modestly, in time, and above all spiritually: "Have an eye to God in every word you sing. Aim at pleasing him more than yourself or any other creature." The modern-day *Trinity Psalter Hymnal* contains helpful advice for pastors, musicians, and the congregation; especially the focus on singing with understanding of the words.[12] Augustine confessed that he "sinned grievously" when he found himself more moved by the singing than what was sung.[13]

The seventeenth-century Englishman Nathaniel Homes set out this encouragement for congregational singing in his pamphlet *Gospell-Musick*: "God hath not given speech to man, but to glorifie him too. . . . And therefore he hath given the naturall gift of Singing (a Musick that excels all instrumentall) to the end to praise and worship him, every man quickning himself and others by symphonie, and singing concent together. . . . By singing we present unto our sences and minds the lively type of heavenly joyes whether to be acted by the Church triumphant in Heaven, or under Heaven at the great restauration."[14]

Words and Music

The words we sing obviously matter for vocal music used in worship. It is the duty of pastors and elders to determine that these are biblically and doctrinally sound. Too many hymns from the latter half of the nineteenth century onwards are more concerned with individual experience rather than theology. They tell the hearers very little about the character of God. When you read a hymn, ask yourself whether the focus is on God or on what he has done for me and my personal feelings about it.

Seek out the best poetry if you want to offer up the very best to God. Poetry, like music, is an art form with objective principles of beauty. William Cowper (1731–1800), author of *Olney Hymns* with John Newton, is widely regarded as one of England's greatest poets. Perhaps his most well-known hymn is *God Moves in a Mysterious Way*. A more overlooked gem is *The Spirit Breathes upon the Word*, and there are many others by Cowper to explore. John Wesley argued that the texts of hymns should reflect nothing other than "the purity, the strength, and the elegance of the English language."[15] But in recent times, the poetry of too many old hymns has been ruined by ill-judged attempts to modernize the words. And for new hymns and metrical psalm translations, zealous Protestants—in their commendable desire for accurate theology—can fail to consider the poetic aspect of English language and so produce dull, lifeless verse.

On a practical level, good accompaniment helps to keep people singing together and in tune. An alert accompanist will not dominate the congregation, but will actively support the singing. A real, acoustic instrument is preferable to playing back recorded sound, which lacks authenticity.[16] Some churches will feature an organ as well as other selected instruments; others use a piano. This may partly depend on the size and nature of the building used for the service. Certainly, if we are to offer high-quality music to God in worship, instruments need to be played by competent, trained musicians.

Associations

For some people, at different times and places in history, certain tunes or styles of music have had bad associations. This was the background to the early church's rejection of instruments in worship, which were prominent in pagan rituals. It can happen on a personal level—if a popular tune was widely played at a difficult time in your life, for example. Music, perhaps because of its potent impact on our souls (mind and emotions), can powerfully connect itself with the context in which it first came to us.

This has implications for church worship and the issue of protecting an individual's conscience. *Austria,* the common tune for John Newton's hymn *Glorious Things of Thee are Spoken,* is also used for the German national anthem. We can understand why survivors of World War II from other countries would not want to sing this tune. We should likewise ask if a new convert would be helped by singing a psalm to an old drinking tune. It is sometimes claimed that Luther used music from the alehouse, but this is false.[17] Moreover, Luther, Calvin, or the Wesley brothers never said, "Why should the devil have all the best tunes?" If anyone said this, it was probably William Booth, the founder of the Salvation Army.[18] (It was later proclaimed in the lyrics of a contemporary Christian music song by Larry Norman.[19]) Leaving aside for a moment the intrinsic musical flaws of rock-infused pop, there is also a strong argument for distancing our worship from pop music as a distinctive Christian witness against all its ungodly associations.

We should remember that mankind is capable of turning anything into an idol. This includes the music he loves. Traditional music can become idolatrous in worship just as much as contemporary music. There are churches in which the choir and organ are idolized and revered in the same way as the band in other churches. Appreciating superb classical music in a church service has an impact on the hearer's soul, but it is not converting. Only the gospel of Christ is the power of God unto salvation (Rom. 1:16). As a choirboy, I sometimes confused the two things, especially when experiencing singing the thrilling climax to a piece. Gene Edward

Veith has commented: "Aesthetic experiences can be very close and are perhaps related to religious experiences, but they are not the same. . . . Properly, the sense of transcendence in a symphony, the sensation of being swept out of ourselves into something high and beautiful, can and should make us mindful of the transcendent realm of the infinite Lord. Yet it need not. Many people are satisfied with the 'richness of life' offered by aesthetic stimulation, which by its nature can make few self-consuming demands."[20]

Wherever the church gathers for worship, in congregations large or small, in remote villages or buzzing cities, persecuted or with religious liberty, whatever the language, whatever the season, we are coming in a special way before God through Jesus Christ. We have so much to praise him for. Our worship looks forward to our eternal worship round the throne of God, where the songs of joy and praise will last throughout eternity (Rev. 5:8–14; 7:9–12). As J.C. Ryle once said, "Praise has been truly called the flower of all devotion. It is the only part of our worship which will never die. Preaching and praying and reading shall one day be no longer needed. But praise shall go on for ever."[21]

Conclusion

Music is a precious gift from God. It has been poetically described as the mosaic of the air. As a mosaic assembles little fragments to form one picture, so music assembles individual sounds to form a single piece. When a composer or performer organizes sounds according to the objective principles of beauty, he makes something to be delighted in. God is the ultimate author of beauty, so we should seek to imitate and please him in creating, performing, and enjoying beautiful music. This is the primary reason you should think about music.

Music in itself does not save anyone from sin; salvation is only found through faith in Jesus Christ (Acts 4:12; 16:31). But playing or listening to the greatest music is healthy for our souls. It brings order to our minds and our emotions—a common-grace blessing for Christian and non-Christian alike. We have a precious and immense inheritance of such pieces in the canon of classical music. There is so much to enjoy, and the widespread availability of recorded music makes it easy to hear it. What Quinlan Terry wrote about architecture is equally true of music: "All our hopes and loyalties, our greatest comfort and our consolation, are only to be found and expressed within a great tradition. We cleave to cities that have endured for centuries with great buildings which have that eternal perspective and historical pedigree. These are the places that we love and feel to be part of us."[1]

However, in the West we live amid the wreckage wrought by atheistic assaults on our cultural heritage. When people turn their backs on the God of beauty, they embrace ugliness instead. The Devil has goaded on composers, as Martin Luther said of some musicians in his own day,[2] to create deformed or savage works which in some cases do not rise above the level of noise. These destructive forces are by no means confined to music—witness the effects on painting, literature, and architecture over the past century. The dreary and ill-formed office blocks around us are the frozen music of our age.

Yet in God's common grace, much good remains possible in music as elsewhere. Christians should step forward to preserve, protect, and defend what is beautiful. The arts are worth appreciating and studying for their own intrinsic, God-given importance. We should resist a utilitarian impulse that demands that everything must be "useful" or generate obvious financial benefit. Clearly, not everyone is called to study music at university. But man is created body *and soul,* and, without those things which delight the soul, life quickly becomes dull and purposeless. Abraham Kuyper wrote: "The world of sounds, the world of forms, the world of tints, and the world of poetic ideas, can have no other source than God; and it is our privilege as bearers of his image, to have a perception of this beautiful world, artistically to reproduce, and humanly to enjoy it."[3]

What place should you give music in comparison to all other aspects of life? The Bible teaches that man's greatest joy should be in God—"man's chief end is to glorify God, and to enjoy him forever"[4]—but secondarily this does not at all rule out enjoying pleasurable, lawful things in this life. After all, God our Creator gave them to us.[5] Each Lord's Day, congregational singing is an integral part of the church's worship—a biblical command that cannot be ignored. Music has a significant place in Christian worship, but can easily turn the direction of worship away from God when it is misused.

Different people will give music a higher or a lower profile in their daily lives, but, whatever our calling, we must think about the music we inevitably hear around us. Shakespeare may have been exaggerating when he said that the unmusical man is fit for only for treasons, stratagems, and spoils.[6] But Lorenzo Valla, the Italian Renaissance humanist, went further, writing in 1431: "He who does not praise music is blind either of soul or of body. If he has eyes, he deserves to lose them, for he does not feel that he has them."[7]

Treasure Trove

The canon of classical music is a treasure trove of objectively beautiful music, granted to us by the providence of God. Great classical music transcends culture and can be enjoyed by everyone; in the same way that great pieces of architecture can be appreciated and are visited by people from all over the world. The great works of classical music should resound across the globe. Learning to appreciate this music begins best in childhood. At any age it requires patience, but it is immensely rewarding. It gets easier and all the more enjoyable over time.

Classical music doesn't come in small packages of instant gratification like the video or audio clips that are so often promoted online today. Simplistic music—like junk food—may be enjoyable at the time but is not ultimately satisfying. Switch it off. Denying yourself immediate pleasure is inimical to modern attitudes, but it has the clearest biblical foundation. At the same time, switch to something better. Remember that there are broad new horizons of music waiting to be discovered. Christians are free in Christ to reject the cultural belief that music choices are integral to your personal identity. There is far more to who you are than the music you listen to. Music is not primarily about expressing ourselves, but rather enjoying good and beautiful things that God has given mankind in creation.

It is a privilege to have easy access to recorded music. We should make discerning and thankful use of this. Yet, there is a subtle danger. The widespread lack of musical taste may be the result of people being consumers of music rather than making music themselves. The thought and action involved in music making develops musical taste. Pursue learning and performing a musical instrument—even if you are an adult and have never picked up an instrument before. Whenever you can, go to live performances (amateur or professional). There is something inescapably energizing and refreshing about live music, and its soul impact far surpasses any recording. The difference between listening to recorded music and live music is like the difference between watching a video of a wedding and actually being there yourself.

A person does not need to be a Christian to write good music, but, when we consider the music of J.S. Bach, we should recognize that the finest music was written by a supremely talented and hard-working Christian who intentionally wrote for the glory of God. As he said: "The ultimate end or final purpose of all music. . . is nothing other than the praise of God and the recreation [or refreshment] of the soul."[8] It should not be a surprise that societies shaped by the Christian worldview produced composers who wrote music of the greatest order, complexity, and beauty. Full-orbed, biblical Christianity recognizes the kingship of Jesus Christ over every domain of life, including the arts.[9] That most definitely includes music.

Martin Luther said: ". . .next to the Word of God, music deserves the highest praise" and when sharpened to an art, "at last it is possible to taste with wonder (yet not to comprehend) God's absolute and perfect wisdom in his wondrous work of music."[10] Music is in a sense mysterious. It is commonplace, yet in some ways it is beyond our comprehension. There are aspects of music and its effects that are hard to explain, and it flows within society's deepest religious, cultural, and philosophical currents. Why is it that Western culture no longer seems to generate great works of classical music? Sir Roger Scruton suggested that the decline in religious faith may *explain* the inability in the West to create new styles of beautiful music.[11] There is a darkening of the soul that occurs when people turn away from God, and this points to the demise of the classical musical tradition that grew and blossomed under the Christian worldview. Yet what could Christian composers—from any country or background—accomplish who are trained to appreciate beauty in music? The palette of musical color in the tonal system is waiting for new brushstrokes from new artists.

Loving the God of Beauty

Why should Christians learn to value what is beautiful? Above all, because God is the source of all beauty. Jonathan Edwards wrote that appreciating beauty in music, as well other aspects of creation, will increase a Christian's love for the God of beauty and our desire to live for him. As Edwards reflected in *The Nature of True Virtue*: "Probably it is with regard to this image or resemblance, which secondary beauty has of true spiritual beauty, that God has so constituted nature, that the presenting of this inferior beauty, especially in those kinds of it which have the greatest resemblance of the primary beauty, as the harmony of sounds, and the beauties of nature, have a tendency to assist those whose hearts are under the influence of a truly virtuous temper, to dispose them to the exercises of divine love, and enliven in them a sense of spiritual beauty."[12]

Music is a common-grace gift of God to all people. Along with other skills and crafts, music has been practiced by godly and ungodly people from the time of Genesis 4 onwards. Yet Christians above all people have reason to enjoy common-grace gifts. As R.B. Kuiper wrote, commenting on this in the context of 1 Corinthians 3:22 ("Whether Paul, or Apollos, or Cephas, or the world, or life, or death, or things present, or things to come: all are yours"):

> The members of Christ's church may justly claim such valuable products of the common grace of God as their very own. While they are warned not to use the world "to the full" (1 Corinthians 7:31 ASV) because its fashion passes away, the fact remains that the world belongs to the children of light in a sense in which it does not belong to the children of darkness. It is theirs to use to the glory of Christ, whose they are, and of God, whose Christ is (1 Corinthians 3:23). And so it is hardly surprising that "the glory and honor of the nations" will be brought into new Jerusalem (Revelation 21:26).[13]

Perhaps one reason for music's special power is that it is an unseen beauty, pointing us to the unseen world of spiritual reality. We cannot yet see that realm, but the Christian mind has an eternal perspective—remembering this world is a "temporary place of refuge, not our true and final home."[14] Let's look ahead and set our sights on the future. God's people look forward to the new heavens and the new earth (Isa. 66; 2 Peter 3; Rev. 21–22). We can expect to enjoy music there which is recognizable to us, but transformed. The vaults of heaven will reverberate with a music that transcends all that we ever heard on this earth. And it will all be to the glory of God.

Music and song are often referenced in Revelation, the final book of the Bible, which describes our eternal home. Christians can confidently look to forward to a musical eternity in the city of God and the new creation. As John Bunyan concluded the second part of *The Pilgrim's Progress,*

> But glorious it was to see how the upper region was filled with horses and chariots, with trumpeters and pipers, with singers and players on stringed instruments, to welcome the pilgrims as they went up, and followed one another in at the beautiful gate of the city.[15]

Musical Examples

From Chapter 7

Example 1— Giovanni Pierluigi da Palestrina, *Super Flumina Babylonis,* ed. Franz Espagne, vol. 5, Opera Omnia (Leipzig: Breitkopf & Härtel, 1875).

Example 2—Orlandus Lassus, *O occhi, manza mia,* ed. Adolf Sandberger, vol. 10, Sämtliche Werke (Leipzig: Breitkopf & Härtel, 1897).

Example 3—Thomas Tallis, *If Ye Love Me, Keep My Commandments,* The Musical Times (London: Novello, 1862).

Example 4—Louis Bourgeois, *Old Hundredth,* Hymnary.org, accessed April 24, 2024.

Example 5—Henry Purcell, *Rejoice in the Lord Alway,* ed. Harry E. Woolridge and Godfrey E. P. Arkwright, The Works of Henry Purcell, vol. 14 (London: Novello, 1904).

Example 6—Antonio Vivaldi, *Concerto in E (Spring),* First movement, ed. Eleanor Selfridge-Field, The Four Seasons and Other Violin Concertos, no. 1 (New York: Dover Publications, 1995 reprint).

Example 7—J.S. Bach, *Brandenburg Concerto No. 5,* First movement, BWV 1050, ed. Wilhelm Rust, Bach-Gesellschaft Ausgabe, vol. 19 (Leipzig: Breitkopf & Härtel, 1871).

Example 8—George F. Handel, "Hallelujah Chorus", *Messiah,* ed. Friedrich Chrysander, Georg Friedrich Händels Werke, vol. 45 (Leipzig: Deutsche Händelgesellschaft, 1902).

Example 9—Wolfgang A. Mozart, *Piano Concerto No. 23,* Second movement, Mozarts Werke, 16.4.23 (Leipzig: Breitkopf & Härtel, 1879).

Example 10—F. Joseph Haydn, "The Heavens are Telling the Glory of God", *The Creation* (London: Novello, 1859).

Example 11—Ludwig van Beethoven, *Piano Concerto No. 5 (Emperor)*, Second movement, Ludwig van Beethovens Werke, 9.69 (Leipzig: Breitkopf & Härtel, 1862).

Example 12—Franz Schubert, *Quintet in A (The Trout)*, Fourth movement, ed. Ignaz Brüll, Franz Schubert's Werke, 7.1 (Leipzig: Breitkopf & Härtel, 1886).

Example 13—Felix Mendelssohn, *Violin Concerto in E minor*, First movement, ed. Julius Rietz, Felix Mendelssohn-Bartholdys Werke, vol. 4 (Leipzig: Breitkopf & Härtel, 1877).

Example 14—Johannes Brahms, *Symphony No. 2*, Fourth movement, 1st ed. (Berlin: Simrock, 1878).

Example 15—Antonín Dvořák, *Symphony No. 9*, Second movement, 1st ed. (Berlin: Simrock, 1894).

Example 16—Sergei Rachmaninov, *Piano Concerto No. 2*, Third movement, 1st ed. (Moscow: Gutheil, 1901).

Example 17—Jean Sibelius, *Symphony No. 3*, Third movement, Opus 52, Copyright © 2020 Robert Lienau Musikverlag, Mainz, Germany. Used by permission of European American Music Distributors Company, sole U.S. and Canadian agent for Robert Lienau Musikverlag, Mainz, Germany.

Example 18—Aaron Copland, *Appalachian Spring*, Copyright © 1958 Boosey & Hawkes, Reproduced by permission of Boosey & Hawkes.

From Chapter 9:

Example 19—J.S. Bach, *Chaconne in D minor for Solo Violin,* from Partita No. 2 in D minor, BWV 1004, ed. Alfred Dörffel, Bach-Gesellschaft Ausgabe, vol. 27 (Leipzig: Breitkopf & Härtel, 1879).

Example 20—J.S. Bach, *Prelude in C major,* BVW 846, ed. Ferruccio Busoni, from the Well-Tempered Clavier vol. 1 (Leipzig: Breitkopf & Härtel, 1894).

Example 21—J.S. Bach, *Fugue in E-flat major for Organ (St. Anne),* BWV 552, ed. Carl Ferdinand Becker, Bach-Gesellschaft Ausgabe, vol. 3 (Leipzig: Breitkopf & Härtel, 1853).

Example 22—J.S. Bach, "Sanctus", *Mass in B minor,* BWV 232, ed. Julius Rietz, Bach-Gesellschaft Ausgabe, vol. 6 (Leipzig: Breitkopf & Härtel, 1856).

Endnotes

Preface

1 Martin Luther, "Preface to Georg Rhau's Symphoniae Iucundae," in *Luther's Works,* vol. 53, *Liturgy and Hymns,* ed. Ulrich S. Leupold and Helmut T. Lehmann (Philadelphia: Fortress Press, 1965), 321-322.

2 Allan Bloom, *The Closing of the American Mind: How Higher Education Has Failed Democracy and Impoverished the Souls of Today's Students* (New York: Simon & Schuster, 1988), 72.

3 Aaron Copland, *What to Listen for in Music,* rev. ed. (Harmondsworth, Middlesex, England: Penguin Books, 1999), 3.

1. Mark the Music

1 Anglicans are known as Episcopalians in the USA.

2 J. Gresham Machen, *The Christian View of Man* (1965; repr., Edinburgh: The Banner of Truth Trust, 2002), 126.

3 John Calvin, *Institutes of the Christian Religion,* ed. John T. McNeill, trans. Ford Lewis Battles (1960; repr., Louisville, KY: Westminster John Knox Press, 2006), 1.15.2-3 (1:184-189).

4 John Flavel, *Pneumatologia, Or A Treatise on the Soul of Man,* Chapter 1.

5 Philippe de Mornay, *The Soules Own Evidence For Its Own Immortality,* Chapter 1.

6 Tinctoris, *De Inventione et Usu Musice,* 1.5, quoting Boethius (the late Roman/early medieval philosopher and politician). Translated by Early Music Theory, accessed April 19, 2024, https://earlymusictheory.org/Tinctoris/texts/.

2. Music in Creation

1 Herman Bavinck, "Of Beauty and Aesthetics" in *Essays on Religion, Science, and Society,* ed. John Bolt, trans. Harry Boonstra and Gerrit Sheeres (Grand Rapids, MI: Baker Academic, 2008), 255.

2 R.C. Sproul, *How Should I Approach Art?* (Sanford, FL: Ligonier Ministries, 2023), 6.

3 Frank McNally, "Ortolan's Symphony: Frank McNally on Beethoven's Feathered Friend," *Irish Times,* April 13, 2019, https://www.irishtimes.com/opinion/ortolan-s-symphony-frank-mcnally-on-beethoven-s-feathered-friend-1.3858768; Paul Barritt, "Birds and Music—A Violinist's View," The Linnean Society of London, May 1, 2021, https://www.linnean.org/news/2021/05/01/birds-and-music-a-violinists-view.

4 Thomas Watson, *A Body of Divinity* (London: The Banner of Truth Trust, 1958), 7, 83.

5 Luther, "Georg Rhau's Symphoniae Iucundae," 322.

6 William S. Plumer, *Psalms—A Critical and Expository Commentary with Doctrinal and Practical Remarks* (1975; repr., Edinburgh: The Banner of Truth Trust, 2016), 928.

7 Stuart Burgess, *Hallmarks of Design—Evidence of Design in the Natural World* (Epsom, Surrey, England: Day One Publications, 2000), 71-73.

8 John Calvin, "Preface to the Genevan Psalter," Christian Classics Ethereal Library, accessed August 29, 2022, https://www.ccel.org/ccel/ccel/eee/files/calvinps.htm.

9 Stuart Burgess and Andy McIntosh, *Wonders of Creation—Design in a Fallen World*, ed. Brian Edwards (2017; repr., Leominster, Herefordshire, England: Day One Publications, 2018), 180-183.

10 Ibid., 183.

11 Sproul, *Art*, 25.

12 E.M.W. Tillyard, *The Elizabethan World Picture* (London: Pimlico, 1998), 56-57.

13 John Rodgers and Willie Ruff, "Kepler's Harmony of the World: A Realization for the Ear," *American Scientist* 67, no. 3 (May-June 1979): 286-292, https://www.jstor.org/stable/27849220; Otto Kinkeldey, "The Music of the Spheres," *Bulletin of the American Musicological Society* 11-13 (September 1948): 30-32, https://www.jstor.org/stable/829272.

14 Sharon James, *How Christianity Transformed the World* (Fearn, Ross-shire, Scotland: Christian Focus Publications, 2021), 150-151.

15 Leon Harkleroad, *The Math Behind the Music* (2006; repr., New York: Cambridge University Press, 2009), chapters 2-4.

16 John Calvin, "Commentary on Genesis," Christian Classics Ethereal Library, accessed July 28, 2018, https://www.ccel.org/ccel/calvin/calcom01.x.i.html.

17 Calvin, *Institutes*, 2.2.16 (1:275).

18 Bavinck, "Of Beauty and Aesthetics," 252.

19 See also *Westminster Confession of Faith*, Chapter 6.

3. Christians and Music

1 Paul Westermeyer, *Te Deum—The Church and Music* (Minneapolis, MN: Augsburg Fortress, 1998), 142-149.

2 Luther, "Georg Rhau's Symphoniae Iucundae," 321-324.

3 Albert Mohler, *The Briefing*, November 20, 2017, podcast transcript, https://albertmohler.com/2017/11/20/briefing-11-20-17/.

4 Sproul, *Art*, 48-49.

5 Quinlan Terry, *The Layman's Guide to Classical Architecture* (Stockholm, Swe-

den: Bokförlaget Stolpe, 2022), 192.

6 Jane Stuart Smith and Betty Carlson, *The Gift of Music—Great Composers and Their Influence* (Wheaton, IL: Crossway, 1995), 62-66.

7 J. Gresham Machen, "Christianity & Culture," *Princeton Theological Review* 11 (1913): 1-15.

4. Thinking about the Arts

1 Gene Edward Veith, Jr., *State of the Arts, From Bezalel to Mapplethorpe* (Wheaton, IL: Crossway, 1991), 30.

2 Ibid., 37-38.

3 Roger Scruton, *Beauty—A Very Short Introduction* (Oxford: Oxford University Press, 2011), 60, 107.

4 Roger Scruton, *The Aesthetics of Music* (Oxford: Oxford University Press, 1999), 466-467.

5 Martin Luther, "Preface to the Wittenberg Hymnal," in *Luther's Works*, Leupold and Lehmann, 316.

6 Abraham Kuyper, *Lectures on Calvinism* (Peabody, MA: Hendrickson, 2008), 140 (six lectures given at Princeton Seminary in 1898).

7 Ibid., 135.

8 John Calvin, "Commentary on Exodus," Bible Hub, accessed April 20, 2024, https://biblehub.com/commentaries/calvin/exodus/31.htm.

9 Kuyper, *Lectures on Calvinism*, 138.

10 Ibid., 139-140.

11 Bavinck, "Of Beauty and Aesthetics".

12 Ibid., 256.

13 Ibid., 259.

14 Ibid.

15 C.S. Lewis, *The Abolition of Man* (London: HarperCollins, 1999), 9.

16 Ibid., 10.

17 Ibid.

18 Bavinck, "Of Beauty and Aesthetics," 259.

5. Objective Beauty

1 R.C. Sproul, *Now That's a Good Question* (Wheaton, IL: Tyndale House, 1996), 419.

2 Sproul, *Art*, 26.

3 Ibid., 27.

4 Charles Moore, "Building Beauty into Housing Will Bring Long-Term Benefits

and Added Value," *Telegraph*, November 3, 2018, https://www.telegraph.co.uk/politics/2018/11/03/building-beauty-housing-will-bring-long-term-benefits-added/.

5 Wladyslaw Tatarkiewicz, "The Great Theory of Beauty and Its Decline," *Journal of Aesthetics and Art Criticism* 31, no. 2 (Winter 1972): 165-180, https://www.jstor.org/stable/429278; Augustine, *Confessions* 4.13, 13.28.

6 Francis Hutcheson, *An Inquiry into the Original of Our Ideas of Beauty and Virtue*, 2.3.

7 Herman Bavinck, *The Wonderful Works of God* (Glenside, PA: Westminster Seminary Press, 2019), 127-128.

8 Jonathan Edwards, *The Nature of True Virtue*, Chapter 3.

9 Richard Taruskin, *The Oxford History of Western Music*, vol. 5, *Music in the Late Twentieth Century* (Oxford: Oxford University Press, 2010), 78-81.

10 John Eliot Gardiner, *Music in the Castle of Heaven—A Portrait of Johann Sebastian Bach* (London: Allen Lane, 2013), 394.

11 Terry, *Layman's Guide*, 14.

12 Scruton, *Aesthetics of Music*, 326-327.

13 Ibid., 465-466.

14 Jay Nordlinger, "Bach, Beethoven and Other Friends of Mankind," *National Review*, December 27, 2021, 35.

15 Veith, *State of the Arts*, 230-231.

16 Bavinck, "Of Beauty and Aesthetics," 259.

6. Thinking about Music

1 Luther, "Georg Rhau's Symphoniae Iucundae," 322.

2 Taruskin, *Late Twentieth Century*, 451.

3 Scruton, *Aesthetics of Music*, 16.

4 Gerald Abraham, *The Concise Oxford History of Music* (Oxford: Oxford University Press, 1985), 64.

5 It is possible that the Notre Dame school's complex use of rhythm drew on Augustine's book *De Musica*, see John MacInnis, "Augustine's *De Musica* in the 21st Century Music Classroom", *Religions* 6, (2015): 216, https://doi.org/10.3390/rel6010211.

6 Abraham, *Concise Oxford History*, 127-128.

7 Ibid., 133-134, 141-142.

8 Tatarkiewicz, "Great Theory of Beauty," 167.

9 Paul S. Jones, *Singing and Making Music—Issues in Church Music Today* (Phillipsburg, NJ: P&R Publishing, 2006), 97.

7. Surveying Composers

1 Copland, *What to Listen for*, 63.

2 The widely used periods for Western music were originally created for art history but must be distinguished from the latter. For example, the Renaissance and Romantic eras both began significantly later in music than in literature or painting.

3 Brian Vickers, "Figures of Rhetoric/Figures of Music?," *Rhetorica: A Journal of the History of Rhetoric* 2, no. 1 (Spring 1984): 16, https://www.jstor.org/stable/10.1525/rh.1984.2.1.1.

4 Claude V. Palisca, *Baroque Music* (Englewood Cliffs, NJ: Prentice-Hall, 1991), 145.

5 Bloom, *Closing of American Mind*, 58.

6 Englishman Hubert Parry memorably set Milton's poem to stirring music for choir and orchestra in 1887.

7 Reinhard G. Pauly, *Music in the Classic Period* (Englewood Cliffs, NJ: Prentice-Hall, 1988), 105-106.

8 Carl Dahlhaus, *Nineteenth-Century Music* (Berkeley, CA: University of California Press, 1989), 24.

9 Patrick Kavanaugh, *Spiritual Lives of the Great Composers* (Grand Rapids, MI: Zondervan, 1996), 75-81 quoting Eric Werner, *Mendelssohn: A New Image of the Composer and His Age* (London: Collier-MacMillan, 1963) and other sources.

10 John K. Novak, "Whole-Tone as Extension of Tonal Harmony in the Music of Debussy: An Underestimated Technique of Conjunction," *International Journal of Musicology* 1 (2015): 79-99, https://www.jstor.org/stable/43858069.

8. Applying the Principles of Beauty to Music

1 Olena D. Chorna et al., "Neuroprocessing Mechanisms of Music during Fetal and Neonatal Development: A Role in Neuroplasticity and Neurodevelopment," *Neural Plasticity* (2019): https://doi.org/10.1155/2019/3972918.

2 Jones, *Singing and Making Music*, 149.

3 Tatarkiewicz, "Great Theory of Beauty," 167.

4 Ibid.

5 Terry, *Layman's Guide*, 20, 126-141.

6 Harold M. Best, *Music Through the Eyes of Faith* (New York: HarperCollins, 1993), 120. Best points out that music is one of the performing arts, along with dance and drama, which are not complete until they have been performed.

7 Scruton, *Aesthetics of Music*, 46.

9. Bach and Beauty

1 Nordlinger, "Bach, Beethoven and Other Friends of Mankind," 36.

2 Gardiner, *Castle of Heaven,* 51.

3 Ibid., 154.

4 Paul T. McCain, "News Flash: J.S. Bach Was a Christian—Why Suzuki Gets Bach," *First Things,* January 8, 2010, https://www.firstthings.com/blogs/firstthoughts/2010/01/news-flash-j-s-bach-was-a-christian-why-suzuki-gets-j-s-bach.

5 The BWV catalog of J.S. Bach's works was assembled and categorized in the twentieth century; the list is by genre, not by date of composition.

6 Instruments in the violin family typically sound one note at a time, so these solo works by Bach feature many arpeggios—a musical pattern in which the notes of a chord are played successively. A string player can also bow two notes simultaneously, which is known as a "double stop". (Although "triple stops" and even "quadruple stops" are written for these string instruments, the notes are usually played in rapid succession incorporating double-stops.)

7 Palisca, *Baroque Music,* 174.

8 Jessica Duchen, "Bach's Monumental *Goldberg Variations*: Masterpiece Guide," udiscovermusic, March 14, 2024, https://www.udiscovermusic.com/classical-features/bach-goldberg-variations-masterpiece-guide/.

9 Palisca, *Baroque Music,* 214.

10 Ivan Hewett, "Bach—The Voice of God in Human Form," *Telegraph,* December 15, 2005, https://www.telegraph.co.uk/culture/music/classicalmusic/3648747/Bach-the-voice-of-God-in-human-form.html.

11 Luther, "Georg Rhau's Symphoniae Iucundae," 323-324.

12 Gardiner, *Castle of Heaven,* 129.

13 J.S. Bach also wrote a *St. Mark Passion,* which sadly does not survive (first performed 1731).

14 Abraham, *Concise Oxford History,* 535-6.

15 Damian Thompson, "God's Messenger," *The Spectator,* March 12, 2016, https://www.spectator.co.uk/article/god-s-messenger/.

10. Reflecting on Bach's Music

1 Gardiner, *Castle of Heaven,* 209.

2 Ibid., 125.

3 Westermeyer, *Te Deum,* 241.

4 Calvin R. Stapert, *My Only Comfort: Death, Deliverance, and Discipleship in the Music of Bach* (Grand Rapids, MI: William B. Eerdmans, 2000), 87-101.

5 Ibid., 219-222.

6 John Ahern, "Contrapuntal Order—Music Illuminates Social Harmony," *First*

Things, April 2020, https://www.firstthings.com/article/2020/04/contrapuntal-order. Needless to say, students of Bach's counterpoint are always taught to avoid parallel fifths and octaves between voice parts.

7 Palisca, *Baroque Music*, 218-219.

8 Stapert, *My Only Comfort*, xi.

9 Uwe Siemon-Netto, "J.S. Bach in Japan," *First Things*, June 2000, https://www.firstthings.com/article/2000/06/j-s-bach-in-japan.

11. What Went Wrong?

1 Francis Schaeffer, *Classical Music and the Loss of Meaningfulness in the Post-Christian West*, recorded July 28, 1961, https://www.labriideaslibrary.org/topics.

2 Dahlhaus, *Nineteenth-Century Music*, 387-388.

3 J. Peter Burkholder, Donald Jay Grout, and Claude V. Palisca, *A History of Western Music*, 9th ed. (New York: W.W. Norton, 2014), 818-819; Alexander Carpenter, "Schoenberg's Vienna, Freud's Vienna: Re-Examining the Connections between the Monodrama Erwartung and the Early History of Psychoanalysis," *Musical Quarterly* 93, no. 1 (Spring 2010): 144-181, https://doi.org/10.1093/musqtl/gdq003; Sharon James, *The Lies We Are Told, The Truths We Must Hold* (Fearn, Ross-shire, Scotland: Christian Focus Publications, 2022), 82.

4 "The First Viennese School" usually refers to Mozart, Haydn, and Beethoven.

5 Burkholder, Grout, and Palisca, *History of Western Music*, 828.

6 William Edgar, *Taking Note of Music* (London: SPCK, 1986), 20-21.

7 Scruton, *Aesthetics of Music*, 283, 305-306.

8 Taruskin, *Late Twentieth Century*, 433.

9 Burkholder, Grout, and Palisca, *History of Western Music*, 830.

10 Ibid., 839.

11 Taruskin, *Late Twentieth Century*, 44, 62; Burkholder, Grout, and Palisca, *History of Western Music*, 940.

12 Taruskin, *Late Twentieth Century*, 20-22.

13 Ibid., 358.

14 Ibid., 56.

15 Sproul, *That's a Good Question*, 418-419.

12. Music as Mass Entertainment

1 Bob Stanley, *Yeah! Yeah! Yeah!: the Story of Pop Music from Bill Haley to Beyoncé* (New York: W.W. Norton, 2015), 1, 341.

2 See, for example, Charles Hamm, *Music in the New World* (New York: W.W. Norton, 1983), 620.

3 “History of the Bass Guitar: From Jazz to Rock”, Musicians Institute, March 5, 2022, https://www.mi.edu/in-the-know/history-bass-guitar-jazz-rock/.

4 Jacquelyn Kulinski et al., “Effects of Music on the Cardiovascular System,” *Trends in Cardiovascular Medicine* 32, no. 6 (August 2022): 390-398, https://doi.org/10.1016/j.tcm.2021.06.004.

5 Hans-Joachim Trappe, “The Effects of Music on the Cardiovascular System and Cardiovascular Health,” *Heart* 96, no. 23 (December 2010): 1868-71, https://doi.org/10.1136/hrt.2010.209858.

6 John Blanchard and Dan Lucarini, *Can We Rock the Gospel?: Rock Music's Impact on Worship and Evangelism* (Darlington, England: Evangelical Press, 2006), 57; Bloom, *Closing of American Mind*, 80-81.

7 Taruskin, *Late Twentieth Century*, 330.

8 “Deafening Music,” *British Medical Journal* 2 (April 18, 1970): 127, https://doi.org/10.1136/bmj.2.5702.127; Tara Patel, “Live Rock is Hardest on the Ears,” *New Scientist*, January 27, 1996, https://www.newscientist.com/article/mg14920140-400-live-rock-is-hardest-on-the-ears/.

9 Blanchard and Lucarini, *Rock the Gospel?*, 136.

10 Marilyn Horne, interview by Jay Nordlinger, *National Review*, August 15, 2022, 43.

11 From Elvis Presley onwards, rock stars have been consciously presented as sexualized figures. Critics such as Allan Bloom have claimed that the prominent beat in this music itself imitates physical intimacy between a man and woman. Also, see secular commentators quoted in Blanchard and Lucarini, *Rock the Gospel?*, 117.

12 Stanley, *Yeah! Yeah! Yeah!*, 79.

13 Taruskin, *Late Twentieth Century*, 312-313.

14 Stanley, *Yeah! Yeah! Yeah!*, 78.

15 Bloom, *Closing of American Mind*, 73, 80.

16 Ibid., 75.

17 Ibid., 76.

18 Hamm, *In the New World*, 654.

19 Michael Walsh, a writer on popular music for *Time* magazine in the 1980s, noted a connection between the minimalist music of Philip Glass (1937-) and rock music: “rock and minimalism share obvious characteristics, including a steady beat, limited harmonies and hypnotic repetition”, see Taruskin, *Late Twentieth Century*, 392.

20 Best, *Through Eyes of Faith*, 42, 71.

13. Taste in Music

1 Goulburn W. Crossley, “St. Augustine's *De Musica*: A Recent Synopsis,” *Musical Times* 92, (March 1951): 127, https://www.jstor.org/stable/933234.

2 Blanchard and Lucarini, *Rock the Gospel?*, 39.

3 Taruskin, *Late Twentieth Century*, 382-383.

4 Scruton, *Beauty*, 112.

5 Bloom, *Closing of American Mind*, 247.

6 Bavinck, "Of Beauty and Aesthetics," 258.

7 Veith, *State of the Arts*, xvi.

8 Ibid., 40.

9 Karen A. DeMol, *Sound Stewardship: How Shall Christians Think About Music?* (Sioux Center, IA: Dordt College Press, 1999), 23.

10 Bloom, *Closing of American Mind*, 74.

11 Trappe, "Cardiovascular Health," 1868-71.

12 Best, *Through Eyes of Faith*, 129.

13 Veith, *State of the Arts*, 49.

14 Scruton, *Aesthetics of Music*, 225 and 230.

14. The Bible and the Soul

1 Gardiner, *Castle of Heaven*, 252.

2 Bloom, *Closing of American Mind*, 173.

3 Ibid., 357 (note the book's subtitle references "souls").

4 Sproul, *Art*, 29.

5 Scruton, *Aesthetics of Music*, ix, 489.

6 Ivan Hewett, "Our Knee-Jerk Fear of Nationalism is Childish—Just Look at Classical Music," *Telegraph*, March 22, 2022, https://www.telegraph.co.uk/music/classical-music/power-pitfalls-nationalism-music/.

7 Machen, *Christian View of Man*, 125-126.

8 Joel R. Beeke and Paul M. Smalley, *Reformed Systematic Theology*, vol. 2, *Man and Christ* (Wheaton, IL: Crossway, 2020), 230.

9 Louis Berkhof, *Systematic Theology* (1958; repr., Edinburgh: The Banner of Truth Trust, 2005), 194; Machen, *Christian View of Man*, 141-143.

10 Beeke and Smalley, *Man and Christ*, 232-4.

11 Paul Helm, *Human Nature from Calvin to Edwards* (Grand Rapids, MI: Reformation Heritage Books, 2018), 29; Beeke and Smalley, *Man and Christ*, 249.

12 Machen, *Christian View of Man*, 126.

13 Calvin, *Institutes*, 1.15.2-3 (1:184-189).

14 Flavel, *Pneumatologia*, Chapter 1.

15 Helm, *Human Nature*, xix.

16 Beeke and Smalley, *Man and Christ*, 252.

17 John MacInnis, "Augustine's *De Musica*," 212.

18 Ibid., 214.

19 Brian Brennan, "Augustine's *De Musica*," *Vigiliae Christianae* 42, no. 3 (September 1988): 267-281, https://www.jstor.org/stable/1584121.

20 Ibid., 275.

21 Helm, *Human Nature*, 14.

22 Ibid., xvii.

23 John Owen, "The Nature, Power, Deceit, and Prevalency of the Remainders of Indwelling Sin in Believers" in *The Works of John Owen*, ed. William H. Goold (1850–53; repr. Edinburgh: Banner of Truth Trust, 1991), 6:170.

24 Beeke and Smalley, *Man and Christ*, 255.

25 Helm, *Human Nature*, 81.

26 Beeke and Smalley, *Man and Christ*, 257.

27 Ibid., 257-258.

28 Paul Helm, "Virtues and Vices," *Helm's Deep—Philosophical Theology* (blog), July 1, 2022, http://paulhelmsdeep.blogspot.com/2022/06/virtues-and-vices-1-july-2022.html.

29 John Owen, *Faith and its Evidences*, in Works, 5:448-49 quoted in Helm, *Human Nature*, 99.

15. Music and the Soul

1 Bavinck, *Wonderful Works of God*, 194.

2 de Mornay, *The Soules Own Evidence*, Chapter 1.

3 Veith, *State of the Arts*, 230-231; Herman Bavinck, "Foundations of Psychology", ed. John Bolt, trans. Jack Vanden Born, Nelson D. Kloosterman, and John Bolt, special issue, *Bavinck Review* 9 (2018): 157-158, 164, https://bavinckinstitute.org/wp-content/uploads/2019/08/BR9_Foundations.pdf.

4 John Calvin, "Preface to the Psalter".

5 Helm, *Human Nature*, 97.

6 Flavel, *Pneumatologia*, Chapter 1.

7 Bavinck, "Foundations of Psychology," 199-200.

8 Matthew Henry, *Commentary on the Whole Bible* (1991; repr., Peabody, MA: Hendrickson Publishers, 2006), 288-289.

9 Luther, "Georg Rhau's Symphoniae Iucundae," 323.

10 Ibid.

11 Quoted in Mishtooni Bose, "Humanism, English Music and the Rhetoric of Criticism", *Music & Letters* 77, no. 1 (February 1996): 14, https://www.jstor.org/stable/737534.

12 Richard Hooker, *Of the Laws of Ecclesiastical Polity*, 5.35.

13 Quintilian, *Institutes of Oratory,* 1.10.

14 Vickers, "Figures of Rhetoric," 6.

15 Ibid., 12.

16 Renaissance humanists advocated the study of classical Greek and Roman texts and many were leading churchmen. In contrast, modern-day secular humanism is a worldview that seeks a world without God.

17 Bose, "Humanism," 2.

18 Vickers, "Figures of Rhetoric," 7-8.

19 Gregory G. Butler, "The Projection of Affect in Baroque Dance Music," *Early Music* 12, no. 2 (May 1984): 201, https://www.jstor.org/stable/3137734; George J. Buelow, "Music, Rhetoric, and the Concept of the Affections: A Selective Bibliography", *Notes* 30, no. 2 (December 1973): 250-259, https://www.jstor.org/stable/895972.

20 Butler, "Projection of Affect," 200-207; Bose, "Humanism," 4.

21 Buelow, "Concept of the Affections," 252; Butler, "Projection of Affect," 204.

16. Bringing Disorder to the Soul

1 Harry Blamires, *The Christian Mind—How Should a Christian Think?* (Vancouver: Regent College Publishing, 2005), 78.

2 Bavinck, "Foundations of Psychology," 204.

3 Nathaniel Warne, "Emotions and the Development of Virtue in Puritan Thought: An Investigation of Puritan Friendship," in *Puritanism and Emotion in the Early Modern World,* ed. Alec Ryrie and Tom Schwanda (New York: Palgrave MacMillan, 2016), 194-200.

4 Helm, *Human Nature,* 96-97.

5 As distinct from the theoretical reason, which is used to evaluate what is true and false. See Bavinck, "Foundations of Psychology," 154-158; Helm, *Human Nature,* 232.

6 Edward Reynolds, *Treatise on the Passions and Faculties of the Soul,* quoted in Helm, *Human Nature,* 99.

7 *Canons of Dort,* 3&4.4.

8 Bavinck, "Foundations of Psychology," 207.

9 Henry, *Commentary,* 288.

10 Alec Motyer, *Isaiah,* Tyndale Old Testament Commentaries (Leicester, England: Inter-Varsity Press, 1999), 63.

11 Owen, "Indwelling Sin in Believers," 6:171-173.

12 Ibid., 6:248.

13 Tom Schwanda writing about Thomas Watson's teachings: Ryrie and Schwanda, *Puritanism and Emotion,* 73-74.

14 Calvin, *Institutes,* 1.11.8 (1:108).

15 Tillyard, *Elizabethan World Picture,* 28.

16 Scott Aniol, *Sound Worship—A Guide to Making Musical Choices in a Noisy World,* (Fort Worth, TX; Religious Affections Ministries, 2010), 91.

17 Beeke and Smalley, *Man and Christ,* 237.

18 It could be argued that atonal music has the opposite effect. It brings anxiety to most people, and therefore stress, rather than pleasure to the body.

19 Bavinck, "Foundations of Psychology," 212.

20 S. Bryn Roberts, "*Milke and Honey*: Puritan Happiness in the Writings of Robert Bolton, John Norden and Francis Rous," in Ryrie and Schwanda, *Puritanism and Emotion,* 98.

21 Keith Condie, "*Light Accompanied with Vital Heat*: Affection and Intellect in the Thought of Richard Baxter," in Ryrie and Schwanda, *Puritanism and Emotion,* 26-27, 34; Helm, *Human Nature,* 98-99.

22 Bavinck, "Foundations of Psychology," 212.

17. Music and Character

1 John Calvin, "Preface to the Psalter".

2 John Calvin, *1 Corinthians,* Calvin's New Testament Commentaries, ed. David W. Torrance and Thomas F. Torrance, trans. John W. Fraser (1960; repr., Grand Rapids, MI: William B. Eerdmans Publishing, 1996), 289, 333.

3 Bloom, *Closing of American Mind,* 70-71.

4 Ibid., 72.

5 Scruton, *Aesthetics of Music,* 118-119, 390-391.

6 Ibid., 502.

7 Luther, "Georg Rhau's Symphoniae Iucundae," 323.

8 Hooker, *Ecclesiastical Polity,* 5.35.

9 Scruton, *Aesthetics of Music,* 379.

10 Luther, "Georg Rhau's Symphoniae Iucundae," 324.

11 Condie, "Vital Heat," 46.

12 Francis Schaeffer, *Art Norms and Thoughts For The Christian Life,* n.d., https://www.labriideaslibrary.org/topics.

13 Sproul, *Art,* 41.

14 Percy Scholes, *The Puritans and Music* (Oxford: Oxford University Press, 1934), 123.

15 Uwe Siemon-Netto, "J.S. Bach in Japan".

18. Three Questions

1 Bavinck, *Wonderful Works of God*, 21.

2 Blanchard and Lucarini, *Rock the Gospel?*, 213.

3 Mickey Hart, *Drumming at the Edge of Music*; *Life*, 3 October 1969; *Hit Parader*, Jan 1968; and *Melody Maker*, 7 October 1967; quoted in Blanchard and Lucarini, *Rock the Gospel?*, 54, 140.

4 Blanchard and Lucarini, *Rock the Gospel?*, 87.

5 Donald Jay Grout and Claude V. Palisca, *A History of Western Music*, 5th ed. quoted in Blanchard and Lucarini, *Rock the Gospel?*, 213.

6 Scruton, *Aesthetics of Music*, 388.

7 Veith, *State of the Arts*, 51.

8 Scruton, *Beauty*, 159-160.

9 Luther, "Georg Rhau's Symphoniae Iucundae," 322.

10 John Calvin, "Preface to the Psalter".

11 Veith, *State of the Arts*, 63.

12 Scholes, *Puritans and Music*, 4-5, 144-145.

13 Hooker, *Ecclesiastical Polity*, 5.38.

14 William Perkins, *Whole Treatise of the Case of Conscience*, 3.4.4.

15 Scholes, *Puritans and Music*, 246-247.

16 Ibid., 55.

17 Ibid., 49-50, 282-286.

18 Ibid., 52, 105, 384-5.

19 George M. Marsden, *Fundamentalism and American Culture* (Oxford: Oxford University Press, 2006), 36, 254-255; Scholes, *Puritans and Music*, 52.

19. Music in Church History

1 Westermeyer, *Te Deum*, 43; Calvin, *1 Corinthians*, 293.

2 Westermeyer, *Te Deum*, 66-67, 120.

3 Johannes Quasten, *Music and Worship in Pagan and Christian Antiquity*, trans. Boniface Ramsey (Washington: National Association of Pastoral Musicians, 1973), 67; quoted in Westermeyer, *Te Deum*, 62-63.

4 Derek W. H. Thomas, *Let Us Worship God: Why We Worship the Way We Do*, (Sanford, FL: Ligonier Ministries, 2021), 96; Scott Aniol, "Early Church Hymns," Religious Affections Ministries, August 18, 2010, https://religiousaffections.org/articles/hymnody/early-church-hymns/.

5 Westermeyer, *Te Deum*, 120.

6 Ibid., 82-89; 141-160.

7 Ibid., 23, 82-84. Westermeyer notes that Ambrose, like the rest of the early church, opposed instrumental music in worship.

8 Augustine, *Confessions* 10.31.

9 Westermeyer, *Te Deum*, 84-86.

10 Ibid., 106-108.

11 Scholes, *Puritans and Music*, 215-216.

12 Robin A. Leaver, "Luther on Music," *Lutheran Quarterly* 20 (2006): 125-127.

13 Luther, "Georg Rhau's Symphoniae Iucundae," 323.

14 Leaver, "Luther on Music," 132-133.

15 Martin Luther, in *Luther's Works*, Leupold and Lehmann, 53-57, 149-150.

16 Erik Routley, *The Music of Christian Hymns* (Chicago: G.I.A Publications, 1981), 21 quoted in Westermeyer, *Te Deum*, 148-149.

17 Westermeyer, *Te Deum*, 160.

18 Ibid., 151.

19 W. Robert Godfrey, "Reforming the Church's Singing," Westminster Seminary California, accessed November 26, 2022, https://www.wscal.edu/resource-center/reforming-the-churchs-singing.

20 Diarmaid MacCulloch, *Thomas Cranmer: A Life* (New Haven: Yale University Press, 1996), 330-331.

21 Westermeyer, *Te Deum*, 170-172.

22 Scholes, *Puritans and Music*, 219.

20. Calvin and Corporate Worship

1 Sproul, *Art*, 8.

2 Calvin, *Institutes*, 3.20.31 (2:894-895).

3 Ibid., 3.20.32 (2:895-896).

4 Nick Needham, *2000 Years of Christ's Power*, vol. 3, *Renaissance and Reformation*, rev. ed. (2016; Fearn, Ross-shire, Scotland: Christian Focus Publications and London: Grace Publications Trust, 2023), 229; Diarmaid MacCulloch, *Reformation: Europe's House Divided* (London: Allen Lane, 2003), 307-308.

5 Godfrey, "Reforming the Church's Singing".

6 Westermeyer, *Te Deum*, 154.

7 Quoted in Plumer, *Psalms*, 413.

8 John Calvin, "Preface to the Psalter"; Westermeyer, *Te Deum*, 158.

9 Herman J. Selderhuis, ed., *Handbook of Dutch Church History* (Göttingen, Germany: Vandenhoeck & Ruprecht, 2014), 244-245, 314.

10 Cotton Mather, *The Great Works of Christ in America—Magnalia Christi Americana* (1852; repr., Edinburgh: The Banner of Truth Trust, 1979), 2:266-267.

11 Iain H. Murray, *The Forgotten Spurgeon* (1973; repr., Edinburgh: The Banner of Truth Trust, 1998), 212-213.

12 John W. Keddie, *Sing the Lord's Song—Biblical Psalms in Worship* (Pittsburgh, PA: Crown & Covenant Publications, 2003), 52.

13 *The Directory for Public Worship of the Westminster Assembly.*

14 Article 32 of the *Belgic Confession* has the same theological perspective.

15 *Westminster Confession of Faith, 1.6.*

16 Thomas, *Let us Worship God,* 32.

17 Brian Norton, "Worship—an Inquiry Into the Question 'What Are We Doing In a Service'?", (unpublished paper, 2001), 5-6.

18 Keddie, *Sing the Lord's Song,* 33, 49-50.

19 Westermeyer, *Te Deum,* 101-102.

20 Plumer, *Psalms,* 412.

21 Thomas, *Let Us Worship God,* 35.

21. Worship or Entertainment?

1 R.B. Kuiper, *The Glorious Body of Christ—A Scriptural Appreciation of the One Holy Church,* (1967; repr., Edinburgh: The Banner of Truth Trust, 2006), 348.

2 Keddie, *Sing the Lord's Song,* 17-18.

3 Jeremiah Burroughs, *Gospel Worship—Worship Worthy of God* (1990; repr., Grand Rapids, MI: Soli Deo Gloria Publications, 2021), 31-34.

4 R.C. Sproul, *Truths We Confess: A Systematic Exposition of the Westminster Confession of Faith,* rev. ed. (Sanford, FL: Reformation Trust Publishing, 2019), 464.

5 Burroughs, *Gospel Worship,* 28.

6 D.G. Hart and John R. Muether, *With Reverence and Awe—Returning to the Basics of Reformed Worship* (Phillipsburg, NJ: P&R Publishing, 2002), 20-22.

7 Ibid., 12.

8 Lester Ruth and Lim Swee Hong, *A History of Contemporary Praise & Worship—Understanding the Ideas that Reshaped the Protestant Church* (Grand Rapids, MI: Baker Academic, 2021), 215-216.

9 Norton, "Worship," 3. Rev. Norton argued convincingly that in Romans 12:1 the Greek word latreia is better translated "service" in English than "spiritual worship".

10 Hart and Muether, *With Reverence and Awe,* 147-158.

11 Burroughs, *Gospel Worship,* 80, 128.

12 Hart and Muether, *With Reverence and Awe,* 48.

13 Ibid., 73.

14 J.C. Ryle, *Knots Untied* (Edinburgh: The Banner of Truth Trust, 2016), 314.

15 Hart and Muether, *With Reverence and Awe,* 17.

16 Veith, *State of the Arts,* 202.

17 Ruth and Hong, *Contemporary Praise & Worship,* 100.

18 Ibid., 291.

19 Ibid., 133.

20 Ibid., 137-138.

21 Ibid., 169.

22 Sproul, *Truths We Confess,* 462-463.

23 Jones, *Singing and Making Music,* 191.

24 Ryle, *Knots Untied,* 328.

25 Scott Aniol, *Worship in Song—A Biblical Approach to Music and Worship,* (Winona Lake, IN: BMH Books, 2009), 318.

26 Hart and Muether, *With Reverence and Awe,* 165.

27 Best, *Through Eyes of Faith,* 214.

28 Blanchard and Lucarini, *Rock the Gospel?,* 187-188.

29 Westermeyer, *Te Deum,* 75-76.

30 Thomas, *Let us Worship God,* 37.

22. Reforming Church Music

1 Hart and Muether, *With Reverence and Awe,* 185.

2 Blanchard and Lucarini, *Rock the Gospel?,* 190.

3 Norton, "Worship," 10.

4 Riemer A. Faber, "John Calvin on Psalms and Hymns in Public Worship," Christian Study Library, accessed November 26, 2022, https://www.christianstudylibrary.org/article/john-calvin-psalms-and-hymns-public-worship.

5 Derek Kidner, *Psalms 1-72,* Tyndale Old Testament Commentaries, (Leicester, England: Inter-Varsity Press,1973), 4, quoted in Keddie, *Sing the Lord's Song,* 25.

6 Aniol, *Worship in Song,* 297-298.

7 Leaver, "Luther on Music," 130-131.

8 Jones, *Singing and Making Music,* 42.

9 Armin Haeussler, *The Story of Our Hymns—The Handbook to the Hymnal of the Evangelical and Reformed Church* (St. Louis, MO: Eden Publishing House, 1954), 7-8.

10 Calvin, *Institutes,* 3.20.32 (2:895-896).

11 The last verse usually sung to *Amazing Grace* was added from another source by a nineteenth-century hymnbook editor. The original by John Newton is:

The earth shall soon dissolve like snow,

The sun forbear to shine;

But God, who called me here below,

Will be for ever mine.

12 *Trinity Psalter Hymnal,* A Joint Publication of The Committee on Christian Education of the Orthodox Presbyterian Church and The Psalter Hymnal Committee of the United Reformed Churches in North America (Willow Grove, PA: Trinity Psalter Hymnal Joint Venture, 2018), xii-xiv.

13 Augustine, *Confessions* 10.31.

14 Quoted in Bose, "Humanism," 15-16.

15 Westermeyer, *Te Deum,* 210.

16 Jones, *Singing and Making Music,* 50-56.

17 Sproul, *Art,* 44.

18 Westermeyer, *Te Deum,* 288; Ruth and Hong, *Contemporary Praise & Worship,* 176.

19 Jones, *Singing and Making Music,* 173-175.

20 Veith, *State of the Arts,* 139.

21 Ryle, *Knots Untied,* 323.

Conclusion

1 Terry, *Layman's Guide,* 192.

2 Luther, "Georg Rhau's Symphoniae Iucundae," 324.

3 Kuyper, *Lectures on Calvinism,* 141.

4 *Westminster Shorter Catechism,* Question 1.

5 Roberts, "Milke and Honey," 120.

6 Shakespeare, *The Merchant of Venice,* Act 5, Scene 1.

7 Valla, L, *De Voluptate, Opera,* 915, quoted in Tatarkiewicz, "Great Theory of Beauty," 170-171.

8 Gardiner, *Castle of Heaven,* 252.

9 Kuiper, *Glorious Body of Christ,* 243.

10 Luther, "Georg Rhau's Symphoniae Iucundae," 323-324.

11 Scruton, *Aesthetics of Music,* 505-506.

12 Jonathan Edwards, *The Nature of True Virtue,* Chapter 3.

13 Kuiper, *Glorious Body of Christ,* 278.

14 Blamires, *The Christian Mind,* 67.

15 John Bunyan, *The Pilgrim's Progress from This World to That Which is to Come,* Part 2.

Index

Music to the Glory of God

Aberystwyth, 211
a cappella singing, 186, 194, 206
accompaniment, 213
acoustics, 24
Adagio for Strings (Barber), 94
aesthetics, 33–34, 36, 215
see also beauty
affections, 37, 155, 158, 172
Ahern, John, 121
Amazing Grace (Newton), 212
Ambrose, 187, 210
American String Quartet in F major, Opus 96 (Dvořák), 86
A Midsummer Night's Dream (Mendelssohn), 81
Andante Festivo (Sibelius), 92
angelic beings, singing of, 18
Anglicans, 183, 196
Aniol, Scott, 167, 211
Appalachian Spring (Copland), 94
appreciation of music, 55, 98, 146, 174–75, 219
architecture, 30–31, 40, 41–42, 99, 133, 138, 217
Aristotle, 24, 33, 154, 156, 172
art music, 71
artist, 30
arts, 30, 32–38, 142–43
Asaph, 185
atheism, 30, 123, 126, 149
atonality, 78, 88, 124–26, 130, 143, 166, 178
At a Solemn Music (Milton), 70–71
Augsburg Confession, 81
Augustine, 21, 25, 36, 37, 40, 141, 152–53, 187, 206, 212
Austria (tune), 214
autonomy, 124
avant-garde movement, 128–30, 142

Bach, Carl Philipp Emanuel, 77
Bach, Johann Christian, 77
Bach, Johann Christoph, 105
Bach, Johann Sebastian, 29, 30, 42, 64, 65–66, 67, 77, 78, 80, 84, 89, 101, 102, 103, 104, 105–17, 123, 149, 175, 182, 189, 219–20
balance or symmetry in music, 100
see also proportion
Barber, Samuel, 94–95, 127
Baroque era, 62–71, 108, 149, 161
Barry, John, 96
bass guitar, 134
Bavinck, Herman, 26, 36–37, 38, 45, 157, 163, 164, 168, 177
Baxter, Richard, 168
Bay Psalm Book, 190
beat, 133–34, 172
see also rhythm
Beatles, 133, 136, 137
beauty, 21–22, 34–38, 39–45, 220
appreciation for, 45, 146
as "in the eye of the beholder," 44
objective principles of, 39–40, 56, 97, 98, 104, 122, 142, 144, 147, 178, 180
overthrown concept in music, 123
Beeke, Joel, 155
Beethoven, Ludwig van, 22, 29, 31, 34, 42, 77–79, 84, 101, 122, 124, 134, 178
Berg, Alban, 125
Berio, Luciano, 134
Berkhof, Louis, 151
Best, Harold, 138, 145, 206
Bezaleel and Aholiab, 35
Bible, and Western culture, 43, 70
big beat, 133–34, 178–79, 205
Billings, William, 77
birdsong, 22–23
Blamires, Harry, 163
Blanchard, John, 135, 141
Bloom, Allan, 70, 137, 143–44, 149, 172
Bluegrass, 132
Boccherini, Luigi, 77
body and soul, 150–52, 218
Bolero (Ravel), 137, 178
Book of Common Prayer, 189
Boulez, Pierre, 128, 129
Bourgeois, Louis, 60–61, 99, 193
Brahms, Johannes, 42, 84–85, 92, 100, 127, 135
Brandenburg Concerti (Bach), 65–66, 67, 107, 108–09, 119
Broadway, 94
Bryn Calfaria, 211
Buddhism, 129
Bunyan, John, 183, 184, 222

Burgess, Stuart, 22–23, 24
Burleigh, Harry, 86
Burroughs, Jeremiah, 199–200, 202
Buxtehude, Dietrich, 64, 111
Byrd, William, 59

Cage, John, 129–31, 141
Calvin, John, 17, 23, 25–26, 35, 60, 152, 157, 166, 171–72, 181, 183, 187, 193–94, 206, 209, 212, 214
Canons of Dort, 164
cantatas, 113–14
celebrity culture, 137
Chaconne in D minor for Solo Violin (Bach), 108
Chalcedonian creed, 151
chamber music, 72
character, 172–73
charismatic movement, 203–4
Charles I, King of England, 195
Chopin, Frédéric, 83, 89, 122
choral music, 113–15
"Christian music," 211
Christian worldview, 43, 124, 130, 175, 220
Christian worship, suitable music for, 182–84
chromaticism, 126
church, marks of, 202
Church of England, 183, 189–90, 197
church history, music in, 185–91
church music, reforming of, 209–15
circumstances of worship, 201
Clarke, Jeremiah, 158
classical music, 34, 71–77, 141, 144, 145, 174–75, 219
Coffee Cantata (Bach), 114, 119
common grace, 25–27, 29, 31, 44, 70, 171, 173, 175, 217, 218, 221
Common Meter, 190
communion with God, 163
complexity, 39, 97, 103–4, 121, 138
concerto, 77
conscience, 156, 173
Constable, John, 98
consumers of music, 143–44, 146, 168, 205–6, 219
contemporary music practices, 201–7
contrapuntal music, 122
Copland, Aaron, 14, 55–56, 94–95, 127
counterpoint, 56, 103, 121
Counter-Reformation, 61
country music, 132
Cowper, William, 190–91, 213
Cranmer, Thomas, 189–90, 193
created order, rebellion against, 126
creation, 21–27
    beauty in, 40
    unity and diversity in, 41
Cromwell, Oliver, 183
Crown Imperial (Walton), 96
cultural supremacy, 142
culture, consecration of, 32
Cwm Rhondda, 211
Czerny, Carl, 22

Darwin, Charles, 123, 125
David, as "sweet psalmist of Israel," 29
Debussy, Claude, 87–88, 126
decadence, 136
Delius, Frederick, 89
democratic culture, 142
DeMol, Karen, 143
Descartes, René, 162
des Prez, Josquin, 56, 161
dichotomy, 151
Dido and Aeneas (Purcell), 62
diet, 143
Directory for Public Worship (Westminster Assembly), 195
discernment, 144
disciplining the emotions, 164
discord, 18, 143, 178
disproportion, 167
dissonance, 78, 84, 124, 126, 127, 128, 130
Dixit Dominus (Vivaldi), 65
Dorian Toccata and Fugue in D minor (Bach), 111
Double Common Meter, 190
drug use, 136
drums, 134–35, 179
Dufay, Guillaume, 56
Dundee, 190, 211
Dunstable, John, 56
Durch Adams Fall ist ganz verderbt (Bach), 111
Dvořák, Antonín, 86, 94, 102, 125

Eastern Orthodoxy, 197

Edison, Thomas, 55
Ed Sullivan Show, 137
Edwards, Jonathan, 26–27, 40, 41, 104, 220–21
1812 Overture (Tchaikovsky), 158
Ein Feste Burg (Luther), 29, 81, 113, 211
electric amplification, 134
elements of worship, 201
Elgar, Edward, 89, 125, 158
Elijah oratorio (Mendelssohn), 80, 81
elitism, 142
emotions, 165, 168–69
Enigma Variations (Elgar), 89
Enlightenment, 129, 161–62
entertainment, 132, 138–39
    in worship, 202–5
Erasmus, 188
Erwartung Op. 1 (Schoenberg), 124–25
Ethan, 185
Ethelred, Abbot of Rievaulx, 188
evolution, 17, 123
Expressionism, 125

false worship, 200
Fanfare for the Common Man (Copland), 94
Fantasia and Fugue in G minor (Bach), 111, 119
Fantasia in G major (Bach), 111
Fantasia on a Theme by Thomas Tallis (Vaughan Williams), 94
fine arts, 33–34
    see also arts
Finlandia (Sibelius), 92
Flavel, John, 17–18, 152, 155, 158
Florida Suite (Delius), 89
folk music, 131–32
folksongs, 93
food analogy, 143–46
Forest Green, 211
forms of worship, 201
Foster, Stephen, 132
Four Last Songs (Strauss), 88
Four Minutes, Thirty-Three Seconds (Cage), 129, 141
Fox, George, 184
Freud, Sigmund, 125
fugue, 110
Fugue in E-flat major for Organ (Bach), 112
Gabrieli, Andrea, 61–62
Gabrieli, Giovanni, 61–62
galant style, 122
Gardiner, John Eliot, 42, 114, 120
Genevan Psalter, 60, 193, 194
George I, King of England, 67
George II, King of England, 67
German Romanticism, 84, 94
Gershwin, George, 94
Glareanus, 161
Glass, Philip, 179
Gloria (Vivaldi), 65
Glorious Things of Thee are Spoken (Newton), 214
God
    as God of beauty, 39, 217, 220–21
    as God of order, not chaos, 40
    holiness of, 200
God Moves in a Mysterious Way (Newton), 213
Godre'r Coed, 211
Goldberg Variations (Bach), 110
gospel, 16, 122, 175, 185, 214
Greek philosophy, 172
Gregorian chant, 188
Grieg, Edvard, 83, 87
guitar, 134

Haeussler, Armin, 211
Haley, Bill, 133
"Hallelujah Chorus" (Handel), 67–70
Hamm, Charles, 138
Handel, George Frederick, 30, 67–70, 80, 81, 103, 141
happiness, 163
harmonizations, 120
harmony, 18, 23, 39, 97, 101–2, 120, 126, 172
Hart, D. G., 200, 202, 206
Hart, Mickey, 179
Haydn, Franz Joseph, 72, 74–76, 78, 80, 86, 103
hearts, fickle and deceitful nature of, 165
heavy metal music, 134, 172
Hebrides overture (Mendelssohn), 81
Helm, Paul, 154, 163–64
Heman, 185
Hendrix, Jimi, 179

Henry, Matthew, 159, 165
Henry VIII, King of England, 189
Herzlich Tut Mich Verlangen (Bach), 111
Hewett, Ivan, 113, 150
hip hop music, 135
Holst, Gustav, 89
Homes, Nathaniel, 212–13
homophony, 62, 103
Hong, Lim Swee, 203, 204
Hooker, Richard, 159–60, 173, 183
Horne, Marilyn, 135
Hutcheson, Francis, 40–41
hymn books, 204
hymns, 206, 210–11

If Ye Love Me, Keep My Commandments (Tallis), 59–60
Ignatius of Antioch, 187
image of God, 17, 35, 40, 150, 218
inclusive psalmody, 210
instrumental music, 183
intellectus, 44
Israel in Egypt (Handel), 67
Italian symphony (Mendelssohn), 81

Jagger, Mick, 179
James, Sharon, 25
Janáček, Leoš, 94
Jennens, Charles, 70
Jesus, sang psalms, 21, 186
Jesus People, 203
Jesus, Thy Blood and Righteousness (Zinzendorf), 191
Joachim, Joseph, 84
Jones, Paul S., 204–5, 211
Joy to the World (Watts), 190
Jubal, 31

Karelia Suite (Sibelius), 92
Keach, Benjamin, 190
Keddie, John, 199
keyboard music, 109–14
Kidner, Derek, 210
kitsch, 145, 166, 180–81
Korngold, Erich, 96
Kuiper, R. B., 199, 221
Kuyper, Abraham, 34–36, 218

Lassus, Orlandus, 58, 99, 103
legalism, 184
leitmotiv, 84
Leoni, 211
Le Rappel des Oiseaux (Rameau), 22
Levites, 29, 185
Lewis, C. S., 37
liberalism, and worship, 201
Liebster Jesu, Wir Sind Hier (Bach), 111
listening to music, 97–98, 146, 174–75, 181, 219
Liszt, Franz, 83
live performances, 219
Llwynbedw, 211
Lobe Den Herren, 211
Lo, How a Rose E'er Blooming (Praetorius), 61
London Symphonies (Haydn), 74
love, 156
Love Divine, All Loves Excelling (Wesley), 190
Lucarini, Dan, 135, 141
Lully, Jean-Baptiste, 64
Lutherans, 189, 196
Luther, Martin, 13, 22, 29, 34, 60, 106, 113, 159, 172–73, 181, 187, 188–89, 193, 211, 214, 217–18, 220

Machen, J. Gresham, 17, 32, 150, 151
McIntosh, Andy, 24
Mahler, Gustav, 88, 94
man-centered worship, 201, 203
marriage, 121
Marvell, Andrew, 13
Mass in B minor (Bach), 42, 103, 114, 115–17
materialism, 17
mathematics, 24–25
Mather, Cotton, 194–95
Mather, Increase, 183
Mattheson, Johann, 161–62
melody, 172
built into creation, 23
Mendelssohn, Felix, 29, 30, 80, 81–82, 103, 111, 122
Messiaen, Olivier, 128
Messiah (Handel), 67, 70, 103, 141
Metastasis (Xenakis), 42
metrical psalms, 190
Michaelangelo, 98, 105
Milton, John, 70–71, 74, 167, 181, 183

mind, as a faculty of the soul, 44
minimalism, 129, 179
"minimalist" music, 104
modern era, 87–96
Mohler, Albert, 30
Monteverdi, Claudio, 62
Moonlight piano sonata (Beethoven), 78
morally neutral, 16–17
Moravians, 191
Mornay, Philippe de, 18, 157
Mozart, Wolfgang Amadeus, 29, 30, 72–73, 101, 122
Muether, John, 200, 202, 206
music
    and architecture, 42
    can become idolatrous in worship, 214
    in church history, 185–91
    coram Deo, 139
    in creation, 21–27
    as gift from God, 217
    and mathematics, 24–25
    not morally neutral, 16–17, 18–19, 138, 179
    power of, 171, 181
    for praise of God, 14
    and the soul, 149, 157–62
    suitable for Christian worship, 182–84
musical education, 212
musical genres, 77, 78
musical instruments, 219
    in worship, 186–87, 194, 196, 197
musical performance, 55
music appreciation, 174–75
    see also appreciation of music
Music for the Royal Fireworks (Handel), 67
My Heart is Inditing (Handel), 67

Nadab and Abihu, 200
naturalism, 17
new creation, 35
New England, 194–95
Newton, John, 190–91, 213
New World symphony (Dvořák), 86, 102
"New Version", 190
nineteenth-century music, 77–87
noise, 128, 130
Nordlinger, Jay, 43, 105
Norton, Brian, 196, 209–10
Nun Danket Alle Gott, 211

Octet for Wind Instruments (Stravinsky), 128
O, For a Thousand Tongues to Sing (Wesley), 190
Old Hundredth (Bourgeois), 60–61, 99, 194, 211
Old Testament, instrumental worship in, 206
"Old Version", 194
O Little Town of Bethlehem, 212
Olivier, Laurence, 96
Olney Hymns, 190, 213
O occhi, manza mia (Lassus), 58
opera, 67, 77, 83, 136
oratorio, 67, 74, 114
Orb and Scepter (Walton), 96
orchestra, orchestration, 77, 88, 102, 120
    see also symphony orchestra
order, 24, 40, 166
Orfeo (Monteverdi), 62
organs, 110–11, 187
Organ symphony (Camille Saint-Saëns), 13, 87
Osiander, Lucas, 189
Owen, John, 154, 156, 163, 165, 184

Paganini, Nicolò, 83
painting, 98
Palestrina, Giovanni Pierluigi da, 56–57, 100, 103, 121, 141
Palisca, Claude, 64, 109
Pambo, 187–88, 189
pantheism, 125
Paradise Lost (Milton), 74, 183
Passacaglia and Fugue in C minor (Bach), 111
passions, 158
Pastoral symphony (Beethoven), 22, 43, 78
Peacham, Henry, 175
Perkins, William, 183
Petrushka (Stravinsky), 127
phonograph, 55
Piano Concerto in A minor (Grieg), 83, 87

Piano Concerto in A minor (Schumann), 83
Piano Concerto in F (Gershwin), 94
Piano Concerto No. 1 (Brahms), 84
Piano Concerto No. 2 (Brahms), 84
Piano Concerto No. 2 (Rachmaninov), 89–91, 101
Piano Concerto No. 5 (*Emperor*) (Beethoven), 78–79
Piano Concerto No. 23 (Mozart), 73, 101
piano sonata, 78
pietism, 184
Pilgrim's Progress (Bunyan), 183, 222
pipe organ, 111
Piston, Walter, 121
Plato, 13, 24, 37–38, 151, 171–72, 189
Pliny the Younger, 186
Plumer, W. S., 22, 197
poetry, 181
polyphony, 62, 103, 121, 188
Pomp and Circumstance marches (Elgar), 89
poor-quality music, 180–82
pop music, 131–39, 142, 144, 203, 214
Porgy and Bess (Gershwin), 94
practical reason, 164
Praetorius, Michael, 61
Prelude in C major (Bach), 109
Preludes (Chopin), 83
Presley, Elvis, 133
"program music," 43
proportion, 39, 97, 99–101, 104, 138, 143
psalm singing, 16, 21, 157, 159, 183, 186–90, 193–97, 206, 210
Purcell, Henry, 62–63, 67, 102, 190
Puritans, 163, 183–84, 195, 196
Pythagoreans, 153

Quadrivium, 25
Quakers, 184
Quintilian, 160, 161

Rachmaninov, Sergei, 89–91, 101
Rameau, Jean-Philippe, 22, 64
randomness, 128
rap, 135
ratio, 44
rationalism, 162
Ravel, Maurice, 88, 102, 126, 137, 178
recorded music, 131, 219
Reformation, 60, 123, 182
    on place of music in worship, 188–89
Reformation symphony (Mendelssohn), 81
regulative principle of worship, 195–97, 207
Reich, Steve, 104, 179
Rejoice in the Lord Alway (Purcell), 62–63
relativism, 44, 141
Rembrandt, 98, 105, 124
Renaissance, 56–62, 99, 103, 161
resurrection of the body, 151
Resurrection symphony (Mahler), 88
reverence, 206
Reynolds, Edward, 164, 165
Rhapsody in Blue (Gershwin), 94
Rhapsody on a Theme of Paganini (Rachmaninov), 89
rhetoric, 161
rhythm, 100, 128, 172, 178
Ring cycle (Wagner), 84
Rochberg, George, 126
rock music, 133–35, 136, 143–44, 167, 172
    targeting children, 136–37
    in worship, 203, 205–6
Rock of Ages, 212
Rolling Stones, 133, 136
Roman Catholic worship, 181
Romantic movement, 77, 83
Rossini, Gioachino, 80
Rhuddlan, 211
Russian composers, 87
Ruth, Lester, 203, 204
Ryle, J. C., 202, 215

St. Anne Prelude and Fugue in E-flat major (Bach), 111
St. Flavian, 211
St. John Passion (Bach), 42, 114, 119
St. Matthew Passion (Bach), 81, 114, 119–20, 122
St. Paul oratorio (Mendelssohn), 80
St. Paul's Cathedral (London), 30–31, 42, 103
Saint-Saëns, Camille, 13, 87

sanctification, 156, 174
Schaeffer, Francis, 124, 174
Schelling, Friedrich Wilhelm Joseph, 42
Schoenberg, Arnold, 124–26, 128, 130
Scholes, Percy, 183
Schubert, Franz, 29, 80
Schumann, Robert, 83
Schütz, Heinrich, 29, 62
Scottish Psalter (1615), 190
Scottish Psalter (1650), 190, 195
Scottish symphony (Mendelssohn), 81
Scruton, Roger, 34, 43, 101, 126, 142, 150, 172, 173, 180, 181, 220
SDG (*Soli Deo Gloria*), 106
Second Viennese School, 125
secularism, 40, 149
"seeker-sensitive" worship, 203
self, 149
Serenade for Strings (Elgar), 89
serialism, 124, 128
Sermon on the Mount, 27
Shakespeare, William, 15, 218
shape-note music, 77
Shore, Howard, 96
Sibelius, Jean, 92–93, 125
simplicity, 39, 97, 102–3, 120–21
singing, in Christian worship, 185–86, 193
Smalley, Paul, 155
Söderblom, Nathan, 122
Solomon (Handel), 67
sonata form, 71, 100
Sospiri Op. 70 (Elgar), 158
soul, 17–18, 44, 149, 218
    darkening of, 220
    disorder of, 163–69
    faculties of, 154–56, 157
    and music, 149, 157–62
Spem in Alium (Tallis), 59
spiritual maturity, 173
Sproul, R. C., 22, 24, 30, 39, 130, 150, 174, 193, 200, 204
Spurgeon, C. H., 195
Stamitz, Johann, 71
Stanley, Bob, 133, 136
Stapert, Calvin, 120, 122
Steiner, Max, 96
Sternhold and Hopkins Psalter, 190
Stockhausen, Karlheinz, 128, 129
Strauss, Richard, 88–89
Stravinsky, Igor, 127–28, 178
string quartet, 72, 77, 86
Super Flumina Babylonis (Palestrina), 57, 100
Suzuki, Masaaki, 106, 115
symmetry, 104, 138, 166
    see also proportion
symphony, 43, 71, 77–78, 84, 103, 133
symphony orchestra, 52, 72, 74, 87, 88, 96
syncopation, 205

tabernacle, 99
Tallis' Canon, 60, 211
Tallis, Thomas, 59–60, 99
Tartarkiewicz, Wladyslaw, 98–99
Taruskin, Richard, 130
taste in music, 141–47
Tate and Brady psalter, 190
Tchaikovsky, Pyotr, 87, 158
technology, 141
Te Deum No. 2 in C major (Haydn), 74
temple, 99
Terry, Quinlan, 43, 99, 217
The Art of Fugue (Bach), 110
The Carnival of the Animals (Saint-Saëns), 87
The Creation (Haydn), 74–76
The Firebird (Stravinsky), 127
The Four Seasons (Vivaldi), 64–65
The Planets (Holst), 89
The Rite of Spring (Stravinsky), 127
The Spirit Breathes upon the Word (Cowper), 213
The Trout Quintet for piano and strings (Schubert), 80
Thirty-nine Articles of Religion, 197
Thomas Aquinas, 44, 154
Thomas, Derek, 196, 197
Tin Pan Alley, 94, 132
Toccata and Fugue in D minor (Bach), 111
tonality, 64, 78, 84, 103, 104, 109, 120
transformed by renewal of the mind, 146, 169
Treatise on Harmony (Rameau), 64
trichotomy, 151
Trinity, unity and diversity in, 41
Trinity Psalter Hymnal, 212

Tristan and Isolde (Wagner), 84
Trivium, 161
true, good, and beautiful, 21, 36
tunes, for psalms and hymns, 210–13
Twelve Grand Concerti (Handel), 67

ugly music, 130, 143, 166–68, 178, 180, 217
understanding, 155
unity in diversity, 40, 120
unwholesome lyrics, 179, 181

Valla, Lorenzo, 218
Varese, Edgar, 128
Vaughan Williams, Ralph, 62, 94, 127
Veith, Gene Edward, 33–34, 44, 143, 145, 182, 203, 214–15
Veni Emmanuel, 211
Verdi, Guiseppe, 80, 83
Vermeer, Johannes, 98
Very Flesh, Yet Spirit Too (Ignatius), 187
Vespers of 1610 (Monteverdi), 62
Vickers, Brian, 160
Victoria, Queen of England, 81
Violin Concerto (Barber), 94
Violin Concerto in D major (Korngold), 96
Violin Concerto in D minor (Sibelius), 92
Violin Concerto in E minor (Mendelssohn), 81–82
violin family of instruments, 107–8
Virgil, 161
Vivaldi, Antonio, 64–65, 108
voice and verse, 181

Wagner, Richard, 80, 84, 126, 179
Walton, William, 96, 134
Water Music (Handel), 67
Watson, Thomas, 22
Watts, Isaac, 190
Webern, Anton, 125
Well-Tempered Clavier (Bach), 83, 102, 109, 122
Welsh hymns, 211
Wesley, Charles, 190, 214
Wesley, John, 190, 191, 212, 213, 214
Westermeyer, Paul, 120, 187
"West Gallery Music," 190
Westminster Abbey, 74
Westminster Assembly, 195
Westminster Confession of Faith, 150–51, 195
"When I am Laid in Earth" (Purcell), 62
When I Survey the Wondrous Cross (Watts), 190, 212
Widor, Charles-Marie, 87
will, 154–55, 157–58
Williams, John, 96
words, 102, 120, 122, 146, 175, 181, 189–90, 193
worldview, 18, 29, 30–32, 40, 44, 123, 129, 138, 141
see also Christian worldview
worship, 199–207, 209
worship leader, musician as, 204
Wren, Christopher, 30

Xenakis, Iannis, 42, 128

Young, La Monte, 129

Zadok the Priest (Handel), 67
Zanchi, Girolamo, 154–55
Zinzendorf, Count von, 191
Zwingli, Ulrich, 187, 189, 193

About Shepherd Press Publications

They are gospel driven.
They are heart focused.
They are life changing.

Our Invitation to You

We passionately believe that what we are publishing can be of benefit to you, your family, your friends, and your work colleagues. So we are inviting you to join our online mailing list so that we may reach out to you with news about our latest and forthcoming publications, and with special offers.

Visit:

www.shepherdpress.com/newsletter

and provide your name and email address.